DRIVING AMBITION

DRIVING AMBITION

My Autobiography

Andrew Strauss

HODDER &
STOUGHTON

First published in Great Britain in 2013 by Hodder & Stoughton
An Hachette UK company

1

Copyright © Andrew Strauss 2013

A CIP catalogue record for this title is available from the British Library

Hardback ISBN 978 0 340 84068 9
Ebook ISBN 978 1 444 72216 1

Typeset in Minion Pro by Palimpsest Book Production Limited,
Falkirk, Stirlingshire

Printed and bound by Clays Ltd, St Ives plc

Hodder & Stoughton policy is to use papers that are natural, renewable and
recyclable products and made from wood grown in sustainable forests.
The logging and manufacturing processes are expected to conform to the
environmental regulations of the country of origin.

Hodder & Stoughton Ltd
338 Euston Road
London NW1 3BH

www.hodder.co.uk

For Ruth, Sam and Luca

CONTENTS

ACKNOWLEDGEMENTS

Writing a book is not unlike playing cricket. As an author you need to show a fair amount of discipline to get a book finished, just as a cricketer needs to spend hours experimenting and honing a technique. More importantly, to be successful, any cricketer needs a strong support network, from coaches and team-mates right the way through to an understanding family, and an author is no different.

Many thanks have to go to everyone at Hodder, especially Roddy Bloomfield, for the gentle prodding, advice and persuasion they have given me along the way. It was certainly needed.

Given that I have had the opportunity to look back at my formative years while compiling the book, it would be remiss of me not to thank my parents for all the help, advice, nurturing and taxiing they bestowed upon me over so many years. They have lived and breathed every moment of my career, almost certainly going through more anguish and stress than I ever did.

I am also immensely grateful for the endless hours put in by the many coaches who worked with me over my career. Philip Spray, Andy Wagner and latterly Duncan Fletcher and Andy Flower deserve particular mention.

For anyone who is fortunate enough to play international cricket, team-mates become something of a surrogate family during the many weeks away on tour. I have been particularly fortunate to share a dressing room with not only some fantastic players, perhaps some of England's finest ever, but more importantly some great blokes. They have all played a positive role of some sort in forming my career.

Last, and certainly not least, I would like to mention Ruth, my wife. Luckily, neither she nor I had any idea just how difficult it would be to combine the job of an international cricketer with a 'normal' family life. It takes a special person to deal with all the ups and downs and significant commitment required to be a successful cricketer. She has been a fantastic source of help, advice, solace and sympathy, while all the time having to put up with the considerable needs of our two young boys, Sam and Luca. Hopefully I will be able to share some of that burden now that I have retired, and finally finished the book!

PHOTOGRAPHIC ACKNOWLEDGEMENTS

The author and publisher would like to thank the following for permission to reproduce photographs:

Hamish Blair/Getty Images, Russell Boyce/Reuters/Action Images, Andrew Boyers/Livepic/Action Images, Philip Brown/Reuters/Action Images, Philip Brown/Reuters/Corbis, Andrew Brownbill/Press Association, Caldicott School Archives, Graham Chadwick/Daily Mail/Rex Features, Gareth Copley/Press Association, Peter Cziborra/Livepic/Action Images, Mark Dadswell/Getty Images, Adrian Dennis/AFP/Getty Images, Ede & Ravenscroft, Matthew Fearn/Press Association, Stu Forster/Getty Images, Paul Gilham/Getty Images, Julian Herbert/Getty Images, Ian Kington/AFP/Getty Images, Clive Mason/Getty Images, Marty Melville/Getty Images, Graham Morris/Cricketpix, Indranil Mukharjee/AFP/Getty Images, David Munden/Popperfoto/Getty Images, Rebecca Naden/Press Association, Jason O'Brien/Livepic/Action Images, Punit Paranjpe/Reuters/Action Images, Steve Parsons/Press Association, Altaf Qadri/AP/Press Association, Carl Recine/Livepic/Action Images, Rex Features, Clive Rose/Getty Images, Stephane de Sakutin/AFP/Getty Images, Jewel Samad/AFP/Getty Images, Ross Setford/AP/Press Association, Tom Shaw/Getty Images, Sports Inc/Press Association, Darren Staples/Reuters/Action

Images, Rui Vieira/Press Association, William West/AFP/ Getty Images, Tim Wimbourne/Reuters/Action Images, Lewis Whyld/Press Association.

The publisher acknowledges the trademarks of Cricket Australia in some of these photographs and where used notes that they have been reproduced with the approval of Cricket Australia.

All other photographs are from private collections.

1

OPENING UP

On an isolated farm in the rugged, bleak highlands of the Orange Free State, a young midwife is tenderly looking after her baby when she hears a knock on the door. She is immediately nervous. Her country is at war with the British, her husband has been captured and sent to Ceylon as a POW, and there are reports of women and children being rounded up by British soldiers to be taken into holding camps. Their farms are usually then scorched to the ground to ensure that the guerrilla forces combating the British are unable to replenish supplies.

She hesitantly opens the door. Immediately her worst fears are confirmed. A young British officer stands in front of her. He announces curtly that she is to pack up any belongings that she can carry and prepare to be moved out of her farm the next morning. She has until then to get things in order.

As soon as she closes the door, a feeling of panic rises within her. What should she do? There have been rumours that the conditions in the camps are harsh and that food is in short supply. The alternative, though, seems just as unappealing. She could load up her horse and cart, take her young baby and attempt to make the journey to a town thirty miles away, where there are friendly faces. However, it is getting dark and, *in the high altitude of the veldt, temperatures can easily drop to minus 5 degrees centigrade. It is a long shot, to say the least.*

She looks at her young son, barely two months old, and shudders at the thought of him in a camp, completely at the mercy of his captors. She makes her decision. She is going to risk the night-time journey.

She rushes to gather as much clothing as possible and proceeds to strap the young boy to her body. She goes to the stables to ready the horse and pack the cart, and within an hour she sets off from her farm in the middle of nowhere. She will have to navigate by the stars, hoping all the time not to be disturbed by British patrols. She is risking her life, and that of her young son, in the hope of remaining free.

I often wonder what would have happened if that young woman had decided against making such a difficult journey. She was my great-grandmother and the young son in her arms was my grandfather on my father's side. Over the course of the next two years, more than 26,000 women and children were to perish in those holding camps, as malnutrition and disease swept through them. It is very likely that neither she nor my grandfather would have survived. It would have spelled the end for this particular line of the Strauss family.

Perhaps unsurprisingly, after such a bitter conflict, the relationship between the British settlers in South Africa and the Afrikaners has never been an easy one. There has been too much blood, too much conflict. I find it very surprising, therefore, that my grandfather, who was brought up for long periods solely by his mother while her husband was in exile in Sri Lanka and St Helena, would choose to marry an Englishwoman. I am certainly not sure what his father, who had spent the majority of his life fighting the British, would have made of it. Nevertheless, that is what my grandfather did. My grandmother's family had come from Kent to manage a sugar estate in South Africa and she met my grandfather when she started working for the bank in Durban of which he was the manager.

Somewhat bizarrely, as it was really quite rare, my mother's family was also a mixture of English and Afrikaner. Her mother's family was of Scottish and German descent, an interesting combination, to say the least, and they had decided to bring up their children at English schools and with English customs. Her father's family, however, had sailed to South Africa in the mid-seventeenth century, probably from France, and had become as Afrikaans as you could get. The surname Botha, somewhat akin to the English name Smith, gives you an appreciation of his lineage.

I suppose my family were mongrels at a time when tensions between the English and Afrikaners remained high. Throughout the second half of the twentieth century, political debates in South Africa centred on two main parties. The Nationalists, who were to introduce apartheid to South Africa, represented the interests of the Afrikaans speakers, whereas the United Party espoused more moderate, Anglophile politics. There were great debates in parliament and on the streets about where the country was heading, but for the majority of white South Africans, that was where their political lives ended. The plight of the majority native black population was not a subject for serious discussion.

My parents met, as I suppose many couples did in those times, through an introduction by mutual friends. My mother was training as a teacher, whereas my father, being a few years older, was already making his way in the insurance industry. It might seem strange nowadays, but my father had to buy my mother out of her teacher-training contract in order to get married. Married women were not allowed to work full-time and so choices needed to be made.

They were both keen on their sport. The climate and the physical South African culture meant that sport was encouraged by the family and in schools. Rugby, football and cricket were the games of choice for my father, while my mother concentrated on tennis. I get the impression that neither thought of taking their sport more seriously than playing for club teams and socially, but nonetheless it was very much part of their lives and, by osmosis, the lives of their children.

I came into the world on 2 March 1977 in Johannesburg. Being the youngest of four children, I was almost guaranteed plenty of attention. My three sisters, Gillian, Sandra and Colleen, were eight, six and five respectively, and they were no doubt delighted to have a little baby brother to play with. The novelty soon wore off, but by and large we all got on well. It was, it has to be said, a comfortable upbringing. The house we moved into when I was aged two was spacious and came complete with tennis court and swimming pool. It probably sounds like a privileged existence, but it was not all that uncommon for white South Africans, who tended to spend most of their time outdoors, to have facilities of that nature.

A South African childhood revolved around three things: school, outdoor activities and holidays within the country. The television channels only came on air at 6 p.m., and the lack of programmes for children, and the fact that the language alternated between English and Afrikaans, meant that television played little part in our lives. Most of the time was spent swimming in the pool, hitting balls on the tennis court and running around in the garden.

The annual trips to the Kruger National Park, the largest wildlife reserve in South Africa, and down the coast in Natal were always highlights. Every time I go back to South Africa and visit the wildlife parks, I have a strange sense of déjà vu. My childhood visits must have indented my soul in some way, and as a result I have developed a real passion for the vast wilderness of the African bush.

My father and mother were both fairly strict. South Africans have a straightforward attitude to most things and they call people out on bad behaviour. Although none of us children could be considered to be truly rebellious, there were plenty of scoldings from my father, in particular, who fulfilled the main role of family disciplinarian.

I remember my first school very well, not least because it was a girls' school. My sisters all attended the junior school of St Andrew's in Johannesburg and for some unknown reason they allowed boys for the first year of preschool. I was one of a handful, all of whom had sisters at the school. My report from that year highlighted the fact that I was good with balls, but that my concentration tended to wane when it came to handwriting. When you combine that with a report from my swimming teacher that I 'seemed to prefer winning to adopting the correct technique', I think it is quite easy to see that my character was pretty well developed by the age of four.

All in all they were happy days: a comfortable lifestyle, a great climate and plenty of innocent fun, especially when I finally joined a boys' school, St John's, at the age of five. I tended to concentrate on sport when I could, playing football for a local club and doing plenty of swimming at school and at home. We were settled, my father was doing well at his insurance company and we seemed to have the world at our feet.

*   *   *

On the surface, at least, it seems a somewhat strange decision on the part of my parents to leave the country when I was seven years old. Perhaps they were influenced by their own nomadic childhoods, when they both moved around the country frequently. They no doubt also saw it as the last opportunity to take the family abroad while all the children were relatively young.

While the decision was not driven by the political situation in South Africa, it is true that by the mid-1980s the world's attention was increasingly turning to the policy of apartheid and the minority white population's treatment of the other, majority, ethnicities. Things were getting fraught, with international sanctions as well as frequent demonstrations putting more pressure on the government to address the concerns of the black population. As is so often the case, though, if you weren't directly involved in it, your life continued pretty much as normal.

My father's job was the practical reason we left South Africa and made the long journey to Melbourne. His company were looking to branch out into the Australian market and my dad was given the opportunity to set things up over there, with the option of coming back to South Africa two years later. For young South Africans, who in those days didn't get the opportunity to travel the world in the way it is possible today, it must have seemed like an opportunity too good to miss.

For most people, the idea of living in Australia sounds like a dream come true: blue skies, barbecues, a relaxed lifestyle and a carefree existence. For us, having come from a way of life that was very similar, Melbourne didn't seem quite as exotic. For starters, the weather was not all it was cracked up to be. Johannesburg surely has one of the best climates in the world: hot, but not unbearably so in the summer, with frequent thunderstorms in the afternoon to freshen things up. The winter is one long stretch of blue skies and no rain, with the temperature remaining at a comfortable 20 degrees centigrade. Melbourne, however, more than lived up to its reputation for having four seasons in one day – with temperatures sometimes swinging between 45 and 10 degrees centigrade. For the first time in our lives, we also had to deal with unpleasant, rainy weather in the winter. I think we all found it quite hard to adjust to. God only knows what it would have been like if we had gone straight to the UK from South Africa.

Adjust we did, though, and in many ways living in Australia was an adventure. My parents, who were clearly keen to experience as much of the country as possible, took us on trips as far north as the Queensland rainforest, as well as dragging us up the mountains in Northern Victoria for some surprisingly good skiing. I found the transition from South African to Australian school an easy one to make, and even my sisters, who were at a much more awkward phase in their development, approaching teenagehood, seemed to adapt well to the new surroundings.

Our house was not nearly as grand as the one we had left in South Africa, and there were no maids and gardeners to maintain it, but it was nice enough, in a Melbourne suburb called Balwyn North, and there were plenty of sports facilities nearby. By then, as I approached eight, sport was taking up more and more of my life. Being decidedly small relative to my peers, in South Africa I really hadn't had the size or strength to hit cricket or tennis balls with any real consistency, but over in Australia all that began to change.

At school Aussie Rules football was the sport to play. Victoria was the hotbed of the sport and it was every boy's duty to make sure they kept the game alive and flourishing. The game was a little bizarre to me, with its high tackles and punching the ball to pass it being in complete contrast to the rugby that I had watched endlessly in South Africa. My father, who no doubt saw the game as sacrilege to the holy game of rugby, signed me up to one of the only rugby union clubs in Melbourne and ended up doing the coaching for the team as well. He always took an active interest in my sporting exploits, and it is in Australia that I have my first memories of kicking the ball with him in the garden and practising my cricket shots, trying to emulate Dean Jones or one of the other Aussie cricketers.

Cricket, in truth, played a relatively small part in this sporting paradise. I played for the team at school, but at that age games were few and far between. I have one vague memory of us winning a game with one of my team-mates taking a hat-trick, but I can't remember anything of my own contribution. My strongest memories of the sport came from playing Test Match Cricket, the board game with a little ball-bearing rolling down a chute, to be hit by a batsman controlled by a player flicking a lever. Hours were spent playing Test matches at my house or that of my mate, Christopher. Scoring a fifty or taking a wicket was always accompanied by a wild celebration, copied directly from those we watched on TV from the likes of Allan Border or Bruce Reid.

The time we lived there was neither long enough for us to feel completely at home, nor short enough for it to seem like one big holiday. I think my parents had a much harder time adjusting than the kids did. The change of lifestyle definitely had something to do with it, but another factor was that South Africans were viewed with some suspicion by the Australians. The daily news reports of violent oppression definitely seemed to make an impression on them, and to some extent anyone from South Africa was guilty by association.

* * *

As the end of our time in Melbourne neared, my parents had difficult decisions to make. The straightforward option was to return to the easy lifestyle we had left behind in South Africa. I think by then, though, they had started to become a little concerned about what was happening back there. There were signs that the country might combust as the black majority increasingly flexed their muscles against their white oppressors. The future was far from certain at that time and it would have been a significant risk to go back to South Africa expecting everything to be the same as when we had left. The other option was to sit tight and make Australia our new home.

As my parents were mulling things over, my father was offered another business opportunity. Some of his former colleagues from South Africa were trying to expand their business in the UK and wanted him to come over to help them in their endeavours. Facing a tough choice between staying in a country where they felt like outsiders and going back to a country on the brink of political turmoil, my parents had suddenly been presented with the perfect way out.

There were some logistical difficulties to overcome. My eldest sister, Gillian, was nearing her final school exams and would have to stay in Melbourne for three months longer than the rest of us to complete them, before heading to England to pursue her dream of becoming a vet. My father stayed with her, which left my mother, myself and the two middle sisters, Sandra and Colleen, to forge a path ahead in the UK. We arrived at the end of August 1986, jetlagged and disorientated, and headed out to leafy Buckinghamshire, where we were to start our new life.

My school had already been selected by my parents on a reconnaissance visit several months previously. The headmaster, who was mad about rugby, had been persuaded by my South African lineage and the fact that I had played in Australia to find a place for me, despite having no room on the waiting list. The school was called Caldicott Preparatory School and it sat in forty acres of grounds on the edge of the historic woods of Burnham Beeches.

As its name suggests, it was a genuine prep school. Uniforms had to be smart and hair needed to be cut. Work had to be done diligently and on time. In many ways, it was like going back in time to a bygone age. It was one big institution, full of rules and regulations, but I loved it. For a boy who was becoming increasingly fanatical about sport, the school had everything. A beautifully manicured array of rugby pitches and facilities for basketball, swimming, hockey, athletics, tennis, squash and, of course, cricket. I immersed myself in it all with great gusto.

It was around the time of my ninth birthday that my competitive side really started to reveal itself. I simply had to win at everything. I remember as if it was yesterday the tears of despair that I struggled to hold back if I lost a game of tennis to my sister, Colleen, who was a very accomplished player (and five years older than me). It hurt, and I did not like it. The same went for my new school. I desperately wanted to be the best at everything, even going as far as to demand to be given another chance to audition for the choir when my initial tone-deaf attempt wasn't deemed up to scratch. Fortunately, the school encouraged that competitive attitude. In academic studies, we were all given a finishing position in each subject at the end of term. I always wanted to be number one and was prepared to go through hours of revising Latin verbs or geographical locations in order to get there.

I am sure that my attitude probably grated on a few people, but I was enthusiastic and tried my hardest at everything. On the sporting field, in particular, I was beginning to show some promise. Despite remaining frustratingly small – one competition I could not win – I quickly established myself in all the teams in my age group. I don't think I was significantly better than anyone else at any sport, but I was pretty good at all of them, including cricket.

In my second year, I was captaining the colts side, combining a bit of dodgy left-arm chinaman bowling with my left-handed batting. By the end of my third year, I had made the school's 1st XI, where I stayed till I left the school three years later. When I look back over the end-of-year reports, I am not entirely sure what I did to merit getting into the 1st XI at such a young age. I certainly never scored all that many runs. Perhaps it was my ability to catch the ball and the lack of a wicketkeeper in the years above, because in my first year I set a record for the most stumpings ever (27), thanks to an excellent leg-spin bowler called Richard Toothill.

The cricket coach was my geography teacher, a man by the name of Philip Spray. He had been a decent cricketer himself and was very passionate about the game, while never one to suffer fools gladly. He obviously saw something in me and persisted in making sure that I practised proper shots, rather than just trying to whack the ball around everywhere. I followed his advice, perhaps through fear of disobeying him, and although I could never hit the ball off the square, a solid cricketing technique was eventually developed.

Caldicott, though, was mainly a rugby school. It held the distinction of winning the national prep school sevens tournament, played at Rosslyn Park, more than any other school, and everyone was proud of this record. The headmaster, Peter Wright, was particularly keen to make sure that we kept that record in place and even arranged an exchange scheme with a school in Cape Town called Bishops, in which Caldicott's best rugby players were swapped with the best from Bishops, ostensibly to broaden their education, but in fact to strengthen the rugby team.

Despite my size, I developed into a pretty good fly-half and captained the side in my last year. Unfortunately, we were unable to keep up the tradition of winning the national sevens tournament, coming unstuck in the final against Millfield. I still remember the kick from our full back that was snaffled up by their tearaway winger, who ran in the try to break all our hearts. So near yet so far.

My father, who had rugby running through his veins, loved coming to watch the games at the weekend alongside my mother. He was a passionate supporter and would dissect the whole game afterwards, discussing with me where it had been won and lost, the poor kicks, missed tackles and so on. When it came to cricket, however, he was a less comfortable spectator. Throughout my time at Caldicott, and more so at Radley College later, he would find a private place to watch me batting, such as a clump of trees or somewhere on the far side of the ground. I am not sure if he just got nervous or simply didn't want to be disturbed by the incessant chatter of other parents, but that habit remained with him throughout my career. God knows how he dealt with it during a Test match.

Two incidents stick firmly in my mind about my time at Caldicott. First, when I was eleven I failed to make the Caldicott team for an athletics multi-event tournament because I no-jumped three times in the trial. Though I was far better than my replacement, the athletics coach ignored my pleas to give me one more chance and named the team without me in it. It was a serious blow to my ego, as I wasn't used to being left out of teams. (Perhaps the athletics coach was trying to teach me a lesson.) I then turned up to watch my team-mates in the competition, which was being held in London, only to find that one of the senior team had not shown up. I was hurriedly put in the Under-13s team and managed to come stone last in every event. It was humiliating beyond compare, and although the parents all congratulated me for 'giving it a go', I had experienced my worst nightmare. Losing and me didn't go together very well.

The other, far worse, moment, had to do with boarding. The rules of the school stipulated that at the age of eleven, boarding became compulsory. This was meant to prepare the pupils for life at the senior public school, to which the majority of boys graduated. I was fully aware of the fact and was even looking forward to the 'freedom'. When the moment came, however, I found it extremely hard. My parents lived less than three miles away from the school and I saw them at the end of each week, but they might as well have been on the other side of the world. Plenty of tears were shed in the dormitory over those first few months as I came to terms with living away from home for the first time.

It is quite surprising that I reacted in this way, as two of my sisters had been boarding for a few years and my eldest sister was away at university. Our house had gone from being a very vibrant place, full of energy, fun and sibling rivalry, to somewhere much quieter. In effect, I was an only child during the school term, with just my mum and dad and our faithful dog Zoe for company. I am sure this was one of the reasons that boarding school made sense for my parents – it would allow me to be with friends – but it still took some getting used to.

That is not to say that I didn't enjoy my time at Caldicott immensely. It was a closeted world, but it suited me down to the ground. I loved the sport, I loved the close friendships I made there, and many of life's important lessons concerning respect, treating others fairly, operating as a team and having manners were drilled into me there on a daily basis.

My holidays around this time consisted of either a trip back to South Africa to visit relatives or whatever my exasperated mother could come up with to get me out of the house. For the most part, my sisters were away, supplementing their student loans with holiday jobs, usually involving working in pubs. My father, as always, was working hard, commuting from Beaconsfield to Croydon, where his business was based. He was gone by seven in the morning and was rarely home before the corresponding time in the evening. Great swathes of time, therefore, were spent at home with my mother.

I have never been at my best with nothing to do. Inactivity usually led to lethargy and by the time I reached teenagehood, sleeping until noon was not out of the question. My mum, therefore, went out of her way to make sure I was as occupied as possible. Occasionally, she took me with her into work, teaching disabled adults in Maidenhead, but mainly she arranged for me to play sport. That meant days spent at the tennis club with other kids who had similarly been dumped by their parents, and the pro, a guy called Peter Willetts, became our surrogate guardian for the day. I also gained membership of Burnham Beeches golf club, and with Rob Easton, who had joined the club at the same time as me, I would spend count-less hours on the course or on the driving range trying to emulate the swing of Nick Faldo, who was world number one at that stage.

There were plenty of other activities too, such as trips to Alton Towers. What there was little of at that stage was cricket. Until I was fifteen, cricket largely finished at the end of the summer term, in early July. Two and a half months of holiday were spent doing just about every other sport apart from cricket. I am not entirely sure why that was the case – perhaps it was because I was never really a part of a county set-up, or maybe it was because my parents concentrated on club tennis – but, apart from the odd colts tournament for Gerrards Cross CC, my cricketing education stopped on prize-giving day. Not that it really mattered, though, as the cricketing education I received at my new senior school, Radley College, was first rate.

I arrived at Radley as a young, naive and rather small thirteen-year-old and was immediately intimidated by the place. For starters, the boys around me (there were no girls apart from one, who was the daughter of one of the teachers and unsurprisingly popular) were more young men than boys. They seemed enormous, with broken voices and tree trunks for legs.

The facilities were at once impressive and overwhelming. The school was set in 800 acres of Oxfordshire countryside. Sports pitches extended as far as the eye could see. There was even a nine-hole golf course, as well as some of the best drama and music facilities you could possibly imagine. The school had its own rowing club, young anglers could practise their fly-fishing on 'college pond' and there was even a pack of beagles for those who fancied country sports. All of this was in addition to the extensive main facilities, which were not surprisingly based around academic work and housing for the pupils and teachers.

It was, in short, a huge institution and it had a whole host of rules and regulations. For instance, there were sections of the grass you were not permitted to walk on; there were jobs, or fags, that the first-years had to do on behalf of their boarding houses; and there were academic gowns that had to be worn all day long. We thought nothing of playing cricket in our break times without even bothering to take off our gowns and we never once worried about how absurd we must have looked to a casual passer-by.

In fact, it seems bizarre now how quickly I came to think of all that as normal. I never really considered how fortunate I was to be at a school adorned with such incredible facilities and opportunities. It was just how it was. That was my school, and that was my life. It was only much later, having spent some time at Middlesex with cricketers from far less affluent backgrounds, that I really started to appreciate my good fortune.

And I genuinely was fortunate. Every hobby or passion was catered for, from opera singing to hovercrafting, with schoolmasters ready to spend endless evenings and weekends running extracurricular activities. At the same time, the boys were all being primed to get the requisite GCSEs and A levels to go to university.

On the rugby field, our coach was Steve Bates, who was scrum-half for Wasps at the time and, in the days before rugby union turned professional, made his living from being a schoolmaster/ rugby coach. On the cricketing side, Andy Wagner, who had played cricket for MCC young pros and Somerset, forged an outstanding combination with Bert Robinson, who had been the school cricket pro for over fifty years, since his days of playing for Northamptonshire.

Under their tutelage, my cricket really started to develop. By the time I was in the second year, I was bolstered up to the colts team (in effect, playing for the age group above mine), and by the summer of my third year I found myself in the school 1st XI. That is not to say, however, that I was the real star performer in the school. That label belonged to Robin

Martin-Jenkins, son of the late Christopher, who was in the year above me and was already being talked about as a future England all-rounder. His contributions to the team, with both bat and ball, were often the difference between winning and losing. In fact, I even had some pretty good competition in my own year, with Ben Hutton, who later went on to be my best man and colleague at Middlesex, showing that cricketing talent can indeed run in the genes, from grandfather to grandson.

Although I was not a stand-out like Martin-Jenkins, I made improvements every year, and once I'd managed to get the particularly unpleasant monkey off my back of never having scored a century – against an Australian touring side, at the age of fifteen – I started to come into my own as a cricketer. By this time, with a couple of others from the school, I was starting to represent Oxfordshire Under-19s in the summer holidays, thus extending my cricket season from two months to four months.

When I look back at the cricket I played at school, what surprises me is that I never really dominated. Surely a future England captain should have been head and shoulders above his peers at that level? Certainly the likes of Alastair Cook and Marcus Trescothick were making significant waves before they reached the age of fifteen. I can't really put my finger on why that wasn't the case. Perhaps it was because I was still playing all those other sports, from rugby to golf and everything in between. More likely, though, it came down to motivation. I think that I was always motivated to prove to everyone that I was good enough to deserve to be playing at the level I was selected for, but not beyond that. I wanted to show people that

I was at least as good as my team-mates, but I never looked towards the real stars of my generation, who were donning their county tracksuits, because I didn't really come up against them. In short, I was quite content being a big fish in what was a very small pond, the Radley 1st XI. Maybe I wasn't confident enough in my ability or even bothered enough to push myself harder, but at that stage cricket for me was a recreation, not a future career.

If I have one criticism about my time at Radley, it is that everything was geared to getting good A levels and proceeding along the well-worn path from school to university and then, in many cases, to the City. Pupils who headed into other careers, from music to drama and of course sport, seemed thin on the ground. Also, I was definitely influenced by my parents, who placed great emphasis on attaining the necessary grades to follow in the footsteps of my sisters, who were making their way in their chosen fields of veterinary science, medicine and accountancy. Cricket as a living did not seem to be on the agenda.

At the end of 1995, I left Radley College, after five incredible years, armed with some lifelong friends, many memories and the more than adequate three As and a B at A level. Those qualifications hide the fact that I really didn't work very hard at school. There were too many other things to do, and my attitude was always to do as little as possible, and leave things as late as possible, before attempting my schoolwork.

I am a little embarrassed about it now, as at times both my teachers and my father were forced to rack their brains to find ways of getting me motivated enough to do my work. Academic ability was never the problem; diligence and application, on the other hand, were more of an issue. At one stage, during the year before my A levels, I was forced to hand a sheet of paper, devised by my father, to the teacher at the end of the lesson, who would in turn attest to the level of my attention over the preceding forty minutes. My friends thought the whole thing hilarious. I definitely did not.

Fortunately, however, I managed to pull it off in the end, and my next destination was independence in the form of an economics degree at Durham University.

2

ALL THE GEAR, NO IDEA

I step onto the train at Beaconsfield Station. This is the heart of the commuter belt and it is obvious to everyone that I am hopelessly out of place. Everywhere are suits and laptops; serious City types are preparing for a long day of meetings and deal-making. I manage to find a seat in the corner and, although I am in a jacket and tie, my cricket bag takes up the majority of the corridor, making it very difficult for the overweight stockbroker to get past, holding his newly acquired Chiltern Lines cup of coffee. Trains, rush hour and large sports bags don't seem to go together too well.

As I watch the Buckinghamshire countryside transform into a more urban landscape, with semi-detached houses and industrial estates appearing alongside the track, I allow myself to think about what might lie in store for me today.

It was August 1996 and a few days before I'd had a call from Andy Wagner, my coach from school, telling me that he had put my name forward to someone called Ian Gould at Middlesex, who had invited me down to Lord's for a net session to have a look at me. The message was pretty short and to the point. I was to get down to the ground for an 11.30 a.m. net session, and because the 1st XI were playing a County Championship game that day, I was to wear a jacket and tie.

That was it. My introduction to the world of professional sport awaited.

It wasn't as though I felt completely out of my comfort zone. I had been at Durham for a year and in my first season for the university I had played against enough county 2nd XI players to know that on my day I could match any of them. All my team-mates from the Durham University side were either contracted to or trialling with county sides, and the idea of playing professional cricket was becoming more and more appealing.

My problem, though, was that I was essentially unknown. I had never been part of any of the age-group sides for a first-class county, and although I had managed to play for Oxfordshire Under-19s for a couple of years, with reasonable success, I hadn't been impressive enough to send county scouts scurrying back to report that they had found the next great hope.

The good players in my age group, the likes of David Sales or Owais Shah, were already sampling the delights of first-class cricket. They were being talked about as part of the next golden generation of English batting. They had contracts firmly in place. They looked good in their county tracksuits. They belonged.

I was, in contrast, an outsider. No real pedigree, no real contacts in the county game. My route into the professional ranks depended on nothing other than scoring runs when it mattered. There would be no one to report on a glorious hundred I scored a couple of years back, or the incredible pull shot I managed to hit against an England bowler. My stats up to that point were modest and I was a public school-educated student. In short, I was just the sort of person to put off the rank-and-file county coaches and players. The years of privilege and opportunity that had been afforded to me up to that point were about to be rendered useless.

If I thought the train journey was uncomfortable, getting through Marylebone Station was infinitely worse. In my deep concern not to be late, I had set off too early and was now jostling with the experienced station campaigners. They had been taking this route for years and knew how to find a way past an inept Marylebone first-timer, who had shown enough bad judgement to bring an enormous cricket bag with him.

By the time I emerged from the throng and walked out of the station, I felt completely flustered. I had managed to get the bag stuck in the automatic ticket barrier and the rest of the commuters were less than impressed by my antics. The day was not going well.

Any hopes that things might get a little easier in the slightly more familiar surroundings of a cricket ground were soon dashed. The security team at the Grace Gates were not sufficiently impressed with my jacket and tie and cricket bag to let me in, and a hurried phone call had to be made to Ian Gould to check that I was, indeed, kosher. I could just about hear Ian's Cockney tones on the other end of the phone telling them that 'The bloke is OK. He is just a triallist. Send him up to the dressing room.'

I made my way past the more friendly stewards at the front of the pavilion with a little more ease and was even given some remarkably accurate directions on how to get to the dressing room. I was to 'go through the Long Room, but be careful with your bag; there are plenty of members about. Then, go up one flight of stairs, veer to the right, go through the door marked "players and officials only" and the door to the dressing room will be in front of you.'

In hindsight, I probably should have thought about the timing of my entrance into the dressing room. It was 10.45, and any cricketer would know that interrupting players in the crucial fifteen minutes before the start of a game is not a great idea. The idea is worse still if the side is batting and the openers are going through their elaborate preparation routines, shadow-batting, skipping and the like.

As I opened the door, the extent of my mistake became abundantly clear. The eyes of all the players instantly focused on the anonymous outsider who had the gall and arrogance to interrupt them at such a crucial time. The first face I recognised was that of Mark Ramprakash, Middlesex's most famous player, who had once again found himself out of the England team and was, I subsequently learnt, 'not in a good place'. He showed a fair amount of restraint in doing nothing more than scowl in my direction. The other players, including Angus Fraser and Phil Tufnell, just looked at me, eager to see what I had to say about my intrusion.

'I am really sorry to bother you guys, but I'm here for a trial and was told to report to the dressing room. I think I'm meant to see Ian Gould,' I just about managed to mumble, conscious that my heart felt as if it was going to explode and that my face had turned bright crimson.

'Well, if that is the case, I suggest you ---- off to the second-team dressing room down the corridor and leave us in peace,' came the less-than-friendly response from Angus Fraser, hero of Bridgetown and all-round England stalwart.

It was far from the ideal opening to my long and extremely happy association with Middlesex County Cricket Club.

The trial went well enough, despite a couple of my future team-mates thinking that I showed more promise with my left-arm seamers than my nervy batting. Well enough, in fact, for 'Gunner', the appropriate nickname for Ian Gould, the second-team coach who had once played in goal for Arsenal, to promise that he and Don Bennett, the club's first-team coach, would come and watch me play for Oxfordshire Under-19s against Middlesex Under-19s the following week.

'Then,' he said, 'we will take things from there . . .'

It was hardly a ringing endorsement of my play in the nets, but he hadn't dismissed me out of hand.

Amazingly, little more than three weeks later I found myself in conversation with Ian Gould at Harrow CC. I had just completed my 2nd XI Championship debut, scoring 98 in the second innings, before succumbing to nerves and running myself out. In addition, I had blazed the Middlesex Under-19s attack all over the park for a run-a-ball 84 for Oxfordshire Under-19s and had also impressed in my limited-overs 2nd XI debut, scoring 64 against a strong Warwickshire team that included Paul Smith, one of the important cogs in their successful Championship-winning team, as well as Darren

Altree, who was generally regarded as the quickest second-team bowler around.

'Straussy,' he said with a rare smile on his face, 'I have just spoken to Don Bennett and we have decided to offer you a two-year summer contract. If I was you, I would go down the rub-a-dub-dub and get completely rat-arsed!'

I followed his advice, and despite waking up the next morning with a thumping head to go along with tired muscles that were unused to fielding for a full day, I felt on top of the world. I was now a professional sportsman. It was something that I had always dreamed of being. I was going to get the opportunity to test my skills against the best cricketers in the country. I was going to travel around and play on the country's most hallowed grounds. And more importantly, I was going to get paid for doing it. In addition, I now qualified for those shiny white tracksuits that all my new team-mates were wearing, emblazoned with Hill Samuel Asset Management, the Middlesex sponsors. I could also help myself to brand-new Nike cricket boots and trainers. I was no longer the outsider. I belonged.

Unfortunately, there was one small problem with this potential sportsman's paradise. In short, I had all the gear and no idea. The end of the summer meant a return to Durham University for my second year, and as lovely as it was to be able to tell my team-mates that I was now a professional cricketer, I didn't have the first idea about what that actually meant. As far as I was concerned, all I had to do was turn up and play, and my natural ability and cool temperament would see that I was successful. After all, it had worked in my trial matches.

Anyway, there was so much other stuff to do at university. I was still playing rugby and looked as if I might make the 1st XV that year, and I was still jumping headlong into the obvious student pitfall of sampling the delights of north-eastern night-life. For some unknown reason, I had also managed to get sucked into smoking excessively, and it was only a massive asthma attack towards the end of my time at university that prompted me to kick my twenty-a-day habit. Somewhere near the back of my priorities lay my economics degree, with its ludicrously lax demands on my time of eight hours a week in lectures. There didn't seem to be any time left for training and over the long, cold winter, as my mental discipline drained away, my waistline expanded accordingly.

'---- me, you look like the Michelin man,' said Ian Gould as I returned to Middlesex, in July 1997, after a disappointing second season with Durham University. 'Seems to me you've been enjoying that student lifestyle a bit too much. Well, we are about to find out if you have been doing any work. Go and join the lads. We're doing a sprint session.'

Suddenly I felt very nervous, in the same way as someone who turns up at an exam knowing that they haven't revised for it. How was I going to hide the fact that I was incredibly unfit? Would my natural athleticism somehow get me through?

I got the answer to that question at the end of the third set of shuttles. Straining to make sure I wasn't lagging too far behind my team-mates, I pushed myself too hard and, snap, I felt my hamstring go. It is to this day the only time I have had a muscle injury. As I was writhing around on the floor in pain, Gould's face appeared in my blurred vision.

'Just what I thought, you lazy -------.'

I spent five weeks recuperating, but for the rest of the season I was public enemy number one at Middlesex. Everyone seemed to have made up their mind that I was a waste of time. I could do nothing right. My only source of solace came from Ben Hutton, my best mate from school, who Middlesex had picked up on a summer contract earlier in the year. Unfortunately for him, he was tainted by the association and both of us were seen as outcasts: public school-educated softies in a world operated by hard, working-class cricket professionals.

Cricketers have an amazing ability to forgive character flaws (or fitness flaws, for that matter) as long as you go out there and perform. Unfortunately for me, my confidence had taken such a dent from being vilified by my coach and team-mates that scoring runs became next to impossible. I didn't know how to play decent spin bowling, having never really had to face it before, and even my normally strong back-foot game was starting to let me down.

My nadir came in the last game of the season, against Somerset. Among their ranks was a Dutch cricketer by the name of Andre van Troost. He was commonly thought of as the quickest bowler in county cricket, but his pace was in no way matched by accuracy. He was famed for bowling beamers, bouncers, no-balls and wides. Normally you would get a combination of all the above in every over he bowled.

Gunner, in an attempt to, on the one hand, give us the benefit of his considerable experience and, on the other, frighten the life out of us, brought us all together before the toss.

'Van Troost is playing, lads. I have one bit of advice for you. Don't try and hook him. He is too quick, and you will either end up in Taunton infirmary or back in the hut. Leave him well and see him off.'

You can imagine the look on Gunner's face as I trudged back to the pavilion after yet another single-figure score. You guessed it, I had hooked Van Troost with all my might, only to see the ball balloon pathetically to the square-leg fielder. I sat in my corner of the dressing room, hiding my head in my hands. Over the season I had averaged an embarrassingly disappointing 13 with the bat. I had no confidence in myself. I was a broken man.

Barely twelve months on from the joy and exhilaration of becoming a professional sportsman, I was suddenly at a crossroads. I had one year to go on my contract, but if the next twelve months resembled the last in any way, I was toast. For the first time in my life the prospect of failure stared me straight between the eyes, and I didn't like it. There was only one way to go. Somehow I had to become a professional sportsman.

When I look back, I was actually very lucky that the MCC had finally given the go-ahead for six university centres of excellence to be established in order to encourage ambitious young cricketers to finish their studies before committing to the game. Graeme Fowler, the ex Lancashire and England opening batsman, was appointed director of the Durham UCCE.

Paul Winsper (who went on to become fitness coach for Newcastle United) was brought in to give us conditioning advice and we were also given access to psychologists and physios.

Overnight, the Durham University CC had gone from a ramshackle organisation of talented students – one of whom had the unenviable task of captaining, coordinating practices and getting people to turn up to matches on time – to a highly professional set-up. It was just what I needed and, after my repeated failures the previous season, I didn't have to be asked twice about my commitment.

I gave up rugby, got a gym membership and, for the first time in my life, started to put in some serious work. It was all a bit of a struggle, given that I had my final exams to prepare for, but I soon realised that there were actually a lot more hours in the day if I could break the habit of setting my alarm to wake me just in time for the lunchtime edition of *Neighbours*.

I became something of a sponge, listening to Graeme Fowler recounting his days of fending off the mighty West Indians and playing alongside Wasim Akram, and I also started practising properly. Rather than just having a hit and a giggle in the nets, I started treating them as opportunities to hone my game and make progress. Much of this change of focus was probably lost on my team-mates at Durham, who had long since come to the opinion that I was a bit of a joke, more a figure of fun than a potential England cricketer. More importantly, though, I was beginning to look in the mirror and see more mental steel to go with a stronger and healthier body.

* * *

My return to Middlesex in the summer of 1998 was not accompanied by any of the doubt that had consumed me the previous year. I knew that I was well prepared, I knew that I had improved immeasurably as a player and I had also now completed my studies. My 2.1 in economics was in many ways a gold-plated invitation to join one of the financial powerhouses in the City, but for me it was nothing more than a safety net that I had no intention of using.

I was determined – more determined than ever – that I was going to make a success of being a professional cricketer.

Needless to say, with that sort of attitude and confidence, things changed dramatically. I seemed to get runs every time I played for the second team (although getting hundreds was proving a little difficult), and I was enjoying just as much showing off my new-found physical prowess to the rest of the lads. Amazingly, I had gone from being surprised and intimidated by the fitness of county cricketers, to being surprised and disappointed by how unfit they all were in the space of twelve months. I was now one of the fit ones, and as such I was a little frowned upon by those who were likely to be shown up in the communal sessions.

As is often the case in cricket, things moved more quickly and more dramatically than I expected. By July, my name was mentioned as being the next in line if a position became available in the first team, and by August David Nash, one of the talented prodigies and a great mate of mine, was sent back to the second team and I took his place.

Not for the first or last time in my life, the opportunity to show that I could prosper at a higher level brought out the best in me.

The innings I played against a decent Hampshire attack that included Nixon McLean, a highly talented and frighteningly quick West Indian fast bowler, still goes down as one of my finest. I remember hardly playing a false stroke, and I was surprised and astounded when I was out to a freakish catch at third slip for 83. They were my first runs in first-class cricket, and from that moment on I knew that I could make a career as a cricketer.

There were to be no other great successes in the last couple of games of the season, but by the time the nights started drawing in and the sporting public's attention turned towards the football season, I was preparing to take on another great challenge: going out to Australia to play cricket.

Throughout the season I had been making arrangements with Luke Sutton, one of my mates from university who was making decent progress at Somerset as a keeper/batter, to spend the winter out in Sydney playing Grade cricket. For me it promised to be a great adventure. At the age of twenty-one, it would be my first chance to travel independently, having missed out on the fabled gap-year that many students embark upon to learn about the world (and women and alcohol) before starting their studies. I would also be able to play cricket in a great climate and hone my skills. All in all, the prospect sounded like a dream come true. The reality, as always, was slightly different.

In 1998, an Englishman arriving at Sydney Airport with a cricket bag on a trolley was a common and amusing sight for the locals. Just as promising young actors are drawn to the bright lights of Los Angeles to find fame and fortune in Hollywood, so cricketers by the bucketload were making their way to Australia, all intent on making their mark in the toughest cricketing environment of all.

In some ways, it was a little like being part of the gold rush that brought so many people to Australia in the nineteenth century. I was aware that most Pommie cricketers came back broken men, using excuses like 'the wickets do too much' or 'you don't play enough to get in decent nick' to justify the embarrassment of being a professional player but not outperforming the plumber who opened the batting with them. Some, however, did manage to make their mark and the gold dust they received came in the form of either hard-earned Aussie respect or invaluable experience of what it takes to perform in Australia. Just as important, it seems to me now, and far less recognised, was the challenge of having to fend for yourself, earn some money, meet new people and deal with the abrasive Australian style.

I was up for the challenge, though. My club side was going to be Sydney University. In some ways it was an atypical Grade club, as many of the players were students and so there was a far higher turnover of players than in most. Also, the club didn't have much money and had no rich benefactor to attract big-name state players, so it had to rely on finding young talent and then nurturing and developing that talent.

All in all, it sounded like the perfect place for an ambitious English first-class cricketer. The fact that I had made my first-class debut prior to arriving meant that I walked about with a little more swagger than before. I was young, but I reckoned I had already proved myself in the world of professional cricket. I was sure that my team-mates and the coaches would be duly impressed.

Well, they were so impressed that on the first weekend I was selected for the 3rd XI. Here I was, a professional player who a couple of months earlier had been spanking a West Indian international bowler around in a first-class game, playing for a club third team in Sydney.

The one Englishman in the club, a teacher by the name of Tim Lester, assured me that they always did this with the new players. It allowed you to find your feet, get over jet lag and ease yourself into the Aussie way of playing the game. I, however, was less than impressed and thankfully showed my displeasure by scoring a hundred on the first Saturday.

I enjoyed the Aussie attitude to cricket. They definitely did not rate anyone in other teams, and that view was particularly pronounced when there was a Pom in the opposition ranks. Their default position was that they were better than everyone else, and every Saturday they would go out there eager to prove their superiority. They played an ego-driven form of the game, in which admitting to weakness was akin to admitting to having an affair with your brother's wife. It just wasn't on. That attitude allowed people to go out and play outrageous innings, whacking it from the first ball, or, in the case of one player from Bankstown, taking on Brett Lee without a helmet. The country was renowned for having the best players, the best structure and the best coaches in the world, and by God did they know it.

All of this was in marked contrast to England, where players were always wary of saying anything that might be regarded as tempting fate. If a player in England said something about an opposition bowler being poor or slow or not being able to turn the ball, he would be shot down in flames by irate team-mates: 'Don't mess with the cricketing gods, mate. He's bound to get you out tomorrow.'

Similarly, in England there was far more respect for other teams. If you were a first-class cricketer, you had earned your stripes, you were part of a fraternity and would be accorded respect. International players were put on a pedestal, as though they were the equivalent of cricketing deities. Players would invariably scour the opposition team news on Ceefax, hoping that their star bowler was injured, otherwise the likes of Glenn McGrath or Courtney Walsh were bound to win the game for the other side. 'Oh no, we've got Warney next week for Hampshire. I'd better get a few this week' was a typical county cricketer's comment.

Within a few weeks of being in Australia, and throughout the three winters I spent there, it was apparent why English players tended to struggle in that environment. It was genuinely uncomfortable. If you were a Pommie professional player, you would have a bounty on your head. Fielders who had appeared semiconscious in the blazingly hot southern-hemisphere sun would suddenly spring to life as you walked out, in the same way as a lion gains enormous energy at the sight of a wounded antelope limping around. Bowlers would be desperate not only to get you out, but also to humiliate you in the process.

I still remember one of my team-mates in my second year

in Australia stopping the whole game when a young Glamorgan player arrived at the crease. He walked towards his potential prey, stood about halfway down the wicket and addressed not just the player, but everyone on the pitch.

'Listen here, Pom,' he said. 'I know you are shit, you know you are shit and so does everyone else. Look me in the eye when I tell you that I will get you out first ball.' He then proceeded to walk backwards back to his mark, continuously mouthing, 'I will get you out first ball.'

The umpires seemed more amused than anyone else about this bit of on-field theatre and were not in the least bit inclined to bring it to an end. Unfortunately, as if it had been pre-ordained, the young Glamorgan player duly obliged, getting out lbw, much to the delight of my team-mates and the umpire, who gave the decision with a smirk on his face. So the image of English players being soft, overrated and overpaid was reinforced, and it made it more and more difficult for the next piece of prey that they came across.

I was hardly immune from all of this. My season never really got going. I was promoted to the second team for a few games, not impressing all that much, but I also knew that my route to the first team was blocked by Jimmy Ormond, the bulky Leicestershire opening bowler, who was doing moderately well for the side. With only one overseas player allowed in each team, I understood that my first season was more about watching, learning and hopefully impressing enough to be thought of as a potential first-team player for the following year.

Everything was turned upside down, however, when I was dropped back into the third team to accommodate a player who had come back from injury. I still proudly thought of myself as a solid first-class opening batsman, and it was just too much of an affront to my ego. When insult was added to injury and my subsequent hundred was not deemed good enough to warrant an elevation back to the second team, I finally threw the toys out of the pram. I declared myself unavailable, had a huge row with the coach and walked out of the club.

When I look back on it now, I am still embarrassed that I took that action. It made no sense. I was out there to learn about Australian cricket, and here I was declining to play. God knows what the powers that be back at Middlesex thought of it.

At the time, though, my priorities were elsewhere. On a random Sunday night out in the run-in to Christmas, I had met a beautiful Australian actress called Ruth McDonald. She was a little older than me, much more worldly and most of all great company. In true Australian style, she called a spade a spade and I was enjoying the idea of walking along Bondi Beach with her on a Saturday far more than getting abused out in the middle. The last three months of my stay were spent almost entirely in her company.

Being an actress, she had plenty of days when she wasn't doing much, and although I had to do a bit of coaching now and then to supplement my meagre savings, most of my time was also free. We explored Sydney, sunbathed constantly on beaches up and down the eastern suburbs, ate loads of ice cream and watched movies and talked in the evenings. I had just about enough time left in the day to squeeze in a bit of fitness work and the odd net session with a few of the other English pros, but my focus was on Ruth, and it was probably one of my better decisions.

I don't think that you can overestimate the role that is played by the partner of a professional sportsman. In Ruth's case, over my career she has had to deal with all sorts of emotions. Sometimes I would come back from a ground completely uncommunicative, despairing at a lost match or a low score. At other times, I would be full of the joys of spring, content with my standing in the world, deeply satisfied about my performance. Mostly, I was riding somewhere in between, giving little away about my state of mind. Ruth, therefore, always had to tread carefully around me during a game. She has been exceptional in that regard. Conscious of my feelings and mindful of my focus, she has brought up two boys mainly single-handedly and has always been there to support me. She is truly a remarkable woman.

My relationship with Ruth also ensured that I returned to Sydney for the next two winters, plying my trade for Mosman, a rival Grade club situated in the affluent suburbs of the North Shore of Sydney. Over the course of my time there, I did manage to play and stay in the first team. I wasn't particularly successful, and there were plenty at the club and elsewhere who thought I was just another of the stereotypical English players, but I did at least show glimpses of my potential, scoring some important runs on occasion. The Aussies also liked my pugnacious back-foot game, the one area where I really felt I could dominate most Aussie club bowlers, who loved nothing more than sending down bouncer barrages as a means of intimidation.

My winters in Australia taught me a huge amount about the game, about different styles of play and conditions. They also taught me about the Australian people. I learnt what made them tick, what they respected and where they were potentially vulnerable. Above all, though, I met some great people, many of whom are still friends to this day.

While I was slowly making my mark as a player, Middlesex was going through a very public and very painful transformation. When I had first stumbled through that dressing-room door in 1996, the club was still living healthily off its reputation as one of the heavyweights of the English game. The Championship had last been won in 1993, but the players still had the mindset and belief that further success was close at hand. Very soon, however, confidence, that fragile intangible that is so hard to gain but so easy to lose, had vanished, and with it went Middlesex's chances of continuing their successful dynasty.

What went wrong? Well, as is so often the case, it all started with a change of leadership. Don Bennett, the outstandingly successful and astute coach, retired at the end of the 1997 season. He had spent twenty-nine years as a coach and was fully deserving of his extra time on the golf course. Under his tenure the club had won seven Championships (one shared), as well as the Gillette Cup (four times), the Benson & Hedges Cup (twice) and the Sunday League.

My only real involvement with him came towards the end of my first season with the club, in 1997. I turned up at the ground to be twelfth man for a first-team one-day game and was fully enjoying the sight of Mark Ramprakash in full flow. Suddenly my admiration was interrupted by a tap on my shoulder. I looked up to see Don, who had a well-deserved reputation as a tough old-school coach who had dealt with everyone from Phil Edmonds to Phil Tufnell and been respected by them all.

'There's no point in you sitting there daydreaming,' he said. 'I'm going down to the nets. Get your gear on. I'll send down a few throw-downs and have a look at you.'

Eager to impress, I raced off to my black Ford Fiesta, lovingly referred to as the milk float by my team-mates, who couldn't understand why anyone would have an automatic car with a 1.1 litre engine. I opened the boot to get out my kit, only to find it horrifyingly empty. I had left my kit by the door of my flat.

As I arrived at the nets, Don was already looking slightly irritated by the length of time it had taken me to get there, and his irritation was about to up a notch or two.

'Sorry, coach,' I mumbled. 'I don't have my kit here. I left it at home. I could do some bowling instead if you like,' I added hopefully.

'Bowling? You must be kidding me. You really are the useless public school ----- that Gunner said you were.' With that he turned his back on me and headed off to the pavilion.

Don's retirement represented a seismic change for the club. That was matched, and probably even surpassed, by Mike

Gatting's decision to stand down as club captain. By this time he was forty years of age and had been at the helm for fourteen years, having had the unenviable job of taking over the reins from Mike Brearley. Although he had been incredibly successful, and was very much part of the furniture of the club, there was a feeling that he had done his time and that Mark Ramprakash would benefit from the extra responsibility of leading the side.

This precipitated a depressingly unsettling period of pass-the-parcel with the twin jobs of coach and captain. From the end of the 1997 to halfway through the 2002 season we had four captains (Ramprakash, Justin Langer, Angus Fraser and myself), complemented by three coaches (John Buchanan, Mike Gatting and John Emburey). It was not the sort of stability to ensure any type of success on the pitch, and inevitably it didn't.

What caused this period of upheaval at the club is a moot point. Did the on-field performances fall away so far that the coach and captain had to go? Or did the lack of stability lead to the poor performances? My gut feeling was that it was a combination of both, but if the club had stuck for longer with Don's replacement, John Buchanan, we might have avoided the downward spiral.

Buchanan arrived at Middlesex with a reputation as an enlightened, new-age coach. He was among the first to use analysis and take lessons learnt from business to push players forward, and he had been immensely successful with Queensland in the Sheffield Shield competition. Looking back, probably even he would admit that he tried to change things too quickly and too dramatically at the club, but his efforts to break down the club hierarchy, encouraging all the players to use the same dressing room and doing away with single rooms for senior players during away matches, caused resentment straight away.

In the same way as Kevin Pietersen and Peter Moores would later never see eye to eye, Buchanan and Ramprakash never seemed to get close to singing off the same song sheet. Ramprakash had the support of several unhappy senior players, and Buchanan was bundled off back to Australia after only one unsuccessful season.

To me, it was a missed opportunity. Here was a man who had the ability and qualifications to revolutionise the club, but instead the administrators at Middlesex, perhaps worried about unsettling the senior players, opted to stick to the old ways. Barely a year after his retirement from playing, Mike Gatting was brought back as coach, an appointment that ultimately did not succeed in either improving performances or keeping the team happy.

As a young player, you are not really aware of the politics of the club. You are striving to make a name for yourself, and your opinion is neither warranted nor required when it comes to the weightier matters surrounding the game. I am thankful, therefore, that I never became embroiled in the agendas and manoeuvring that some of my more established colleagues had to face. Instead, I tried to learn from whoever was coaching at any given time.

Mike Gatting was fantastic with me. He helped me transform my game, always imploring me to 'Get back and across, and hit the ball back from where it has come from.' I think he enjoyed my boyish enthusiasm and saw me and Ben Hutton, my best mate, as potentially the next lynchpins of the Middlesex batting line-up in future years.

Others, who had perhaps spent too much time with Mike Gatting the player, found it hard to take orders from someone who had been a team-mate so recently. Gatt probably didn't do himself many favours by allowing himself to be laughed at for various comedic moments. The most notable came when he conducted a meeting about one-day tactics dressed in nothing but a towel, spending the majority of the session shovelling an incredible Gatt-style portion of spaghetti bolognaise down his throat. Ultimately, though, he was just being himself, and the club should have known what type of coach he was likely to be.

One leader that I count myself very fortunate to have worked with during this time was our Australian import, Justin Langer.

Somewhat strangely, in 1999, once I had established myself in the side to the degree that I was accorded the privilege of choosing a seat in the dressing room, I found that the only place left was next to Justin Langer, right in the corner. It was one of the marquee seats, usually only available to those who had spent years 'doing their time' in the first-class game. I couldn't understand why no one wanted to sit there. Here I was, sitting next to a successful international left-hander, who was passionate, committed and eager to help out youngsters. This was like manna from heaven.

It was only when I spent my first game in my new position that I understood my team-mates' reluctance. As soon as Langer was dismissed just before tea, I noticed players scurrying out of the dressing room at an alarming rate. I was sitting comfortably in my seat, reading the paper, having been dismissed much earlier in the day, and saw no real need to move.

A little tension rose inside me as I heard Langer swearing to himself on the way up the stairs that led to the dressing room, but I understood the convention by which players who had just got out had the right to vent a little anger for a minute or two, before calming down and rejoining the rest of players, who were watching the game, reading magazines or playing cards.

As the door slammed open, I watched in bewilderment as the Aussie left-hander stormed through, looking like someone who had exceeded a safe dose of steroids. He swore loudly as he stalked around the room. On eyeing a delicious array of cakes, lovingly prepared by the kitchen staff as a special treat for the tea break, he picked up the tray and smashed it down as hard as he could into a nearby rubbish bin. 'We don't -------deserve these cakes. We are ----,' he shouted at the top of his voice while the cakes flew in all directions.

Shortly afterwards, I displayed far better reflexes than I had earlier in the day, out in the middle, and narrowly avoided being hit by his helmet, which was flung from the other side of the dressing room, roughly in the direction of his place in the corner. It was soon joined by his bat, his pads and his thigh pad, before Langer stormed out of the dressing room, heading for the makeshift gym in the physio room to punish himself for his indiscretions.

It was a baptism of fire, and I would never again make the mistake of staying in the room when he was dismissed. In less volatile moments, I came to admire, respect and immensely like this gritty little fighter from Western Australia. He was passionate, he was driven, he hated the lazy, in-your-comfort-zone attitude displayed by so many county cricketers. He demanded hard work and commitment and then went about setting the right example. Perhaps he was a little intense, and maybe it scared some of the players enough for it to affect their performances, but I couldn't help but be impressed by his attitude.

It was also scarcely believable that he was prepared to spend his rare days off, away from his wife and young daughters, feeding balls into the bowling machine for myself and Ben Hutton. He was desperate to succeed as a Middlesex captain and would stop at nothing to achieve that aim. If that meant trying as hard as possible to hone the techniques of two talented but extremely inconsistent youngsters on his day off, then so be it. The fact that he was ultimately unsuccessful in his aim had as much to do with the prevailing culture at the club, which tended to shun hard work and commitment in favour of nights out, alcohol and not being seen to try too hard, as it did with Langer's methods.

By the beginning of the 2001 season, both Langer and Mark Ramprakash, his predecessor as captain, had left the club, leaving a huge hole in terms of run-making and experience. The daunting task of captaining a side which had been rooted to the bottom of the table the previous season, and without its only two consistent batsmen, had been assigned to Angus

Fraser, the highly popular ex-England medium-pacer, who was very much in the autumn of his career.

Gus was a Middlesex legend. No one had ever questioned his commitment, and even though he was renowned for being grumpy, he was well respected by team-mates and opposition alike. He also sowed the seeds of a Middlesex revival and in doing so showed me what leadership was really about.

Although he was not quite the bowler he once was, he was able to lead by example because he was so passionate about the club. For him, wearing the three sea axes of Middlesex was just as important as brandishing the three lions of England. Where he really excelled, though, was in his empathy with the other players. He genuinely cared about those who were playing under him. He was interested in them as people and not just as commodities that could be traded depending on their output. After the poor returns of the previous few seasons, he wanted to make people proud to be playing for the county again and to foster a happy dressing room.

He cared enough, however, not to be frightened to have the difficult conversations, or to remind people when they didn't perform to the expected standards. All in all he was, and still is, a tremendous example of what a professional cricketer should be like. Unfortunately his tenure was cut short by an opportunity to take over the cricket correspondent's job at the *Independent*, but he has always been a great source of help and advice to me, whether at Middlesex or as I made my way into the England ranks. It is no surprise to me that he has done so well in his new role as Middlesex Managing Director of Cricket.

Angus Fraser's departure meant that a successor was required to captain the club. The decision faced by the committee at Middlesex was far from simple. On the one hand they had a couple of seasoned veterans, no doubt keen to fulfil one last challenge in their careers, in the form of Paul Weekes and Phil Tufnell (OK, Tuffers probably wasn't exactly the type to captain the club). On the other hand, there was the young, ambitious, slightly naive vice-captain, who had only been in the side for a couple of seasons.

I was twenty-four years old, barely established in the side and had no real experience of captaining any team since school. Looking back, it was quite a risk on the part of the club, and I was blissfully unaware of quite how unprepared I was to take on the job, but in June 2002 I was appointed Middlesex captain.

3

A TASTE OF CAPTAINCY

I am dripping in sweat. The notorious Monday-morning preseason fitness session has just finished. Today we were put through our paces in my least favourite exercises. The instructors call them SAQs (short for speed, agility, quickness), but what they really are is a number of sets of gruelling shuttle runs. They vary in distance, but there is very little rest in between and the constant changing of direction has given me sizable blisters on the balls of my feet.

Usually, around this time, the endorphins start pumping through the body and the warm afterglow of knowing you have put 'gas in the tank', to be used later in the season, kicks in. Today, however, I am feeling frustrated and angry. The source of my displeasure is not my performance in the session, nor for that matter my team-mates, all of whom are looking fit and eager for the season to begin. No, the real problem I have is that Phil Tufnell, our most experienced player, has called in sick for the third Monday in a row.

No one has ever mistaken Tuffers for a fitness freak, and at the age of thirty-seven the thought of running up and down a sports hall in Finchley is unlikely to motivate him to get his ageing bones out of bed. The problem for me, though, is that everyone has noticed him not being there. The trainers are concerned that he is likely to risk injury if he is not fit enough at the start of the season. The players are all rolling their eyes, shaking their heads and muttering comments like 'He is taking the ----.'

Captaining Middlesex for the first full season, I am not only keen that the players should be fitter than ever, but also that everyone should be treated equally. If you treat some people as if they are special or different, you are sowing the seeds of your own downfall.

Faced with this unsavoury situation, there is only one course of action available to me. I decide to bypass the offer of the coach, John Emburey, to give Phil a buzz, as I feel it will be more powerful if it comes from me.

I pick up the phone.

"Allo,' comes the weary and slightly irritated voice of Phil Tufnell. 'Who is this?'

'Tuffers, it's Straussy here, mate. I'm ringing to find out why you weren't at training this morning,' I say, trying to keep calm but sound sufficiently annoyed at the same time.

'I'm not feeling well,' he replies in a completely unconvincing manner, as though we both know that it isn't the reason for his non-appearance.

'Well, mate, it looks like too much of a coincidence to me. Listen, I desperately want the team to move forward, and getting fit and doing the hard yards together is an important part of that. I understand that you are never going to be the fittest on the staff, and I also understand that this is probably the last thing you feel like doing at the moment. We need you to be here, though, even if you aren't going to be at the front of the pack.'

I begin to gain a little confidence, the more I speak.

'It is really important,' I go on, 'that the younger players under-stand and realise that everyone is in this together, and if you aren't here, then it is impossible for us to do that.'

There is a pause at the other end of the line, as if he is taking it all in. I am curious to see how he is going to answer.

'---- off, Straussy,' comes the response, and with that the phone goes dead.

Welcome to the joys of captaining Middlesex at that time.

The reason for including this story in the book is not to settle a score with Tufnell. I knew him well enough by then almost to expect the reply I got. Tuffers had challenged all the captains he had played under. He certainly didn't respond well to authority, and successive captains, from Gatting all the way through to Fraser, had made their minds up that the on-field performances just about made up for the odd bit of hassle you had to deal with along the way. Also, it had to be said that Tufnell could be genuinely brilliant in the dressing room. He was interesting and funny, the sort of guy that team-mates loved having a bit of banter with, and when bowling, in partic-ular, he had a surprising amount of passion in his performance.

Shortly after this episode, and thankfully before things really came to a head, Tuffers got the infamous call from the producers of *I'm a Celebrity, Get Me Out of Here*. It was an offer he couldn't refuse, knowing full well that his cricketing career was almost over, and he made the wise and merciful call that he was, indeed, a celebrity and that he should get out of the Middlesex dressing room just before the 2003 season started. It proved a smart move on his part, allowing him to go on to a very successful career in the media.

What the story illustrates, though, is quite how difficult it can be for a twenty-four-year-old, whose credentials for the job are shaky to say the least, to establish himself as a leader.

Looking back, I probably relied too much on John Emburey early in my tenure. Embers is truly one of the best people I have ever met in cricket. He is kind and generous, and hardly anyone I have met has a bad word to say about him. I like him immensely. However, his philosophy on the game was formed through watching and playing in the incredibly successful Middlesex sides of the 1970s and 1980s. He was generally suspicious of newfangled ways and tended to take comfort in old-school values and traditions. I, on the other hand, had seen Australia get to the top of the world rankings and stay there. My time playing Grade cricket had affected my thoughts and I was certain that we had to do things differently and drag the club forward. I liked the idea of Middlesex leading the way in innovation, with other coaches looking at us, nodding their heads and scribbling notes to remind them of our well-thought-out way of going about things. Embers and I were probably never destined to be the most natural of bedfellows. Deep down our philosophies were too different. Also, I have to admit that although I had a strong idea of *where* I wanted to get to, I was far less clear about *how* to go about it.

If you throw into the mix the disparate group of players we had at our disposal, the situation became even more

My parents, David and Dawn, celebrating New Year in 1984.

Going on a hike with my dad in 1982.

My sisters, Colleen, Gillian and Sandra, looking after their little brother in 1980.

Left: Not content with his son playing Aussie Rules football, my rugby-mad father enrolled me at Waverley Harlequins rugby club in Melbourne.

Above: Exploring the Australian bush with my friend Christopher in 1985.

Below: Receiving a trophy for winning a sevens tournament with Caldicott prep school. Rugby was definitely the school's priority.

Every sport was catered for at Caldicott. Here I am in the tennis team.

Caldicott 1st XI in my final year. My first taste of captaincy was a good one.

With my rugby coach, Richard Greed, in my final year at Radley College. He succeeded ex-Wasps and England player Steve Bates in 1995.

Playing fly-half for Durham University. I was forced to give up the game in 1998 as my cricket became more serious.

My last day at Radley, in the summer of 1995.

Graduating from Durham University in 1998 alongside Luke Sutton, with whom I travelled to Australia the following winter. He went on to have a successful career at Somerset and Derbyshire.

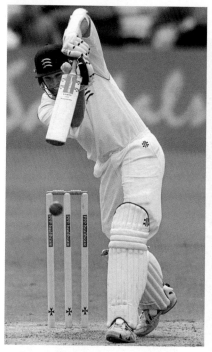

Making my way at Middlesex. My early efforts were not always successful.

Ben Hutton, my great mate from school, university and Middlesex. He was also best man at my wedding.

Justin Langer captaining Middlesex in 2000. A great influence on me and an excellent left-handed opener.

John Emburey, Middlesex coach during my captaincy stint. The county was going through difficult times.

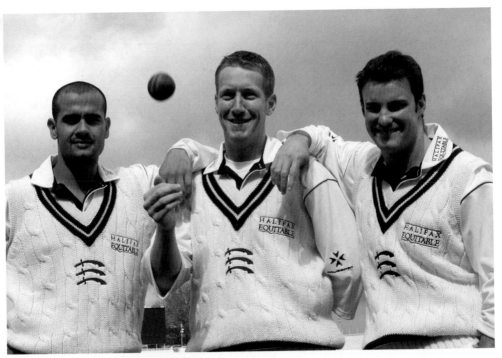

Owais Shah, Tim Bloomfield and myself at the start of the 2001 season.

I learnt a huge amount about captaincy at Middlesex, although captaining Phil Tufnell was not always easy!

My wedding day, 18 October 2003. Ruth has been a pillar of support, for both me and the kids.

complicated. Our two nominated overseas players, Joe Dawes and Ashley Noffke, were steeped in the Queensland way of doing things, and both felt that the club had to drag itself into the twenty-first century. Many of the older players in the club, however, were less convinced of the need to move away from what we had always done, despite the lack of success in recent years. Caught between these conflicting groups were plenty of young, impressionable players who were just looking for a sense of direction.

Nothing was simple, and in those days I probably didn't have the skills or the ideas to make things happen. It was a stressful period. There was so much to learn in a short space of time: man-management, tactics, how to give an inspiring talk in public, how to deal with your own time. I had no training in any of these things and unsurprisingly I didn't get it all right.

One of the more intriguing aspects of the job was enduring the monthly Cricket Committee meeting. Beforehand, John Emburey and I would meet to prepare a report into how the side were doing and to outline our plans for the coming month. John would then present the report at the meeting and we would have to answer questions from an array of past players or interested members. The ages of the committee members ranged from forty-five to ninety, although unsurprisingly there was a strong majority of the older, retired brigade.

Discussion usually drifted away from questions about what was going on with the side to lectures about how we ought to play, followed by nostalgic reminiscences about how good the game used to be. On more than one occasion I was dumbfounded when committee members decided that the reason for all our ills was either that we used helmets (which meant that we 'neglected to watch the ball closely enough') or that we were playing on covered wickets (which meant that our techniques were 'not up to scratch'). I understood that the members were trying to help and were passionate about the club, but the notion that we were somehow going to win the Championship by discarding our helmets or lobbying the ECB to bring back uncovered wickets was absurd.

I came out of those meetings feeling as if I had just lost two hours of my life for no reason, and I am delighted that the club has now moved away from the committee system, which was antiquated and past its sell-by date to say the least, to a more dynamic executive board structure, in which the Director of Cricket is given free rein but is accountable for his performance.

All in all, it was a steep learning curve, which served me extremely well in the years to come. In fact, if there was one experience that I had in county cricket that prepared me for Test cricket more than any other, it was captaining Middlesex. I had to learn to deal with distractions; I had to learn to speak coherently; I had to learn to think about the game in a different way; and I had to learn to understand that my team-mates were all different and treat them accordingly. In short, I had to grow up.

That is not to say that times were all bad. For the most part, we got on very well. Our wives and girlfriends all became good friends and would regularly come to Lord's to support us while we plied our trade on the field and then meet us in the Tavern after the game. We were becoming a family again and our performances on the pitch were promising. In 2002 we managed to achieve promotion into the first division for the first time since the two divisions had been introduced. We would also manage to avoid relegation in 2003, finishing sixth, and thus on the surface at least things were going in the right direction.

People unaware of what was going on behind the scenes would no doubt have described my captaincy as 'leading from the front'. Over the two seasons, I scored over 2,700 runs, showing that my game was developing and also that the captaincy was not weighing me down too much. In this I was helped by some remarkably consistent performances from a number of other batsmen at the club. Sven Koenig had come in from the highveld of Gauteng and taken to English cricket like a duck to water. Ed Joyce was beginning to make waves as an elegant, Gower-esque left-hander, and the likes of Owais Shah, Ben Hutton and David Nash were all contributing on a regular basis.

Our bowling, though, was far more of a concern. Angus Fraser and Phil Tufnell had both left big boots to fill, and our young bowlers were struggling to make inroads on flat Lord's wickets. We drew far too many games as we weren't able to force results and, looking back now, some of my tactics, such as bowling wide of off stump to 7–2 fields, were never likely to yield great results.

More than our inability to take wickets, however, I was increasingly irked by the *way* we were going about our business. By the end of the 2003 season, I knew deep down that if Middlesex wanted to start challenging consistently at the top of the first division, then we had to make some difficult changes. It was not a task that I was particularly relishing, as it would no doubt knock a few noses out of joint, but I was determined that over the winter we would take the necessary steps.

In the space of a few short months, however, my life was about to change.

4
ONE GLORIOUS DAY IN MAY

*My heart is beating too fast. I am struggling to subdue the rapidly
rising feeling of panic. Desperately trying to keep myself in check,
I repeat to myself quietly, 'Think of the process, Strauss, think of
the process.'*

*I am shadow-batting now, going through the complete array of
shots. Forward defence is quickly followed by a cut shot, then a
pull. All the time my feet are bouncing up and down, like a boxer
prancing around the ring. I feel the adrenalin running through
my veins. I am alert and alive. I vaguely remember a sports
psychologist saying that 'nerves should be welcomed; they are your
body's way of telling you that you are ready.'*

*Well, if that is the case, then I am definitely ready. I am more
than ready. I play a couple of imaginary leg glances, while at the
same time taking some deep breaths. My team-mates, with one
exception, are busy taking off their boots or changing into tracksuits. For the bowlers, in particular, their job is done. New Zealand
have been bowled out. It is time to relax.*

*I glance at Marcus Trescothick, my opening partner. He looks
tense. He is not moving around like I am, but rather sitting
down, staring into space, as though he is going through a mental
checklist. I know, having seen him on television many times, that*

he keeps his emotions in check. This is his way of preparing for battle.

Shortly there will be nowhere to hide. The warmth and comfort of the dressing room is about to be replaced by the cold, harsh reality of Test cricket. My mind wanders briefly. The question 'What will it be like out there?' drifts into my consciousness. I force myself not to think about it. I will find out soon enough.

I spent most of last night thinking about that very question. In between the tossing and turning, self-interrogations such as 'Am I really good enough for this?' and 'Am I going to be able to cope with the pressure?' constantly played out in my mind. I assured myself that I could deal with it all, but as the night wore on, my conviction diminished somewhat.

I continue to jump around, conscious now that some of my team-mates are looking in my direction. Players make judgements on their peers in many different ways and for many different reasons. They are looking at me, evaluating how calm and ready I look. If I fail, I know that there will be a dinnertime comment along the lines of 'He looked too pumped up before he went out. I knew he wasn't going to get any.' Again, I can't dwell on this sort of stuff now. I have to keep my mind on the job.

I hear the sound of a bell in the background. 'That's the worker, lads,' one of the bowlers calls out.

'The worker' refers to the bell that sounds in all grounds to tell players and umpires that the game is starting in five minutes. I look at Trescothick, he gives me a nod and we both start moving towards the dressing-room door – the same door that I nervously entered for the first time at Middlesex seven years previously.

'This is it,' I tell myself. 'This is what you have been waiting your whole life for.'

Marcus, adopting the role of the senior player, takes the lead down the stairs and into the Long Room. I am amazed by how little space there is. In county games, this area is usually sparsely populated – there may be ten or fifteen members on chairs, with copies of the Daily Telegraph open, settling in for a long day of snoozing and polite applause. Today it is different. I can't even see the seats. The room is packed with MCC members, all eager to see how England respond to New Zealand's first innings of 386. There is only a very narrow corridor for us to make our way towards the outfield. As we navigate through this walkway, I am acutely conscious of faces very close to mine, looking at me with a mixture of interest and passion.

'Come on England,' someone shouts on my left. 'Go for it, Strauss. You can do it,' comes another anonymous voice from somewhere behind me. I feel my emotions coming to the surface. The hairs on the back of my neck are standing up like rigid soldiers. This feels too intense. I have to keep calm.

We go through the pavilion door and down the steps. Now, for the first time, I feel the full force of the atmosphere of a packed Lord's cricket ground. A huge roar erupts as we walk onto the playing surface. The place feels electric.

I glance around at the stands. During a Middlesex game they are bleak and soulless – great big white elephants that can be intimidating. Now, though, they are alive. There are colours every-where. There are sounds, chants, smells. Although I have played here all my career, this is a different cricket ground.

We are halfway to the wicket now and gradually I am

beginning to calm down. This part of the ground is no different. The New Zealanders have just completed their pre-session huddle and are making their way to their fielding positions. Stephen Fleming, their inspirational captain, is in conversation with Daryl Tuffey, their barrel-chested opening bowler, who is about to send down the first over.

'Go well, mate,' Trescothick murmurs to me as he heads to the far end, where he is due to face the first ball. 'You too,' I mumble in reply.

Before I know it, the first ball has been bowled. Trescothick lets it go through to the keeper. Five balls later, the over is finished. It is a maiden. Now it is my turn.

'Two, please,' I call out to the umpire, with my bat held upright in front of middle and leg stump. I try to say it in as confident a way as possible.

'That's it,' returns the voice of Rudi Koertzen, the South African umpire.

I look around at the field that Fleming has set for me. Three slips, a gully, backward point, mid off, mid on, square leg and fine leg. I count each fielder to make sure that I haven't missed anyone. The field is regulation. There are no surprises, even though Fleming knows my game pretty well after a spell for Middlesex in 2002.

I look down at the ground and tap my bat on the crease. I am solely concentrating on the process now. There are no more thoughts. I bring my eyes up to see Chris Martin, a tall, gangly swing bowler who can get them down there quite quickly, starting his run-up.

'Watch the ball,' I whisper to myself. 'Watch the ------- ball.'

Martin accelerates as he nears the crease. He jumps and lets go of the ball.

It is 21 May 2004 and it is my first ball in Test cricket.

Anyone who says that luck doesn't play any part in sport clearly has not played at the highest level. Professional sport is littered with people who chose the wrong moment to have an off day or got injured just as they were about to hit the big time.

What about the boxer who is on the receiving end of a one-off knockout punch from a far inferior opponent? What about the footballer who hits an excellent penalty, only to see the goalkeeper guess the right way and tip it against the goalpost? What about the Olympic athlete who wakes up with food poisoning on the morning of the biggest day of their career? The list could go on and on. Everywhere lie tales of misfortune that prevented sportsmen and sportswomen from reaching their potential.

I know the old sporting maxim 'you make your own luck' contradicts this argument, but that maxim is there because both coaches and players know that you can't control luck and so it is futile to worry about it. Far better to concentrate on getting your training right or making sure you are in the best frame of mind to deliver your skill. All that we can really control is the percentages. If you have talent, train hard and are as prepared as you possibly can be, then the percentages shift in your favour. If you are not, then they drift away from you. Luck is still around there in the background, so that players and spectators can never be sure of a result until the final wicket, whistle or bell. That is part of the attraction of sport.

The England cricket team analyst, Nathan Leamon, who unsurprisingly loves to look at numbers, came up with the remarkable statistic that if an England cricketer makes his debut in England, he is 40 per cent more likely to have a long and successful career than someone who makes his debut away from home. I suppose there is some logic to this. If you start at home, you are more comfortable with the surroundings and you know the conditions. Moreover, the team is more likely to be successful and thus there is less pressure on your shoulders. Conversely, away from home everything becomes more difficult. Unfamiliar foreign conditions, combined with lonely hours in hotel rooms with team-mates you don't know, make the chances of instant success much less likely. Unfortunately, cricketers have no control over when they make their debut. If a spot becomes available on an overseas tour, your chances of a long and successful career are immediately shortened.

The reason I mention all this now is that I feel incredibly lucky that I made my Test debut when I did, in May 2004. Five days before the start of the Test match, I had no idea that a Test debut was even a possibility. The England cricket team were riding high after giving the West Indies a walloping in their own backyard, mainly on the back of some outstanding bowling from Steve Harmison. They had a settled batting line-up, with experienced campaigners like Mark Butcher and Nasser Hussain being counterbalanced by younger, more exciting talents. Marcus Trescothick,

Michael Vaughan and Andrew Flintoff were all making waves on the international circuit. It certainly didn't look as if a gap was going to open up any time soon, especially at the top of the order, with Trescothick and Vaughan complementing each other so well.

Fate, however, intervened. During the nets before the first Test against New Zealand, Vaughan slipped awkwardly while attempting a sweep shot and twisted his knee. As he was writhing around in agony, it was apparent to everyone present that he was unlikely to be fit to play the Test match.

It must be stated that I wasn't suddenly picked from complete obscurity to make my debut on the game's greatest stage. I had been part of the England set-up, but only in the one-day format. During the previous winter, I had been selected to tour Bangladesh, Sri Lanka and the West Indies, and although much of my time was spent on the obligatory drinks-carrying duties, I had impressed enough in the nets to be selected for five games. My results had been patchy, with a couple of fifties in the last two games against the West Indies just about proving that I was better than my returns of 3, 29 and 10 had suggested up to that point. Also, over the two months away from home, I had got to know many of the players in the team and felt a little more comfortable in their presence.

On the back of those performances in the Caribbean, I was next in line for an opener's spot. Ironically, if the injury had been to anyone but an opener, it was likely that Paul Collingwood, who had been part of the set-up for far longer than me, would have got the nod. Thankfully, I felt in the form of my life. I had come back from the ODI tour feeling extremely confident and had taken it onto the pitch for Middlesex. A couple of hundreds in my last two innings meant that I was in prime touch with the bat.

The other piece of the jigsaw was that I was playing at Lord's, my home ground. Obviously, I knew the ground and the wicket very well, having played hundreds of innings there, but Lord's in the early 2000s was also a batsman's paradise. If you could just get through the new ball, there were generally no demons to unsettle you, from either seam or spin.

All in all, it was the perfect situation for a debut. The gods had smiled upon me.

The ball leaves his hand. I pick it up early. It is on a good length, with a touch of gentle swing away from me. I play a little outside the line of the ball with my defensive shot, knowing that the Lord's slope is likely to deflect the ball a little from its intended path. The ball hits the middle of the bat and dribbles back towards the bowler.

'Good start, Straussy,' I murmur to myself.

The second ball is similar to the first. This time, though, it is a little straighter. The bowler has committed the cardinal sin of drifting onto the new batsman's pads. If I were Stephen Fleming, I would be cursing under my breath. I close the face of the bat on the ball, feel the solid thump of willow on leather and look up to see where the ball has gone. The square-leg fielder sets off to retrieve it. I call 'Yes' to my partner and set off for what would be an easy two. I am up and running.

There is no doubt that there is a distinct feel to Test cricket. It is the big league. From the moment that I arrived at the team hotel, two days before the Test, I could tell that the atmosphere was very different from my recent ODI experiences.

My first duty as a prospective England Test player was to sit, as if in court, at a substantial round table while journalists from all the major newspapers and cricketing magazines fired questions at me and then furiously scribbled down my replies in a series of squiggles that bore no relation to written English. I think they call it shorthand, but I still have no idea how they decipher it when they get home.

'It looks as if you are likely to play. How does that make you feel?' one of the journalists asked.

I patted back the question as if it was a gentle half-volley, knowing all the time that our media relations officer, Andrew Walpole, was hovering in the background, ready to pounce if I wandered into any dangerous territory.

'Well, if I am selected, I would be incredibly excited. It's everyone's dream to play for England, and if you do get the chance, you want to make a success of it.' I tried my hardest not to sound too robotic, as if my answers were written down in front of me.

'Do you think your introduction into the team will put some pressure on Nasser Hussain and Mark Butcher?' one of the tabloid journalists asked, trying to lure me into an obvious trap.

'I haven't been selected yet,' I answered, wary of saying anything further.

Over the years, I have come to realise that press conferences are a game in their own right. Print journalists, in particular, are keen to get you to say something even a tiny bit controversial. They have articles to write and readers to entertain. The odd juicy quote here and there definitely helps them.

Back then, I could sense that they were dying for me to say something about Hussain or Butcher that might be construed as disrespectful or imply that their best days were behind them. It would have been a good story. I could imagine the headlines: 'Debutant slams ageing stars.'

Later in my career, I came to enjoy those verbal jousts with the journalists. We all knew the rules of the game and their probing questions were usually met with a wry smile and a stubbornness to stick to my prearranged script. The journalists, in turn, seemed to be as interested in how I managed to wriggle my way out of saying the wrong thing as they were in writing down what I said.

Before my debut, however, I didn't know the journalists all that well, so I was guarded and careful. That attitude resulted in the sort of bland quotes that you hear from most sportsmen: clichéd waffle that impresses neither the journalists nor the public. It all comes from having to watch what you say too carefully.

If my first press conference was a step into the unknown, the preparation time before a Test match was almost equally surprising for me. I was coming from a system where volume was the name of the game. In county cricket, if you weren't playing, you were travelling. The time for practice was in preseason and the odd morning session the day before a game. The prevailing wisdom was, and still is, that you are employed to play and so you must play. Comments such as 'We used to play twenty-eight matches in 1963 and it never did us any harm' seemed to sum up the attitudes of county chief executives.

There were, of course, some benefits to this system. We were never short of opportunities to play, and if you got in a good run of form, the volume of cricket meant that you were usually able to make the most of it, either in four-day or one-day cricket. Bowlers, as is often the case, got the short end of the stick, having to operate at about 85 per cent for most of the season in order to avoid overuse injuries.

What was either completely missing or simply paid lip service to was high-quality, deliberate practice, in which the aim of the game is to challenge, push, experiment and improve your game. Practice in county cricket wasn't practice, it was warming up. In the nets or at fielding practice players went through the motions, knowing that conserving energy was the priority.

In the England set-up, that notion was turned on its head. Fielding practices were high-intensity affairs, where one mistake was frowned upon and two mistakes were almost unforgivable. There was a whole host of cones, balls, stumps and routines, as well as plenty of support staff to run the sessions. The players knew that this was their opportunity to push themselves and impress, and so they bought into the idea, for the most part. The result was that standards increased, and did so quickly. I had always prided myself on being one of the best fielders at Middlesex. In the England set-up, I was average at most.

The same attitude prevailed in the nets. Gone were the county bowlers trundling in off short runs, bowling at 50 per cent. In their place were England's finest steaming in with new balls, determined to win the battle with the batsman down the other end. It was a genuine challenge, and from the point of view of someone who had to face Flintoff and Harmison most of the time, not always a pleasant one.

Duncan Fletcher was constantly surveying the scenery from behind his sunglasses, making mental notes about players' strengths and weaknesses. He had an incredible eye for cricketing detail and would as a matter of course notice small things that were picked up by no one else.

Although there was no place for cruising in this new practice regime, it was surprisingly empowering. To be able to focus on improving your game, to be challenged by a number of different coaches, to feel as though you were being stretched, to finish a session feeling genuinely exhausted – all this was especially motivating. I could feel myself improving by the minute, and it all left me wondering why the county system could not replicate that sort of preparation.

Duncan Fletcher always used to complain that 'I should just be putting the roof on the house, but I find myself having to build the foundations as well,' and I could see how frustrating it must have been for him to deal with players either not ready for Test cricket or too steeped in the traditions of county cricket to buy into his philosophy.

His answer to this frustration was largely to turn his back on county cricket. He identified some talented players who he thought had the temperament to thrive in Test cricket, picked them consistently and then worked to turn them into the genuine article. Batsmen like Vaughan, Trescothick, Collingwood and myself definitely benefited from this approach, but even Fletcher himself would admit that it was far from ideal. The county system – the system that was meant to be producing England players, which millions of pounds of ECB money was propping up every year – was largely being disregarded by the England set-up, on the basis that it wasn't doing its job.

'That's lunch, gentlemen,' announces Rudi Koertzen.

I turn and head towards the dressing room. The previous thirty-five minutes have passed in a blur. Never before have I concentrated so hard on batting. I have been out of my comfort zone, but my temperament has not let me down. The attention, the crowd and the chirps from the opposition have all combined to make me focus more, not less. I have made it through to the lunch interval on 15 not out, and the relief as I unstrap my pads is palpable. Most importantly, however, I feel as though I am playing just another game now. I know that I can handle the bowling, I feel comfortable with the conditions and my focus is turning towards getting a decent score, rather than dealing with the distractions of Test cricket.

I give the magnificent three-course meal at Lord's a miss and instead opt for a couple of ham and cheese rolls. I never feel hungry during an innings, but recognise that it is important to get some fuel on board. Trescothick and I make our way out of the dressing room just as the weary bowlers are stumbling out of the dining room with bellies full of rack of lamb and treacle sponge. Players love playing at Lord's more for the lunches than anything else.

The post-lunch session starts with a few more nudges and nurdles, then, bang, I middle an overpitched ball from Oram to the midwicket boundary. I have reached 30. Daniel Vettori, regarded by most as the best left-arm orthodox spinner in world cricket, comes into the attack. Surprisingly, he bowls from the Pavilion End, where his natural spin is negated to a certain extent by the Lord's slope.

'Be careful not to play at balls wide of off stump,' I tell myself as he comes in to bowl.

New Zealand are forced to set a reasonably defensive field after our positive start, so there are plenty of gaps to work the ball into. A few sweeps and back-foot pushes and I have got myself to 44. Martin returns to bowl. Wide of off stump, I middle it through extra cover off the front foot. Two balls later, short and wide, I throw the bat at it and it whistles away to the boundary for another four. I have scored my first Test fifty.

I raise my bat to the pavilion and acknowledge the applause from the crowd. This is where playing in front of a full house is brilliant. Gone is the concern about making a fool of myself in front of thousands; now my mind is focused on getting a big score, and having a large number of people supporting you, as well as the honour of playing for your country, helps concentrate the mind.

Oram sends a couple of full balls down the leg side, which I get down to the fine-leg boundary. Easy runs. Vettori is proving more difficult, bowling from the other end. He seems to have settled on a line which makes it difficult to score singles, and the presence of two fielders around the bat unnerves me.

I have a decision to make. Either I suck up the pressure and play out a couple of maidens, or I take the game to him, hit one over the top and hopefully open up more options if Fleming changes his field. A well-known cricketing cliché is 'If your heart and your head say to go for a big shot, then do it. If your heart says yes, but your head no, then refrain.' I size up the situation. We are 160–0. Marcus Trescothick is on 72 and I am on 76. We don't want to lose a wicket now, but it is important to keep the momentum going. I know that I only have to get half a bat on the ball and it should go over midwicket for four. I decide to take on Vettori.

The ball is well flighted. I skip down the wicket, get to the pitch and middle it over midwicket for a one-bounce four. Adrenalin surges through my body. I have taken the risk and it has paid off. Fleming hastily positions a man at deep midwicket and takes out one of the men around the bat.

Scoring is starting to prove more difficult now. The fields are defensive and the ball is getting softer. It takes me ten overs to get from 80 to 90 and I am getting edgy. I am frustrated about scoring slowly and the thought of getting a hundred on debut is starting to consume me. I am thinking too much about the final result, getting a hundred, and not enough about the process, *getting ten runs. I resolve to play every ball on its merits, but the adrenalin is flowing.*

Martin bowls a length ball wide of off stump. I should leave it, but it seems like the first wide ball I have received in days. I flash at it, only to hear the snick as it catches the inside edge of the bat. There is another sound. I look back to see the ball travelling down to the fine-leg boundary and my stumps intact. 'What was that noise?' I think to myself, but decide to forget about it and concentrate on the next ball. Television replays later show that the ball clipped off stump but did not dislodge the bails.

Three balls later, I think that I see a bit of width on a short ball from Martin. I prepare to cut it. There is no width after all and I end up having to steer it through gully, where Oram dives low but cannot hold on to the catch. I run through for a single, but berate myself for trying to invent scoring shots.

I am now on 96. It has taken an age to get the last six runs and I can feel the anticipation in the crowd. Everyone seems to know that I am going through a difficult patch and is willing me to get through it. I, on the other hand, am hating the pressure. The emphasis has changed from he could get a hundred to he should get a hundred, and that makes things much more difficult. It is now a battle with myself and my emotions. The bowlers have been trying to get me out in vain for hours and are now resigned to waiting for me to do something to get myself out. All I have to do is wait patiently and score off the bad deliveries, but I am finding it difficult to keep concentrating. I have an almost uncontrollable urge to hit a boundary. Scoring a four is going to relieve all the pressure and take me to a hundred, but I have to wait for the right ball.

Tuffey bowls me one short of a length. I see it early and play my favourite pull shot. I feel the ball come off the middle of the bat and look up, expecting to see the ball whistling to the square-leg boundary. I have got it a little fine, though, and the fine-leg fielder moves swiftly to his right to cut it off. I am now on 98. Martin starts another over.

'Surely,' I think to myself, 'it has got to happen this over.'

I let a couple of length balls go through to the keeper, but now adrenalin is really coursing through my veins. I am so close. Another length ball. This time I try to take a risk by hitting through the line, but the ball bounces more than I anticipate and I am fortunate that it finds the splice of the bat rather than the edge.

Mark Butcher casually walks down the wicket. He has seen this all before. 'Keep watching the ball, Straussy. In a minute he is going to bowl you a wide one, and you are going to smack it through the covers for four. Be patient.'

I nod in reply. Martin runs in again and lets go. The ball is full and wide, just as Butcher said. I slash at the ball and feel solid contact. The ball has gone between the two cover fielders, and as I look up, I realise that I have just brought up my hundred. I sprint to the other end, knowing that the ball is going for four, but I'm not sure how to react. I punch the air and wave my bat with so much force that I nearly fall over.

In one moment, all the tension, adrenalin, fear and nerves leave my body, to be replaced by pure unadulterated joy. I *raise my bat to my team-mates, all of whom are on the balcony cheering me on. I look around the ground. Everyone is on their feet cheering. The giant scoreboard displays a message: 'Congratulations Andrew Strauss on scoring 100 on debut.' I cannot believe this is happening to me.*

England v New Zealand
(1st Test)

Played at Lord's Cricket Ground, London, on 20–24 May 2004

Umpires:	DB Hair & RE Koertzen (TV: MR Benson)	
Referee:	CH Lloyd	
Toss:	New Zealand	

NEW ZEALAND

MH Richardson	lbw b Harmison	93		c GO Jones b Harmison	101
SP Fleming*	c Strauss b SP Jones	34		c Hussain b Harmison	4
NJ Astle	c GO Jones b Flintoff	64	(7)	c GO Jones b Harmison	49
SB Styris	c GO Jones b SP Jones	0		c Hussain b Giles	4
CD McMillan	lbw b Hoggard	6		c Hussain b Giles	0
JDP Oram	c GO Jones b Harmison	67		run out (Hussain)	4
DR Tuffey	b Harmison	8	(10)	not out	14
CL Cairns	c Harmison b Flintoff	82		c Butcher b Giles	14
BB McCullum†	b SP Jones	5	(3)	c GO Jones b SP Jones	96
DL Vettori	b Harmison	2	(9)	c GO Jones b Harmison	5
CS Martin	not out	1		b Flintoff	7
Extras	(b 9, lb 6, w 2, nb 7)	24		(b 14, lb 16, nb 8)	38
Total	(102.4 overs)	**386**		(121.1 overs)	**336**

ENGLAND

ME Trescothick*	c McCullum b Oram	86		c and b Tuffey	2
AJ Strauss	c Richardson b Vettori	112		run out (Cairns/McCullum)	83
MA Butcher	c McCullum b Vettori	26		c Fleming b Martin	6
MJ Hoggard	c McCullum b Oram	15			
N Hussain	b Martin	34	(4)	not out	103
GP Thorpe	b Cairns	3	(5)	not out	51
A Flintoff	c Richardson b Martin	63			
GO Jones†	c Oram b Styris	46			
AF Giles	c Oram b Styris	11			
SP Jones	b Martin	4			
SJ Harmison	not out	0			
Extras	(b 4, lb 18, nb 19)	41		(b 7, lb 12, w 5, nb 13)	37
Total	(124.3 overs)	**441**		(for 3 wkts) (87 overs)	**282**

ENGLAND	O	M	R	W		O	M	R	W
Hoggard	22	7	68	1	(3)	14	3	39	0
Harmison	31	7	126	4	(1)	29	8	76	4
Flintoff	21.4	7	63	2	(2)	16.1	5	40	1
SP Jones	23	8	82	3		23	5	64	1
Giles	5	0	32	0		39	8	87	3

NEW ZEALAND	O	M	R	W		O	M	R	W
Tuffey	26	4	98	0	(2)	10	3	32	1
Martin	27	6	94	3	(4)	18	2	75	1
Oram	30	8	76	2	(1)	15	4	39	0
Cairns	16	2	71	1	(6)	6	0	27	0
Vettori	21	1	69	2	(3)	25	5	53	0
Styris	4.3	0	11	2	(5)	13	5	37	0

Fall of wickets:

	NZ	Eng	NZ	Eng
1st	58	190	7	18
2nd	161	239	180	35
3rd	162	254	187	143
4th	174	288	187	–
5th	280	297	203	–
6th	287	311	287	–
7th	324	416	290	–
8th	329	428	304	–
9th	338	441	310	–
10th	386	441	336	–

Close of play:	Day 1:	NZ (1) 284–5 (Oram 64*, Tuffey 2*, 88.2 overs)
	Day 2:	Eng (1) 246–2 (Butcher 22*, Hoggard 0*, 74 overs)
	Day 3:	NZ (2) 134–1 (Richardson 46*, McCullum 72*, 39 overs)
	Day 4:	Eng (2) 8–0 (Trescothick 1*, Strauss 6*, 5 overs)

Man of the match:	AJ Strauss
Result:	**England won by 7 wickets**

It didn't matter how bland I was in the post-play press conference because the expression on my face said it all. I had just achieved the boyhood dream. How many times have aspiring young cricketers found themselves in their back gardens, or on a quiet residential street, with a bat in hand, pretending that the next ball they are about to face is going to bring up a hundred at Lord's on debut. I know that I did it many times.

People sometimes say that achieving your dreams can be anticlimactic, as though the realisation is like reaching the end of a book. You want more but know that it is impossible – the journey is finished. Well, in my experience, that certainly wasn't the case. Maybe it was because I knew that my journey had not finished. In fact, it had just started. The warm glow in my stomach told me that I had achieved something fantastic. I had graduated to the next level in the most emphatic style. I had proved to myself that I could handle the pressure of the occasion. I had made my friends and family proud. I was part of a new 'Test cricket centurions' club, whose members included all the greatest players. And I had done it all on one glorious Friday afternoon in May.

New Zealand in England 2004

1st Test. Lord's, London. 20–24 May 2004
New Zealand 386 (M.H. Richardson 93, C.L. Cairns 82;
   S.J. Harmison 4–126) and 336 (M.H. Richardson 101, B.B. McCullum
   96; S.J. Harmison 4–76)
England 441 (**A.J. Strauss 112**, M.E. Trescothick 86) and 282–3
   (**A.J. Strauss 83**, N. Hussain 103*)
England won by 7 wickets.

2nd Test. Headingley, Leeds. 3–7 June 2004
New Zealand 409 (S.P. Fleming 97, M.H.W. Papps 86; S.J. Harmison 4–74)
   and 161 (M.H. Richardson 40; M.J. Hoggard 4–75)
England 526 (M.E. Trescothick 132, G.O. Jones 100, A. Flintoff 94,
   A.J. Strauss 62) and 45–1 (**A.J. Strauss 10**)
England won by 9 wickets.

3rd Test. Trent Bridge, Nottingham. 10–13 June 2004
New Zealand 384 (S.P. Fleming 117, S.B. Styris 108) and 218 (A.F. Giles
   4–46)
England 319 (M.E. Trescothick 63, M.P. Vaughan 61, **A.J. Strauss 0**;
   C.L. Cairns 5–79, J.E.C. Franklin 4–104) and 284–6 (G.P. Thorpe 104*,
   M.A. Butcher 59, **A.J. Strauss 6**; C.L. Cairns 4–108)
England won by 4 wickets.

England won the series 3–0.

5
TOURING

To me there has always been something wildly exciting about the word 'touring'. At school, I somehow missed the opportunity to go on one of those overseas adventures organised by the teachers and followed, with great enthusiasm, by the parents. I think I was just plain unlucky.

In fact, the closest I ever came to going on a fully fledged tour while at school was with my prep-school rugby team and the destination was Scotland. A week of freezing weather ensued and although we played against the cream of the crop as far as Scottish schoolboy rugby was concerned, I arrived back in the safety of the Home Counties a little underwhelmed by the experience. I was younger than most of the other boys, I had not established myself in the team and supporting from the touchline for most of the games was not a pleasant pastime by any means. If I learnt anything from that particular tour, it was that going on tour and being a bit-part player is certainly not all it is cracked up to be.

In truth, I longed to be able to go on a cricket tour as a schoolboy. Radley College had made the journey to Barbados a couple of years before I had made my way into the XI, and the combination of warm winter sun, exotic beaches and good competitive cricket in alien conditions sounded like bliss. Alas, it was never to be, but the thought stayed with me.

Once I graduated to the professional ranks, touring became an even more intriguing proposition. Sitting in the bar, listening to Angus Fraser or Phil Tufnell talking about the '1994 tour to Australia' or the '1998 tour to West Indies' got the juices flowing very quickly. Some of the stories were hilarious, filled with details of incredible highs and lows on the field, but also intriguing behind-the-scenes information. Anecdotes over a beer about celebrations, partying with the rich and famous and nightmare journeys on the subcontinent were far more interesting than anything that happened in the middle.

What really made me envious, though, was the way they could casually switch from one tour to another. A typical conversation would go along the lines of:

'Gus, remember that night in Jamaica in 19-- after we won the Test match. What a night that was!'

'Tuffers, you muppet, we didn't win the Test match in Jamaica that year. You are obviously talking about the tour before in 19--. Either that, or you went out celebrating after we lost by an innings and plenty.'

'Oh yeah . . . I always get confused about tours to the West Indies. Can't think why!'

The room would then fall about in laughter.

Cricketers around the country would have given an arm and a leg to get on each and every one of those tours. (Well, maybe a couple of those West Indies tours in the early 1990s might not have had such a long list of volunteers. Walsh and Ambrose still carried a venomous reputation.) By talking about them, they were, probably unknowingly, showing everyone just how good they were. They had been part of the inner sanctum, the holy of holies of English cricket, so often that they couldn't remember which series they were talking about. That made me both full of admiration and jealous at the same time.

What also intrigued me about touring was just how hard the cricket seemed to be. During my formative years, throughout the 1990s, I would religiously turn on *Test Match Special* during the overseas tours and hear the difficulties the English team were having dealing with the pace of the West Indian quicks in Antigua, or the guile of Mushtaq Ahmed on a turner in Karachi, or for that matter the canniness of Eddo Brandes, the chicken farmer, in Zimbabwe. In truth, we were just like Guinness. We didn't travel well. The odd victory raised hope that perhaps this tour might be different, but by and large we got beaten up by the top teams. South Africa, the West Indies, India, Pakistan and, of course, the impregnable Australia all sent us home with our tails between our legs. Oh, I should probably also add Sri Lanka and New Zealand to that list.

I couldn't work it out. We were usually competitive at home, but as soon as we took on opposition teams in their own backyards, the cream of English batting disintegrated under a barrage of bouncers, googlies, reverse swing and dodgy umpiring. Clearly something mysterious went on in those faraway lands.

It goes without saying, therefore, that there was more than a little trepidation in my mind as I packed my bags for my first ever Test tour with England, in 2004–05. The destination was to be South Africa, with a little stop-off in Zimbabwe for four highly contentious ODIs. I was particularly excited about going to South Africa. Clearly, it was a country that I knew extremely well, and although there was bound to be a bit of stick directed at me for my South African roots, I had a sneaky suspicion that one of my new ODI team-mates, Kevin Pietersen, complete with his blue hair, strong Durban accent and three lions tattooed on his arm, would most likely act as a lightning rod as far as the South African public were concerned.

I knew, though, that South Africa were a particularly tough proposition at home. The last tour had started in the most pitiful of fashions, as a new-look England side, under the guidance of Duncan Fletcher, had subsided to two runs for four wickets on the opening day of the first Test, en route to a series defeat. This time, however, things were different. We had won our previous seven Test matches in a row, had a genuinely hostile bowling attack for the first time in decades and had left English shores with bucketloads of the most precious and elusive ingredient of success, confidence.

First, however, we had a difficult tightrope to walk in Zimbabwe. For those in the side who had been part of the 2003 World Cup debacle, when the England team eventually decided against going to Zimbabwe and in doing so lost the opportunity to win the World Cup, the situation seemed all too familiar. Whether cricketers liked it or not, politics and sport did mix. There were far too many examples from the past, such as the sporting boycotts of South Africa in the 1970s and 1980s or the decisions by the USA and Russia not to compete at the Olympics in 1980 and 1984 respectively, to see that the two were inseparable.

The political issue for the UK government was a tricky one. Clearly, things had gone horribly wrong in Zimbabwe. In what was once dubbed the breadbasket of Africa, the population was struggling to sustain itself as forced farm seizures and mismanagement had rendered the agricultural industry ineffective. Inflation was running into the realms of fantasy, as the Zimbabwe dollar became completely worthless. The historic close ties between Zimbabwe and the UK meant that our government was under pressure to do or say something to show that what was going on over there was unacceptable. Unfortunately, the government knew that heavy sanctions, or sporting boycotts, would add fuel to Robert Mugabe's assertion that Zimbabwe's tribulations were the result of an imperial conspiracy.

The result was that the UK government on the one hand said that the cricket team should not go to Zimbabwe, but on the other hand were unwilling to step in to give the order not to go. The England Cricket Board, in turn, ran the risk of financial disaster if it chose not to undertake a tour without express objection from the government. The outcome was that the cricketers were unwitting pawns in a great big game of politics and they were the ones who had to answer the difficult questions.

Eventually, we all trudged our way into Zimbabwe for a ten-day period. It was one of the bleaker experiences of my life. The games of cricket were largely meaningless. Zimbabwe were shorn of most of their best players, who had left the country to follow their careers elsewhere. The result of the series was never in doubt, but seeing a country being brought to its knees, with looks of complete hopelessness on everyone's faces, white and black, gave me a far better perspective of the situation in the country.

Looking back, the fact that British journalists were allowed into the country for the first time in many years, and also reported back on some of the harrowing scenes, just about made the trip worthwhile in my opinion. We didn't change anything that was going on out there, but perhaps it added a little attention to the proceedings.

As we arrived in Johannesburg from Harare, much of the angst that had accompanied us in Zimbabwe abated. Now we could appreciate and enjoy touring with England as it was supposed to be. There is no doubt that when you are travelling as the England cricket team, you are noticed. Thirty-odd people wearing the same uniform, accompanied by vast amounts of sporting baggage, always causes a stir among the holidaymakers or business travellers at an airport.

Also, being such a large group gives you certain privileges. There is offsite checking-in, usually in an airport hotel, so a lot of the hassle of travelling is taken out of your hands. Certainly in the subcontinent, where cricketers have a far higher profile, special VIP rooms are prepared for the team and the obligatory passport checks take place in a far-off space, while the players are sampling a cup of tea and being waited on hand and foot. On one occasion, travelling in Pakistan, we were sitting on the top deck of a Pakistan Airways Boeing 747 when we were asked if anybody wanted to come to the cockpit and watch as the plane landed in Islamabad Airport. Most of the guys were either asleep or listening to their iPods, so I thought I might as well take them up on the offer.

I was shepherded to the door of the cockpit by the flight attendant. She then knocked on the door, which was unlocked by a particularly unimpressed co-pilot. This was in 2006, five years after the attacks on the Twin Towers, and it was clear that passengers coming into the cockpit of a commercial airliner was against protocol. The co-pilot, who was in his thirties, was no doubt concerned that this was likely to lead to some sort of career-threatening disciplinary matter. The pilot, on the other hand, in his fifties and obviously a cricket nut, was like a giddy schoolboy.

'Mr Strauss, thank you so much for coming. I love the way you play the game. Very good cut shot. Shoaib Akhtar is very quick, no? What about Inzamam, he is the best, I think. Freddie Flintoff is a great player too. How do you like our country? It is an honour to have you in my aeroplane.'

His monologue came thick and fast and I barely had a chance to think of a reply to one question before another barrage of cricket-related probing headed in my direction.

'I loved the Ashes 2005. What about that catch against Gilchrist? Kevin Pietersen very good player. Which is your favourite city in Pakistan? Do you think we are better than India? I think we will beat you 2–1 in the series. English players cannot play leg-spin bowling.'

As this line of questioning continued, I looked through the windscreen and could plainly see the lights of the runway in the distance. We were less than five minutes away from landing. In fact, it was clear that the co-pilot was getting more than a little agitated by the lack of attention being paid by his more experienced colleague. As he was talking into his headset, no doubt communicating with air traffic control, he threw a withering look in the direction of the pilot, who finally got the message.

'Mr Strauss, please take a seat at the back of the cockpit and enjoy the landing.' With that the questioning stopped, and he got back to business.

That was the kind of special treatment on tour that the conversations between Fraser and Tufnell in the bar at Middlesex had led me to expect. What I didn't expect was that this treatment would be maintained for the little things as well. All baggage was looked after by Phil Neale, the tour manager. All you had to do, as a player, was leave it outside your room and it would magically appear outside your room again at the next destination. Your only role in the procedure was to get your luggage outside your room on time, usually by 10 p.m. on the night before departure, and to rip off any old baggage tags in the process. Phil hated doing that himself.

Needless to say, after a few post-match beers, even this task was far too onerous for some players, and someone wandering down the corridor of the hotel would invariably find Phil

with a face like thunder, muttering under his breath, '-------
hell, he couldn't even be bothered to take his tags off. Why
do I bother?'

Bizarrely, we all got used to this treatment far too easily,
and Phil never really got the recognition he deserved for
proverbially mopping up after us all the time.

The tour to South Africa in 2004–05 lived up to my romantic
notion of travelling in every way. Aside from having everything looked after for us, the South African people really
embraced the visit of an English touring side, especially one
that had the potential to be reasonably good.

As far as tours are concerned, there are few better locations
than South Africa. Our off-field time was spent in a multitude
of different ways. Some of the best golf courses in the world
are situated in South Africa, and every city we went to had
a suitable offering, but there was so much else to do. Beaches,
game parks, shopping, white-water rafting and bungee-
jumping were all on the agenda, and the quality of the food,
especially the steaks, was exceptional.

One of the biggest risks for a new England tourist is getting
carried away with the recreational side of a tour. Away from
the cauldron of a Test match, it is easy to feel as though you
are on a holiday. The West Indies, in particular, with its white
sandy beaches, palm trees and copious amounts of rum, always
has the potential to derail young, unsuspecting travellers. The
temptation is at its strongest when you are not in the side,
languishing in the background, carrying drinks.

I was fortunate not to have to go through that too often. I did, however, get a taste of what it was like on my first ODI tour to Bangladesh, in 2003, and later in the 2007 World Cup. You feel like a second-class citizen. You are last to get into the nets, as if you are an afterthought; you are submitted to constant fitness sessions in order to pass the time; and while the international matches are going on, you feel like little more than a waiter to your more illustrious colleagues. If you have to endure a full five months away from home, with little prospect of playing, the temptation to let your hair down becomes almost unbearable.

The problem, though, is that the management of the side has nothing to judge you on as a person or as a player other than the way you conduct yourself off the field at those moments. Because you aren't getting a game, you can't rescue yourself with inspired performances on the pitch, so you had better be careful not to be seen to be enjoying the ride too much.

Many of the young players that came into the England side in my time and then sank back into county obscurity without ever getting a decent run in the side did so because they couldn't handle the tough challenge of touring but not playing. While I was captain we tried, as far as we could, to let those that weren't playing have designated 'on' and 'off' days, so that they could at least let their hair down legitimately, but it was, and never could be, as satisfying as being in the side, performing for your country.

*   *   *

My first Test away from home came in Port Elizabeth in December 2004 and, if anything, I was able to outdo my magical home debut by scoring a century in the first innings, followed by an unbeaten 94 to see us home to victory, our eighth in succession and an England record. By the end of the series, I had amassed nearly 700 runs at an average of 72.88. Clearly, at that stage, the unfamiliar conditions of playing abroad had not affected me in the slightest. Looking back, however, I can see that I was helped enormously by my naivety.

Having played all round the world now, more than once, it seems to me that the conditions in which you play are not the real reason that overseas cricket is so difficult. The real challenge is dealing with your own attitude towards those foreign wickets. For example, if we were touring India, all the focus before the series would be on how we played spin. The media would focus on it, the Indian players were bound to say something about it and we would spend hours formulating plans to contend with all the many spin bowlers we were likely to encounter. By the time the first Test started, as a batsman you already felt as though you were in a do-or-die situation. If you started well and were able to score runs early in the series, then you knew you had overcome your own personal trial by spin and could settle in to bat as normal. If, however, you got a couple of low scores against spin bowling, then it was impossible to get away from the torment. Net sessions would be arranged especially to help you overcome your 'problem'. One or two of your team-mates would come up to you with suggestions as to how to play the different varieties of spin. The media would constantly ask why you were so weak in this area. Worst of all, though, when you

South Africa v England
(1st Test)

Played at Sahara Oval, St George's, Port Elizabeth, on 17–21 December 2004

Umpires:	DB Hair & SJA Taufel (TV: IL Howell)
Referee:	CH Lloyd
Toss:	South Africa

SOUTH AFRICA

GC Smith*	c Strauss b Hoggard	0	(2)	c SP Jones b Flintoff	55
AB de Villiers	lbw b Flintoff	28	(1)	c and b Hoggard	14
JA Rudolph	c GO Jones b Flintoff	93		c Trescothick b Giles	28
JH Kallis	b Harmison	0		lbw b SP Jones	61
HH Dippenaar	c Trescothick b SP Jones	110		b Giles	10
Z de Bruyn	b Flintoff	6		c Trescothick b Flintoff	19
SM Pollock	c Trescothick b Hoggard	31		c GO Jones b SP Jones	0
AJ Hall	b Hoggard	6		run out (Thorpe/GO Jones)	17
TL Tsolekile†	c Flintoff b Giles	22		b SP Jones	0
M Ntini	not out	2		lbw b SP Jones	4
DW Steyn	c Strauss b Giles	8		not out	2
Extras	(lb 13, w 4, nb 14)	31		(b 4, lb 3, w 1, nb 6, p 5)	19
Total	(110.4 overs)	**337**		(69.1 overs)	**229**

ENGLAND

ME Trescothick	b Steyn	47	c Tsolekile b Pollock	0
AJ Strauss	c De Villiers b Pollock	126	not out	94
MA Butcher	c Tsolekile b Ntini	79	c Smith b Ntini	0
MP Vaughan*	c Smith b Hall	10	b Steyn	15
GP Thorpe	b Smith	4	not out	31
A Flintoff	c Rudolph b Ntini	35		
GO Jones†	c Dippenaar b Ntini	2		
AF Giles	c Hall b Pollock	26		
MJ Hoggard	c Tsolekile b Hall	0		
SP Jones	c and b Steyn	24		
SJ Harmison	not out	15		
Extras	(lb 21, w 1, nb 35)	57	(lb 3, nb 2)	5
Total	(126.5 overs)	**425**	(for 3 wkts) (40.4 overs)	**145**

ENGLAND	O	M	R	W		O	M	R	W
Hoggard	20	4	56	3		12	2	38	1
Harmison	25	2	88	1		14	1	54	0
SP Jones	16	4	39	1	(5)	13.1	3	39	4
Flintoff	22	4	72	3		15	2	47	2
Giles	27.4	8	69	2	(3)	15	2	39	2

SOUTH AFRICA	O	M	R	W		O	M	R	W
Pollock	32	14	61	2		11	2	36	1
Ntini	28	6	75	3		6.4	1	24	1
Steyn	25.5	2	117	2	(4)	6	1	29	1
Hall	22	1	95	2	(3)	9	1	14	0
De Bruyn	9	1	31	0					
Smith	10	3	25	1	(5)	8	0	39	0

Fall of wickets:

	SA	Eng	SA	Eng
1st	0	152	26	0
2nd	63	238	64	11
3rd	66	249	152	50
4th	178	267	168	–
5th	192	346	201	–
6th	253	353	201	–
7th	261	353	217	–
8th	324	358	218	–
9th	327	394	224	–
10th	337	425	229	–

Close of play:	Day 1:	SA (1) 273–7 (Dippenaar 79*, Tsolekile 6*, 90 overs)
	Day 2:	Eng (1) 227–1 (Strauss 120*, Butcher 24*, 66 overs)
	Day 3:	SA (2) 99–2 (Smith 33*, Kallis 10*, 23 overs)
	Day 4:	Eng (2) 93–3 (Strauss 51*, Thorpe 23*, 31 overs)

Man of the match:	AJ Strauss
Result:	**England won by 7 wickets**

were alone in your hotel room, you would still not be able to escape the pressure – and in some cases, the dread – of having to go out there again in the next game and perform. All of this after a couple of low scores that could happen to anyone.

Retaining the perspective that, whatever anyone else might say, you have no real weakness against that type of bowling, and that things are likely to turn in your favour soon, is the hardest task for an international player. This is especially true away from home, where it is impossible to get away from everything. The best and most experienced players learn to deal with it, but even then a couple of poor collective performances, of the kind we displayed in the UAE against Pakistan in 2012, would have us all scratching our heads and experimenting to find new ways to contend with the spin bowlers. Whoever said that cricket is played 90 per cent in the head definitely knew what they were talking about.

Clearly one of the real delights of touring is that you are able to see the world. By that I mean that you go to places that you would never dream of visiting on holiday and meet people whose paths you would never cross otherwise. Bangladesh, Pakistan and Sri Lanka were all fascinating places to visit, although I am sure that in this day and age the opportunities for real exploration are far more limited than in the past. The idea of going up the Khyber Pass, for example, as England players of the past used to do, would be thought of as suicidal in today's climate.

The country that really stood out for me, though, was India.

When I first went to Mumbai for a week-long training camp with Middlesex in 2003, I was shaken, as most newcomers are, by the assault on my senses. Noise from the non-stop hustle and bustle continued all through the night and was accompanied by strange and mysterious aromas, originating from either local spices or open sewers. In daylight, it was hard to cope with the multitude of visions in front of me. People had built ramshackle houses on the fast lane of the motorway to the airport; there were beggars everywhere; and alongside all the squalor lay incredible colonial buildings and five-star hotels. It was almost too much to take in.

Over the years, Mumbai has changed enormously, as have many of the built-up areas of India. Economic success has brought with it many Western-style comforts. Shopping centres, fantastic hotels, good food and sanitation are commonplace everywhere now, although you never have to venture too far from your hotel to see the India of the past.

Despite the somewhat challenging travel arrangements in India, where what could be a one-hour flight often takes a whole day as you travel from one hub to another and then on to your final destination, I particularly enjoyed going to some of the less well-known areas of the country. On my first tour there, in 2006, we played seven ODIs in places like Faridabad, Kochi, Goa, Guwahati, on the edge of the Chinese border, and Indore.

It was in Indore that I experienced one of the more surreal moments of my life. Quite bizarrely, Indore is the proud recipient of a Pizza Hut franchise. Quite why there is a restaurant there, when there are very few throughout India, is a very interesting question. On finding out this news, and having been feasting on various curries for the best part of three months, we decided that a team pizza night was in order.

It is fair to say that the manager of the restaurant was somewhat taken aback to see the whole of the England cricket team, including Andrew Flintoff and Kevin Pietersen, walking into his pride and joy. He hurriedly arranged for the best table in the joint to be prepared, situated in front of a large panoramic window, and we all sat down, looking forward to our meat feast and Hawaiian pizzas.

As our drinks arrived, we were vaguely aware that a few people were hanging around outside the window looking in at us, but thought nothing of it. By the time our pizzas arrived, however, there must have been at least 2,000 people staring at us as we tucked into our food, all mesmerised by the sight of famous cricketers in their midst.

Nothing prepares you for the passion of the Indian people for the game of cricket.

Aside from the obvious delights of touring, there can also be a far more sinister, unseen side. On your first few tours, you are unlikely to see it. Everything is too new, too intoxicating, too full of exhilarating experiences. Over time, an increasingly dark cloud accompanies some Test cricketers when they go away from home.

For starters, leaving home becomes far more difficult. The constant grind of travelling around the UK during the summer, followed by months away from home in the winter, is especially hard on families. Those players with young children find it particularly difficult to maintain a 'normal' relationship with their offspring. Of course, there are plenty of people in other jobs who have to travel around the world, but few are likely to say goodbye to their children in October, knowing full well that the next time they will all be together, at their own house, will be in April the following year. As your career progresses, saying goodbye becomes a more and more difficult task.

Then there are those soulless hotel rooms in cities you may have visited several times, which can be incredibly demoralising. There have been two high-profile cases of players suffering from depression while I have been in the England side: Marcus Trescothick and Mike Yardy. Both found the hours alone in their hotel rooms at night, with nothing but satellite TV and PlayStations for company, extremely hard to endure. Although most players never quite reach the stage where they cannot physically continue, many, including myself, have found the combination of being away from support networks, in far-off hotels, while suffering from bad form, to be particularly difficult to overcome. It is ironic that what seems the most enthralling aspect of playing international cricket when you start can become the most significant reason for finishing playing the game.

I am not sure exactly what can be done about it. Perhaps it is just the natural progression that every cricketer goes through in their careers. Certainly some deal with it better than others. I would like to think, however, that in the long term there may be ways around it. I get the feeling that tours will become shorter, with home and away fixtures, in the mould of a Champions League football game, being an option. Or it may become more common for players to specialise more in one form of the game. How all this might fit into an already crowded cricketing calendar, with host cricket boards eager to find new ways of raising revenue, remains to be seen.

England in South Africa 2004–05 – The Basil D'Oliveira Trophy

1st Test. St George's Park, Port Elizabeth. 17–21 December 2004
South Africa 337 (H.H. Dippenaar 110, J.A. Rudolph 93) and 229
(J.H. Kallis 61, G.C. Smith 55; S.P. Jones 4–39)
England 425 (**A.J. Strauss 126**, M.A. Butcher 79) and 145–3 (**A.J. Strauss 94**)
England won by 7 wickets.

2nd Test. Kingsmead, Durban. 26–30 December 2004
England 139 (**A.J. Strauss 25**; S.M. Pollock 4–32) and 570–7 dec (**A.J. Strauss 136**, M.E. Trescothick 132, G.P. Thorpe 118, G.O. Jones 73, A. Flintoff 60)
South Africa 332 (J.H. Kallis 162) and 290–8 (J.A. Rudolph 61, A.B. de Villiers 52)
Match drawn.

3rd Test. Newlands, Cape Town. 2–6 December 2005
South Africa 441 (J.H. Kallis 149, N. Boje 76, G.C. Smith 74; A. Flintoff 4–79) and 222–8 dec (J.H. Kallis 66)
England 163 (**A.J. Strauss 45**; C.K. Langeveldt 5–46, M. Ntini 4–50) and 304 (S.J. Harmison 42, R.W.T. Key 41, **A.J. Strauss 39**; S.M. Pollock 4–65, N. Boje 4–71)
South Africa won by 196 runs.

4th Test. New Wanderers Stadium, Johannesburg. 13–17 January 2005
England 411–8 dec (**A.J. Strauss 147**, R.W.T. Key 83, M.P. Vaughan 82*; M. Ntini 4–111) and 332–9 dec (M.E. Trescothick 180, M.P. Vaughan 54, **A.J. Strauss 0**)
South Africa 419 (H.H. Gibbs 161, M.V. Boucher 64; M.J. Hoggard 5–144) and 247 (H.H. Gibbs 98, G.C. Smith 67*; M.J. Hoggard 7–61)
England won by 77 runs.

5th Test. Centurion Park, Centurion. 21–25 January 2005
South Africa 247 (A.B. de Villiers 92; A. Flintoff 4–44, S.P. Jones 4–47) and 296–6 dec (J.H. Kallis 136, A.B. de Villiers 109)
England 359 (G.P. Thorpe 86, A. Flintoff 77, G.O. Jones 50, **A.J. Strauss 44**; A. Nel 6–81) and 73–4 (M.P. Vaughan 26*, **A.J. Strauss 0**; M. Ntini 3–12)
Match drawn.

England won the series 2–1.

6

HEROES

I have never known what it is like to be a hero. OK, I have landed the odd conversion in the last minute of a rugby game and scored some important runs when it mattered, but to be a genuine hero, in the mould of Roy of the Rovers, is not something I have ever experienced or imagined.

Now, on 13 September 2005, I am a hero. Not just me; so are my team-mates. Not just them, but also the coach, Duncan Fletcher, and the support staff. Not just all of us, but also Gary Pratt, the substitute fielder, who ran out Ricky Ponting at Trent Bridge. I know I am a hero because I am standing on an open-top bus slowly making its way through the centre of London. Around me are tens of thousands of people, all looking up at us and waving. Some are cricket fans, many are not. They are all basking in our accomplishment of prising the Ashes urn from the relentless grip of the Australian cricket team for the first time since 1986. There are flags of St George draped over buildings. Patriotic tunes like 'Jerusalem' are blaring out of Tannoy systems around Trafalgar Square. The sun is shining. People are smiling. No one is working. All this is happening because of us.

After waiting patiently for the completion of our lap of honour around the city, the Prime Minister, Tony Blair, welcomes us to

10 Downing Street for a reception. It is unbelievable to be standing around while politicians and distinguished guests gush about our achievements.

In the heady days that follow there are all sorts of opportunities to explore. The Weakest Link, the game show hosted by Anne Robinson, puts on an Ashes special. Sponsors Red Bull offer to take us all to their headquarters in Salzburg, before whisking us to Venice for a night of celebration. Transport is taken care of by the company's lavishly restored DC-10 aeroplane. Businesses are falling over each other to be associated with this winning England cricket team. We are the talk of the town; we are celebrities.

Nothing could have been further from our minds eight weeks earlier as we prepared for the start of the 2005 Ashes series.

I had always been led to believe that the Ashes was different. 'Just wait until you play in an Ashes series' was the standard comment from the likes of Vaughan, Butcher and Hussain whenever conversation turned to the pressures of international cricket, the quality of opposition sides, or the media spotlight for that matter.

During the months that followed my debut, when the runs were flowing and my confidence was high, I wasn't completely sure if I believed them. With the innocence of youth, Test cricket didn't seem all that difficult and at least part of me thought that they had much to gain by building up this myth. The harder Ashes cricket was supposed to be, the more they could justify the struggles of the England cricket team over the previous eight Ashes series, and also the more, in Vaughan's case, he could revel in his own magnificent achievements.

To me, at that stage, pressure seemed to be completely self-inflicted. If you were worried about your place in the side, if you were concerned that your team was not good enough to win, if you were secretly dreading letting down your friends and family, then you were bound to feel pressure. However, for someone who had sailed to 1,000 Test runs in ten Tests and won his first eight consecutive Test matches, that didn't seem relevant. I was confident, the team was a well-oiled machine and the Australians were about to meet a completely different type of England cricket team.

As the first Test drew nearer, however, I definitely started sensing something different about this Ashes series. There was a growing feeling amongst the press and the public that this year was our chance. This was the England team who could finally give the great Australians a run for their money. There was genuine expectation, rather than the usual hopes and prayers that luck might just run our way. As someone about to enter his first series against Australia, I was beginning to appreciate the importance of it all.

The closer we got to the start of the series, the more I started thinking about the quality of the opposition. The truth was that the Australian team was full of legends. There was no point in denying it. Hayden, Langer, Ponting, Gilchrist, Warne and McGrath were some of the game's biggest names, and they were more than adequately backed up by the likes of Damien Martyn, Michael Clarke, Brett Lee and Jason Gillespie. There were no weak links. They had bucketloads of experience and collectively they possessed something far more valuable than their individual skills. They had an aura. They had won too many important series and dominated too many great players for that to be discounted. There was a reason they had been all but unbeatable in all conditions bar India for the previous decade, which meant it was almost impossible not to feel intimidated by the prospect of facing up to them. A little kernel of doubt started to invade my mind, which wasn't helped by Shane Warne getting me out cheaply for Hampshire early in the season.

The final days before the series resounded to a chorus of 'good lucks', and 'you can do its', as well as all the usual pre-series media build-up. Having played Australia in seven ODIs before the start of the Test series, the players from both sides were beginning to tire of all the Ashes hype and were keen to get on with it.

My diary entry from 20 July 2005 sums up my feelings pretty well.

So here it is. The Ashes starts tomorrow, and judging by all the media and texts I have been getting, it looks like a lot of people think that this is quite important! In some ways it feels like my debut again – a step into the unknown, and a new challenge. I get goose bumps just thinking about going out there tomorrow. It is going to be an atmosphere like no other . . . It is tempting to let my mind wonder how good it would be to do well in this series, and also how devastating it could be if things don't go well.

That was the prospect for all of us. The stakes were high. Win, and be a hero. Lose, or perform badly personally, and all that hope and expectation could come crashing down, submerging you and your reputation in a tidal wave of broken dreams.

I have many memories of that first Test match at Lord's in July 2005, my introduction to Ashes cricket, but they are strangely brief. It is as if they are a series of pictures, rather than a continuous movie. I suppose it is similar to the memories you might get if you attempt a bungee jump or white-water rafting. The adrenalin means that you are so focused on what is happening at the time that your mind struggles to compute it all.

The first memory that sticks in my mind is that of Ricky Ponting getting hit on the grille of his helmet by a ball from Steve Harmison. It was a huge psychological as well as physical blow. Here was the world's greatest puller of the ball getting hurried up by our opening bowler, who was rated the number-one bowler in the world at the time. All the talk in the team room before the game had centred on us never taking a backward step against the Aussies. We had to show that we weren't going to be intimidated and were ready to give as good as we got. I remember Duncan Fletcher equating it to standing up to the schoolyard bully. That perhaps explains why none of us went to check that Ponting was OK as the blood dripped from his cheek. We were a set of gladiators in the amphitheatre and compassion was not an emotion we were prepared to display. Having said that, however, I think we all have regrets that we didn't go and check on him. It was out of character for all of us. We had got too caught up in the moment, too emotional, and we showed it then. Perhaps we also displayed it again later that day when we came to bat.

Another vivid memory I have is of walking through the Long Room at Lord's on my way out to bat with Marcus Trescothick. We had bowled Australia out for 190, so the members were clearly sensing a famous victory and the reception was mind-blowing. Never have I seen so much passion on so many faces as we walked through that crowded room. This was about more than cricket; this was about England and Australia, and the complicated relationship between the two countries. For more than a decade English sports fans had had to endure the embarrassment of Australia, a much smaller nation, beating us at just about every sport going. Now, retribution was in the air.

Barely forty minutes later, as Andrew Flintoff had his off stump flattened to leave us on 21–5, there was an eerie silence in the ground. There wasn't even the dull murmur of disappointed whispering. The crowd were in shock. Their enthusiasm had collapsed under the weight of Glenn McGrath's unerring accuracy and they were forced to concede that their expectations had once again been misplaced.

We were in a similar state in the dressing room. For the first four and a half hours of the day, we had traded blows with this mighty Australian side, largely dominating, thanks to some intimidatory bowling from Harmison and Flintoff in particular. The final hour, though, had reminded us all of our frailties. It was no surprise that the nemesis, once again, was

Glenn McGrath, who had managed to back up his outrageous pre-series 5–0 prediction with some scintillating bowling.

On the surface, there didn't seem to be too much to worry about when facing McGrath. He wasn't that quick, operating mainly within the 80–85 mph band. He generally didn't swing the ball and was occasionally inclined to lose his rag and start chuntering to himself and others. However, his height, his ability to seam the ball both ways and his deadly accuracy made him one of the game's greatest bowlers. His primary asset was that, like very few others in world cricket, he was able to attack and defend at the same time. Even on the flattest of wickets, it was hard to get on top of him, and there was always the threat of a ball moving off the seam just when a batsman felt settled.

It would be wrong, though, to confuse his accuracy with being one-dimensional. Anyone who saw him play ODI cricket had to marvel at his ability to bowl yorkers under pressure. His record in the subcontinent spoke volumes about his ability to reverse-swing the ball, and on a fast and bouncy wicket his short ball was deceptively hostile and quick.

His secret, I suppose, was that he had all the tools in his armoury but only used them when he needed them. If he didn't, he merely stuck to plan A, which was to hit a length hard on off stump, relying on the combination of his height and any moisture in the wicket to get movement. That combination was more than good enough for most international players. Nothing demonstrated it more than our score of 92–7 at the end of the first day of the 2005 series.

* * *

The final memory I have of the game is the reception the Australian players gave me as I came out to bat in the second innings. We had been set an unlikely 420 to win and we all knew that something akin to a miracle was needed. That, however, was little more than a subplot in the drama between the Australian team and this young, naive England opening batsman.

The day before, Damien Martyn had been given out lbw for a very well-constructed 65 but was clearly unhappy with the decision. He remonstrated with the umpire and I, clearly too pumped with emotion at the time, told him to '---- off back to the pavilion' on my way past to congratulate the bowler, Steve Harmison. It was very much out of character for me, but after seeing the Aussies operate during the ODI series, I was getting increasingly frustrated by the way they walked around as if they owned the place.

That night, Kevin Pietersen, who despite being on debut had already struck up a chummy relationship with Shane Warne, informed me that the Aussies were hacked off with me for getting stuck into one of their players. According to him, they were 'going to let me have it in the second innings'.

And so they did. I was met with a chorus of abuse as I prepared to face the new ball. 'You aren't so loud now, are you?' came from the direction of the slip cordon. 'Come on, Binga, knock this -----'s head off,' came another shout from behind me as Brett Lee started his run-up. Most of it was pretty tame really, and I probably deserved it, but I was impressed by how they all got stuck in together. That, in my mind, was the real strength of that Australian side. They may not have been the best of mates off the field, but on it they came together in the common cause, always probing for opposition weaknesses, searching for an opening. When they found it, they rarely let go.

Overall, I was quite happy about the way I managed to contend with the verbal barrage. It seemed to concentrate my mind and allow me to focus on the ball, rather than any technical worries. The 37 I scored in that second innings was hardly match-turning, and my dismissal precipitated the inevitable slide to defeat, but at least in my mind I believed that I could mix it with the Aussies.

We went away to lick our wounds and learn the lessons from the game, knowing that defeat in the next Test, at Edgbaston, would almost certainly consign our latest attempt to regain the Ashes to the same graveyard as so many other English Ashes campaigns.

The Test match at Edgbaston that followed has gone down in English cricketing folklore as one of the greatest Test matches ever. It was a game full of drama and intrigue. From the moment that Glenn McGrath twisted his ankle just before the toss, right through to the gloved leg-side dismissal of Michael Kasprowicz that concluded the game, it was one of those contests you couldn't take your eyes off. It had everything.

The audacious way in which we started the game, scoring 400 runs in less than eighty overs, was a direct reaction to the defeat at Lord's. In the days leading up to the second Test, all the conversation had been about how badly we had let ourselves down with the bat in the first, and how important it was to go out there, look the Aussies in the eye and take the game to them. If we were going to go down, it would be in a blaze of glory.

Of course, it is always easier to come up with fighting talk in the safety of a dressing room than it is out in the middle against some of the best bowlers in the world. Great credit for our performance has to go to Michael Vaughan, who did much to instil the belief in us that we were capable of slugging it out with the Aussies, but also to Marcus Trescothick, Kevin Pietersen and Andrew Flintoff. They, more than any others, actually went out there and demonstrated what we had been talking about in our team meetings.

Some of the stroke play of Pietersen and Flintoff against Lee and Warne was outrageous. From afar, it almost looked as if they were trying to outdo each other in how far they could hit the ball, as well as in the boldness of their shot selection. In fact, I wouldn't be surprised if there was some sort of competition going on between the two alpha males in the England cricket team. Regardless, it was scintillating to watch and it forced Ricky Ponting, the Australian captain, to deal with a scenario that he and his team had rarely had to contend with before.

That Edgbaston Test, in my opinion, saw Andrew Flintoff's finest performance in an England shirt. His first-innings 68 was followed by a vitally important counter-attacking 73 in the second innings, when we had our backs to the wall at 72–5. His accurate and aggressive bowling had a big impact on the outcome of the match, and his spell against Langer and Ponting at the start of the Australian innings must go down as one of the most lethal I have witnessed. And after all that, he had the presence of mind to get down on his haunches and console Brett Lee when the game was finally won.

'Freddie' was a strangely contradictory character. A salt-of-the-earth lad from Preston, who was media-savvy enough to make sure he was always drinking the right brand of energy drink when the cameras were focused on him. The ultimate team man, who would bowl himself into the ground to try and win a match but on taking a wicket was prone to doing Jesus poses, mouthing his own name, while his team-mates tried to celebrate alongside him. An up-and-at-them cricketer, full of aggressive intent, but also a character prone to self-doubt and insecurity.

I don't suppose we were ever likely to be bosom buddies. We saw the world too differently. He no doubt thought of me as too much of a goody-two-shoes, too aligned with Vaughan and Fletcher, whereas he was much more of an anti-establishment figure, tending to court the disaffected in the side. Yet I admired him greatly for two reasons.

First, he has one of those magnetic personalities that can light up any room. People take notice of him, and at his best on the cricket field he was able to use that to ignite the entire crowd behind the England cause. Many of my most electrifying moments on the pitch occurred when he was either straining his every sinew to take a wicket, or was whacking the likes of Brett Lee around the ground.

Secondly, I was always impressed by how loyal and generous he was to his friends. While he certainly wouldn't go out of his way to help everyone, he would do absolutely anything for his mates, and I am sure that the likes of Steve Harmison would struggle to find anyone more genuinely willing to stand up for them than Fred.

What was without doubt was that he was capable of great things on a cricket pitch. He was a player that opposition teams genuinely feared. As a bowler, his immense stature, awkward bounce and bustling intent made him incredibly intimidating, and left-handers, in particular, always struggled with his round-the-wicket spells. I am glad I didn't have to face him in a Test match.

With the bat, his power and willingness to take on bowlers made him seriously threatening. Perhaps he wasn't able to do it often enough, in the way that Kevin Pietersen has, to be judged as genuinely world-class with the willow. He was good enough, though, and in combination with his bowling and high-quality slip-catching, he was rightly seen as one of England's greatest all-rounders. On his good days, as at Edgbaston in 2005, he seemed able to bend the will of the gods in his favour and turn games on their heads. Very few are capable of that, and his team-mates in that fateful Test will always be grateful.

Perhaps my abiding memory of the Edgbaston game was sitting in the dressing room afterwards, feeling absolutely drained of all energy. The nerves, the emotion and the anguish that accompanied our two-run victory left me completely shattered, and I was not alone. The topsy-turvy nature of the game, where one side dominated, only for the other to come back into the game, continued right to the last. Just when we were beginning to feel we were about to be a part of English cricket's greatest choke, Steve Harmison's desperate short ball found the glove of Michael Kasprowicz's bottom hand, and England were back in the series.

I have always felt that the best innings I ever played for England in a Test match took place at The Oval in 2005 in the fifth Test. There are a few others that came close. The hundred at Lord's in 2009 against Australia, my redeeming century in Napier against New Zealand in 2008 and the second-innings century in Brisbane in 2010 on the back of a first-innings duck spring to mind. However, I am proudest of that innings at The Oval because of what was at stake.

As we headed into the final Test with a 2–1 lead in the series, the expectation of English cricket supporters had reached a crescendo. It was impossible to think about anything other than the five days ahead of us and we all knew that this could be our moment. Seize it, and we would all remember the victory for the rest of our lives. On the other hand, if we succumbed to the pressure and bottled it in front of an expectant nation, I don't think we would ever have been forgiven. It may sound over-dramatic, but that is how we felt.

I remember Ashley Giles appearing in the home dressing room at The Oval on the morning of the first day looking completely spent. The dark circles under his eyes and haunted expression on his face revealed his obvious stress.

'Gilo, you look terrible, mate,' I said, only partly in jest.

'I'm not surprised,' he replied. 'I haven't slept for the past seven weeks.'

'You aren't the only one,' I said, and looking around at the rest of the lads nodding their heads, it was clear that we had all been going through the same anguish in silence.

I have never been more nervous walking out to bat than on that day with Marcus Trescothick. Our destiny was on the line, and on a beautiful sunny day in September, it was our job to build the foundation for our ultimate victory. Perhaps fuelled by adrenalin, we got off to a rollicking start against the seamers on an unresponsive Oval surface, until the team was pegged back by the brilliance of Shane Warne, not for the first time. Four quick wickets transformed our steady start from 82–0 to 131–4, and once again the pressure weighed heavily on my shoulders.

Shane Warne had been something of a bogeyman for us all during the series. For me in particular, playing against him for the first time in a Test series, he had proved quite a handful. Like any armchair cricket fan, I had watched him mesmerise English batsmen for a decade from his infamous 'Gatting' ball at Old Trafford in 1993, but aside from facing him a couple of times in county cricket, I had no real idea of what it would be like to do battle with him in an Ashes series. I felt reasonably confident that I would do all right, given that I thought I had played leg spin well in the past, so it was perhaps a mixture of stubbornness and naivety that allowed me to dismiss Duncan Fletcher's gentle warning that 'You may have to work a bit on your technique against Warne' as nothing more than Duncan trying to keep me on my toes. I was in for a rude awakening.

When you watch Warne on television, it is easy to assess

the technical challenges. You can see the wizardry of his bowling. The subtle variations, as well as the unerring accuracy, are on display. What you can't appreciate, however, is how much of a role his personality, and gamesmanship, play in proceedings. I am not surprised that he has gone on to play poker since retirement, because I always felt that he was trying to look into my psyche in the middle, figuring out what I was thinking by observing my body language and facial expressions – exactly as a poker player does. He is famous for his sledging, of course, but I think that those who put his wicket-taking ability down to having a quick wit and foul mouth are missing the point. He would say all manner of things to you in the middle, but I always had the impression that really he was probing to see how you reacted to what he was saying.

For instance, after I had struggled against him early in the series, he started calling me 'Daryll' after Daryll Cullinan, who had been his 'bunny' in years past. Cullinan never got a run against Warne. As much as I hated being compared to Cullinan by Warne (secretly, I was worried that there was more than a grain of truth in his assessment), I could also see that he was goading me. By saying it, he was tempting me to come out of my shell and try to dominate him – taking matters into my own hands to rid myself of the label. But he was also looking for signs that I was going to cower and submit to his superiority. If he ever reached a stage where he could genuinely intimidate a batsman, then the battle was already won.

By and large, I kept myself to myself and refused to play his games, but Fletcher's warning about my technique came back to bite me. The old-school theory of playing with the spin was getting me into trouble against him. The drift he managed to get on the ball meant that by looking to hit him on the leg side, I was often hitting across the line of balls that were well wide of off stump but were straightening back to hit the stumps. The odds weren't in my favour.

Hours of work in the nets, and against Merlyn, a prototype spin-bowling machine that is now commonplace in every county indoor school, under Fletcher's expert tutelage allowed me to start hitting the ball back to where it came from a little more and saved me from the ignominy of being Warne's next bunny. A century on a turning wicket at Old Trafford in the drawn third Test match had finally proved to me that I could contend with him, although the number of times I got out to him over this and subsequent series displayed that I would never be completely comfortable against his bag of tricks.

Looking back, I suppose I feel fortunate to have been able to lock horns with the player I regard as the best bowler to grace a cricket pitch, certainly in my time and perhaps ever. You can say what you like about Shane Warne the man, but as a bowler he was unparalleled, a superb exponent of the hardest art in bowling.

Thankfully, despite our precarious position on the first day of that final Test match, the wicket remained true and I was able to compile a crucial partnership with Andrew Flintoff to help get us to a position of comparative safety, and just after tea a leg-side flick off Brett Lee brought up my most important century for England.

England v Australia
(5th Test)

Played at Kennington Oval, London, on 8–12 September 2005

Umpires:	BF Bowden & RE Koertzen (TV: JW Lloyds)
Referee:	RS Madugalle
Toss:	England

ENGLAND

ME Trescothick	c Hayden b Warne	43	lbw b Warne		33
AJ Strauss	c Katich b Warne	129	c Katich b Warne		1
MP Vaughan*	c Clarke b Warne	11	c Gilchrist b McGrath		45
IR Bell	lbw b Warne	0	c Warne b McGrath		0
KP Pietersen	b Warne	14	b McGrath		158
A Flintoff	c Warne b McGrath	72	c and b Warne		8
PD Collingwood	lbw b Tait	7	c Ponting b Warne		10
GO Jones†	b Lee	25	b Tait		1
AF Giles	lbw b Warne	32	b Warne		59
MJ Hoggard	c Martyn b McGrath	2	not out		4
SJ Harmison	not out	20	c Hayden b Warne		0
Extras	(b 4, lb 6, w 1, nb 7)	18	(b 4, w 7, nb 5)		16
Total	(105.3 overs)	373		(91.3 overs)	335

AUSTRALIA

JL Langer	b Harmison	105	not out		0
ML Hayden	lbw b Flintoff	138	not out		0
RT Ponting*	c Strauss b Flintoff	35			
DR Martyn	c Collingwood b Flintoff	10			
MJ Clarke	lbw b Hoggard	25			
SM Katich	lbw b Flintoff	1			
AC Gilchrist†	lbw b Hoggard	23			
SK Warne	c Vaughan b Flintoff	0			
B Lee	c Giles b Hoggard	6			
GD McGrath	c Strauss b Hoggard	0			
SW Tait	not out	1			
Extras	(b 4, lb 8, w 2, nb 9)	23	(lb 4)		4
Total	(107.1 overs)	367	(for 0 wkts)	(0.4 overs)	4

AUSTRALIA	O	M	R	W		O	M	R	W
McGrath	27	5	72	2		26	3	85	3
Lee	23	3	94	1		20	4	88	0
Tait	15	1	61	1	(5)	5	0	28	1
Warne	37.3	5	122	6	(3)	38.3	3	124	6
Katich	3	0	14	0					
Clarke					(4)	2	0	6	0

ENGLAND	O	M	R	W		O	M	R	W
Harmison	22	2	87	1		0.4	0	0	0
Hoggard	24.1	2	97	4					
Flintoff	34	10	78	5					
Giles	23	1	76	0					
Collingwood	4	0	17	0					

Fall of wickets:

	Eng	Aus	Eng	Aus
1st	82	185	2	–
2nd	102	264	67	–
3rd	104	281	67	–
4th	131	323	109	–
5th	274	329	126	–
6th	289	356	186	–
7th	297	359	199	–
8th	325	363	308	–
9th	345	363	335	–
10th	373	367	335	–

Close of play:	Day 1:	Eng (1) 319–7 (Jones 21*, Giles 5*, 88 overs)
	Day 2:	Aus (1) 112–0 (Langer 75*, Hayden 32*, 33 overs)
	Day 3:	Aus (1) 277–2 (Hayden 110*, Martyn 9*, 78.4 overs)
	Day 4:	Eng (2) 34–1 (Trescothick 14*, Vaughan 19*, 13.2 overs)

Man of the match:	KP Pietersen
Result:	**Match drawn**

As I soaked up the applause, I was genuinely proud of myself in a way that was never to be repeated. Maybe it was the Australian cricket team's undoubted quality; perhaps it was the fact that I had stepped up to save my team under pressure. I am not sure what made me feel that way, but I still look back at that moment, with my helmet off, sweat dripping down my face, staring up at all the grateful English supporters at The Oval that day, as my best experience as an England batsman.

Perhaps ironically, that first-day century was completely overshadowed by Kevin Pietersen's outrageous last-day heroics. It would be hard to argue that his adrenalin-fuelled machismo was the most sensible way to make sure that we were able to occupy the crease for the last day of the match, thus ensuring the draw we needed. However, it was Pietersen's first demonstration on the Test scene that he was a very special talent, who, unbridled by team directives or predetermined methods, could play in a way of which others were simply incapable. The level of his self-confidence, the quality of the stroke play and the sheer boldness of his innings still stick in my mind today. It was brilliance at a time when brilliance was demanded and required. Above all, it made us all heroes.

Australia in England 2005 – The Ashes

1st Test. Lord's, London. 21–24 July 2005
Australia 190 (S.J. Harmison 5–43) and 384 (M.J. Clarke 91, D.R. Martyn
65, S.M. Katich 67)
England 155 (K.P. Pietersen 57, **A.J. Strauss 2**; G.D. McGrath 5–53) and
180 (K.P. Pietersen 64, M.E. Trescothick 44, **A.J. Strauss 37**; G.D. McGrath
4–29)
Australia won by 239 runs.

2nd Test. Edgbaston, Birmingham. 4–7 August 2005
England 407 (M.E. Trescothick 90, K.P. Pietersen 71, A. Flintoff 68, **A.J.
Strauss 48**; S.K. Warne 4–116) and 182 (A. Flintoff 73, **A.J. Strauss 6**;
S.K. Warne 6–46, B. Lee 4–82)
Australia 308 (J.L. Langer 82, R.T. Ponting 61; A. Flintoff 3–52) and 279
(B. Lee 43*; A. Flintoff 4–79)
England won by 2 runs.

3rd Test. Old Trafford, Manchester. 11–15 August 2005
England 444 (M.P. Vaughan 166, M.E. Trescothick 63, I.R. Bell 59, **A.J.
Strauss 6**; S.K. Warne 4–99, B. Lee 4–100) and 280–6 dec (**A.J. Strauss
106**, I.R. Bell 65; G.D. McGrath 5–115)
Australia 302 (S.K. Warne 90; S.P. Jones 6–53) and 371–9 (R.T. Ponting
156; A. Flintoff 4–71)
Match drawn.

4th Test. Trent Bridge, Nottingham. 25–28 August 2005
England 477 (A. Flintoff 102, G.O. Jones 85, M.E. Trescothick 65, M.P.
Vaughan 58, **A.J. Strauss 35**; S.K. Warne 4–102) and 129–7 (**A.J. Strauss
23**; S.K. Warne 4–31)
Australia 218 (B. Lee 47, S.M. Katich 45; S.P. Jones 5–44) and 387 (f/o)
(J.L. Langer 61, S.M. Katich 59, M.J. Clarke 56)
England won by 3 wickets.

5th Test. The Oval, London. 8–12 September 2005
England 373 (**A.J. Strauss 129**, A. Flintoff 72; S.K. Warne 6–122)
and 335 (K.P. Pietersen 158, A.F. Giles 59, **A.J. Strauss 1**; S.K. Warne
6–124)
Australia 367 (M.L. Hayden 138, J.L. Langer 105; Flintoff 5–78, M.J.
Hoggard 4–97) and 4–0
Match drawn.

England won the series 2–1.

7

DISGRACE

I wake early to the sounds that accompany a summer morning in Australia. Birds are singing, the sun is shining and the city of Adelaide is slowly coming to life. I look out of my hotel window to see the River Torrens beneath me. The embankment is busy with early-morning strollers, joggers and cyclists taking advantage of the relative coolness of the early hours. The forecast is for another scorching-hot day, approaching 40 degrees centigrade. On the far side of the river, I can make out the distinctive floodlights of the Adelaide cricket ground. At that time of the morning it is completely deserted, nothing more than a serene addition to the landscape of the City of Churches.

In less than three hours, though, the scene will be completely transformed. Thousands of home fans, from all corners of South Australia, will make their way to the ground, hoping that their team might just be able to force a result in the second Test match of the 2006–07 Ashes. In addition, almost as many English travelling fans are likely to be heading to the huge grass bank on the far side of the ground. They are no doubt excited about the prospect of a day of Barmy Army songs, copious amounts of beer and the obligatory sunburn. They are also expecting their team to bat at least till teatime to ensure a well-earned draw.

I am a little jaded after four days of intense Ashes cricket in uncomfortable heat, but I am also feeling the best I have for a long time about the team and the state of my own game. Having surrendered the first Test in Brisbane relatively meekly, we need to show everyone that we aren't going to be a pushover for the rest of the series. A double hundred by Paul Collingwood and a sublime century from Kevin Pietersen saw us to a formidable first-innings total of 551. Australia rallied in reply, getting close to our score on the back of a Ricky Ponting hundred, but by ending the fourth day at 59–1 in our second innings, we have overcome the potentially difficult new-ball spell from McGrath and Lee.

I am 31 not out overnight, my first contribution to the series of any size after failures in Brisbane, and I am feeling much perkier about my ability to play on the bouncy wickets of Australia. I hope that today will bring a sizeable score, a winning draw and some real momentum going into the potentially tricky Perth Test match.

Shortly before 11 a.m., I make my way down the steps from the players' viewing gallery with my partner Ian Bell, following the Australian fielders onto the ground. 'What a wonderful day to play Test cricket,' I tell myself as I survey the cloudless sky, the full house of support and the beautiful backdrop of the Adelaide Oval, one of my favourite grounds.

For the first twenty minutes of play, everything seems to go pretty much according to plan. Ian Bell and I are playing ourselves back in, and although we aren't scoring a significant number of runs, there are few moments to worry the travelling fans unduly.

After another six fruitless overs, I am beginning to get concerned. The Aussies have managed to get the ball reversing quite considerably, and the combination of Stuart Clark, with his unerring accuracy, at one end and the ever-present threat of Shane Warne at the other is slowly strangling any scoring intent from Bell and myself. I know that if we keep this up for too long, the pressure will build on us and also on those waiting in the dressing room.

I try to use my feet against Warne, hoping to change his length a little and provide some scoring opportunities. Every time I do, he seems to read my plans and brings his length back. I have no other way of scoring, so I keep to the plan. As he delivers the ball once more I move down the wicket, and once more the ball is agonisingly short of a length to attack. I stick out my pad and bat together, knowing that it is impossible to be out lbw so far down the wicket. The ball hits the pad and balloons to the short-leg fielder. There is a half-hearted appeal from Adam Gilchrist behind the stumps and Matthew Hayden, the slip fielder. It goes without saying that Warne is appealing for a potential bat-pad catch, but then he appeals for everything.

I make sure that I get back into my ground before turning towards the umpire, Steve Bucknor, fully expecting to see his head shaking vigorously, as is his habit when he rules a decision not out. Instead, I know I am in trouble. He hasn't moved yet, but I can see that he is running through the computations in his head. The dreaded moment comes seconds later as he raises his finger. I have been given out caught. There will be no challenge from me – this is before the introduction of DRS. All I can do is head back to the pavilion to curse my bad luck.

I spend the best part of half an hour with my head in my hands down in the dungeon of a dressing room. I can't see the play continuing. There are no windows and the TV is switched off. All the other players are up in the viewing gallery, two storeys above me. From the complete silence of the crowd, however, I can tell that the scoreboard is not ticking over. We are still being strangled. Soon, a great roar erupts. Ian Bell has been needlessly run out attempting a risky single. He is quickly followed by Kevin Pietersen, bowled around his legs by Warne. The situation is getting out of hand. The momentum is swinging violently against us and we desperately need a couple of players to stand up and stem the tide.

Paul Collingwood, fresh from his Herculean first-innings double century, stands firm. Around him, however, no player displays any real permanence at the wicket. Flintoff nicks off, Geraint Jones follows and the English players and supporters alike are suddenly staring at a train wreck. Unless something changes very quickly, we are about to pull off one of the greatest chokes in Ashes history.

As is so often the case when momentum changes so violently, the end of our innings seems inevitable. Giles, Harmison, Hoggard and Anderson all succumb to the mastery of Warne and McGrath. Australia have over a session to chase down the modest total of 168. From the moment that Justin Langer slogs the second ball from Matthew Hoggard over midwicket for four, the result is a foregone conclusion. There is no way that we will be able to restrict the Australian scoring rate enough to hold out for a draw. Hayden, Ponting and Hussey all knock nails in our coffin with some scintillating stroke play.

Finally, with more than three overs left in the match, Mike Hussey hits the boundary that wins the game for Australia. The home fans are ecstatic, having witnessed one of the great Test match wins. The Australian players are jumping up and down celebrating their stunning performance. In contrast, the English fans are in shock. They can't believe what they have just witnessed. In their minds, the series is already over. There is no way back from 2–0 down after such a confidence-sapping performance.

In our dressing room there is a deathly silence. Everyone is sitting in their seats, accompanied by the debris from five hard days of Test cricket. Dirty kit is strewn all over the floor. Dozens of empty Powerade bottles are lying on the benches, constant reminders of the graft we have been through in the heat. None of us, though, have anything to show for it. We have lost. We have capitulated. We have choked. We have blown our chances of winning in Australia. It is over.

Two months earlier the defence of the Ashes, so wondrously won in 2005, had got off to the worst possible start when our captain, Michael Vaughan, was ruled out of the series with his recurrent knee injury. As he'd spent the whole of the previous summer injured, the selectors had at least had a little time to prepare for life without Vaughan. Unfortunately, Andrew Flintoff, his unofficial deputy, had injured himself in the course of the three-Test series against Sri Lanka and so the final series of the summer of 2006, against Pakistan, was captained by the deputy's deputy – me.

After a 3–0 series win, the succession plan had clearly been thrown into doubt. Some of the media were speculating about Flintoff's suitability for the job, citing the difficulties experienced by England's last all-round talisman, Ian Botham. On the other hand, there was plenty of talk about Flintoff's ability to inspire the team, leading from the front. Most people weren't really talking too much about the alternative. I was seen as the safe, slightly uninspired choice, who would probably do a decent job but nothing more. The debate centred around Flintoff, not me.

I have to say that I felt distinctly uncomfortable at the thought of usurping Flintoff from what he regarded as his rightful place. I definitely thought I had the capability and credentials to lead the team, having captained Middlesex and got used to the idea of captaining England during the summer. However, it was clear that Flintoff desperately wanted to do the job. He was next in line and it was not as though we were best buddies in the side. If he was overlooked, it would have been hard for him not to see it as a slap in the face. The selectors, in effect, would have been killing off his chances of leading his country without really giving him the opportunity to show whether he was up to it or not.

At the time, whenever I thought about the idea of captaining the side in the Ashes, the initial excitement was always followed by more than a little dread at the thought of dealing with the immense baggage that would be created if Flintoff was not made captain. It was perhaps this feeling that prevented me from stating my case more forcibly when Duncan Fletcher asked me if I wanted the job. 'You have seen us both captain the side,' I replied. 'It is up to you to decide.'

I am sure he was looking for me to put forward a stronger argument.

The issue was finally resolved when we were going through our annual fitness-testing up at the national academy in Loughborough. It was always a tough day, with the obvious tests – VO2 max, sprint test and strength tests – being complemented by a number of additional scans. Eyes, heart, skin cancer, body composition (otherwise known as the fat test), injuries, flexibility and general well-being were all checked. At the end of the session, Duncan called me into one of the meeting rooms on the top floor of the building.

'Straussy, the selectors met yesterday to discuss who was going to captain the side to Australia. We have decided to give Flintoff the job. There are a number of reasons for this that I can't go into at this stage, but I think that the decision might be good for you in the long term.' Fletcher delivered my fate in his usual unemotional manner.

'I think you have made the wrong decision,' I replied, 'but of course I will support Freddie as much as I can.' And that was that. There was nothing more to discuss.

Looking back at the Ashes series that followed, when we got absolutely thumped 5–0, many people jumped to the conclusion that it was the decision to make Flintoff captain that sealed our fate. I don't subscribe to that point of view in the slightest. The truth was that they were a far better side than us, especially in their own conditions. Even with our side from 2005 fully intact and firing on all cylinders, I think we would have struggled to win. The Australians were on their home patch, their ranks filled with some of the greatest cricketers ever to play the game, and they were hell-bent on revenge for 2005.

In contrast, we had lost our captain to injury. Marcus Trescothick, in my opinion one of the great England openers, had been forced to return home with a recurrence of his panic attacks and depression. Ashley Giles was feeling his way back after long-term injury, and Steve Harmison, one of our talismans in 2005, was struggling to hit the cut strip, as he demonstrated with the first ball of the series. We weren't in any position to win that series, no matter who was leading the side.

What became apparent over the course of an arduous tour, which consisted of five Test matches followed by a long ODI tri-series with the hosts and New Zealand, was that it was vitally important for the coach and the captain to see eye to eye. The relationship between Freddie Flintoff and Duncan Fletcher had always been a fraught one. Flintoff had never reacted well to authority, and Duncan had just about resigned himself to the fact that Flintoff was never going to toe the party line. As long as Freddie kept performing, then all was just about OK, but by the time Flintoff was made captain, they really didn't speak very much. In some ways, it was very similar to the situation with Kevin Pietersen and Peter Moores some years later.

In that regard, I found it strange that Fletcher opted to appoint Flintoff captain for the tour. Perhaps he saw it as a way of bringing Flintoff into the bosom of the side, allowing him to appreciate how difficult a job it was and then hoping that it would give him a greater sense of responsibility.

In any event, it didn't work. As the tour progressed, Fletcher and Flintoff became more and more distant from each other. The players, who were almost without exception struggling with poor form and the ignominy of being humiliated by a far better side, tended to stick their heads in the sand and do their best to make sure they weren't the ones who were going to get dropped.

In fact, the entire three-month tour was, without doubt, my lowest moment as an England cricketer. It started with great anticipation and expectation, but once we had been defeated in Adelaide, a dark cloud hung over us for the next two months. We knew we weren't playing well, the media knew we weren't playing well – and the thousands of England fans who had come over to support us were seething at our incompetence.

I still remember getting into a lift going up to my hotel room after the Perth Test, where the Ashes were finally surrendered. As I shuffled my way in, it was obvious that I was sharing my journey with some distinctly unimpressed England fans. The St George crosses that were daubed on their faces, giving them an almost clownlike appearance, were in direct contrast to the sombre and morose expressions beneath the paint. I tried to make myself as inconspicuous as possible, but it was impossible. As we made our way up the many floors of the hotel, the uncomfortable silence was broken by one of the supporters.

'You know, you should be ashamed of yourself. You and your

team-mates are a disgrace. I was embarrassed watching an England team play with so little fight.'

Each word hit home like a dagger to my heart. No one felt more disappointed than me. There was nothing that I could really say in my defence, other than 'We are trying our best, you know.' The words sounded hollow.

I felt incredibly angry with those fans. They did not know all the turmoil we were going through. They did not appreciate the stresses and strains that went into playing an Ashes series. The pressure had certainly contributed to Marcus Trescothick having to go home, in effect ending his England career. What about the sleepless nights worrying about what the next day might have in store? What about walking out to bat with the hopes of your family, your friends, your fellow players and your country on your back? Could they appreciate that?

Of course they couldn't. That wasn't the point. They had saved up their money and travelled 10,000 miles to see a famous English victory on Australian soil. They got the opposite. They were entitled to feel short-changed. I realised that my anger did not actually lie with them; it lay with myself and the rest of the team. We had let ourselves down.

I made a vow that if I ever came back to Australia on a cricket tour, it would be different.

By the time the tour reached Sydney for the fifth Test, the wheels were well and truly off. It was no surprise that Australia won the last game of the series so comfortably. They were so far in the ascendancy that the series was close to being a mismatch. Also, they were in no mood for charity. It was the final game in the careers of both Shane Warne and Glenn McGrath. They were not interested in signing off with a defeat.

The one-day series that followed defied belief. It was clear that as a group we were completely shot to pieces. There was very little hope for us in a series that was supposed to be our final preparation for the World Cup that followed in the West Indies. In order to keep us all vaguely sane, the management of the side, with Michael Vaughan back as captain once more, decided to place our emphasis on just having a bit of fun. That meant turning our back on all the pressure and expectation, trying to enjoy our cricket, having a few beers in the evenings and all in all trying to appreciate Australia as a country.

The change of tactic certainly didn't bring any immediate relief. The way the tournament worked, we would all play each other four times, and then the top two teams would go through to a best-of-three final. Each week we would play New Zealand on a Tuesday and Australia on a Friday. For the first three weeks of the tournament, Friday became our bogey day. We were hammered by Australia in Melbourne and Brisbane – and even faced the acute embarrassment of losing to the Aussies in a day/night game in front of a full house in Adelaide before the floodlights needed to be turned on.

Thankfully the games against New Zealand were much closer affairs. We were like two second-division teams going at it hammer and tongs, playing for second place. We could not hope to compete with our Premier League rival, Australia. At the end of the group games, we had beaten New Zealand twice and lost twice, and we only made it through to the final because we had somehow managed to beat Australia in our final group game in Sydney on the back of a brilliant hundred by Ed Joyce. New Zealand didn't beat Australia at all.

My abiding memory of that final group game is of watching the Australians going through a gruelling two-hour fitness session on the day before, no doubt getting themselves in tip-top shape for the rigours of the World Cup that was about to follow. We, on the other hand, were spending most of our time on the beach or in the bar.

Nonetheless, we made it through to the best-of-three final and proceeded to pull off one of the most outrageous heists in the history of ODI cricket. Paul Collingwood inspired us with a brilliant 120 in Melbourne and followed it up with 70 in Sydney as we surprised everyone, including ourselves, by walking away with the spoils, despite everyone knowing that we were a vastly inferior side. Talk about the unpredictability of sport.

In an eerie omen for what was about to follow in the World Cup, our celebrations that night were curtailed by an armed gang smashing their way into our city-centre hotel in Sydney at about three in the morning, robbing the reception, relieving Dean Conway, our physiotherapist who was standing in the foyer, of his wallet, and sending those of us who were still enjoying a celebratory drink into a blind panic. The gang saw us in the bar area and started to make their way towards us. Reg Dickason, our security man, was forced into action for just about the only time that I was involved with the team. His cunning plan to get us all out of the predicament: to open the back door and tell us all to run as fast as we could. Fortunately the plan worked and we weren't followed by the gang. Perhaps the gods were reminding us that there wasn't much to celebrate after losing all five Tests and five of the ten ODIs we had played.

England have never won a World Cup. There are many reasons for this. Perhaps it is to do with the very different type of limited-overs cricket that is played in England, where the swinging and seaming ball necessitates far more caution than elsewhere in the world. We have always struggled to match the sheer power and positivity of some of the other teams in more benign conditions. Also, it is fair to say that limited-overs cricket in our country is not the main event. Cricket enthusiasts in our country worship Test cricket and endure ODI cricket. In other parts of the world it is the other way around. That emphasis, however, means that limited-overs cricket is relegated to a far lesser status when it comes to scheduling, preparing and practising. County teams still stumble into one-day fixtures, unsure of who they are playing against, often knackered after the completion of a four-day fixture the day before and with only an hour before the start of the game to make the necessary adjustments in mindset and technique to switch into one-day mode. That is certainly not a recipe for high-quality cricket.

It is also true that the schedule – with England teams attempting to cope with the two-month World Cup campaign almost immediately after spending three months playing a tense and fatiguing Ashes series away from home – has to be a significant contributing factor. In both the World Cups I played in, I felt as if we were competing with one arm tied behind our back. As our old psychologist Steve Bull always used to say, 'It is impossible to peak and then peak again.' Olympic athletes structure their training to make sure they come good for one event. They would never contemplate the idea of competing in the Olympics and then at a world championship a month or two later. The body and mind just can't cope.

In March 2007, we arrived in the West Indies after barely a week at home, hopeful that our one-day series victory in Australia may just have inspired us enough to pull off something similar in the World Cup. In truth, though, the feat was always going to be unlikely. The players were running on empty, mentally and physically exhausted, and struggling to cope with the idea of two more months in hotel rooms.

Duncan Fletcher, our coach, was reaching the end of his tether as well. It was clear to us all that his uncomfortable relationship with the media was close to breaking point. He was getting more and more paranoid about what was being said and written, often wondering aloud how certain pieces of confidential information were finding their way into the pages of the tabloids. He was also getting exasperated by what he termed our lack of nous when it came to one-day cricket. He just couldn't understand why we weren't making better decisions under pressure and paying more attention to the little things, such as batsmen backing up properly or fielders making sure they were throwing the ball to the correct end. It was clear that he felt everything he was saying was going in one ear and out of the other.

He was also struggling with discipline. Following the Australian ODI series, something of a drinking culture had been established in the side. There was a sort of reverse logic being clung to that we had won the series in Australia because we had all gone out and had a few drinks – that must have been the secret to our success. Maybe it was, but it was never going to work long-term and it all came home to roost in the World Cup.

Immediately after losing the first match against New Zealand, with forty-eight hours before a vitally important game against Canada, the players really shouldn't have been going out at all, but such was the habit that had been established over the preceding weeks that most of the lads were out and about in the bars of Saint Lucia. No doubt some of the holidaymakers and supporters wouldn't have been overly impressed with our lack of professionalism, but it was only when one of the newspapers got a tip-off that Andrew Flintoff had been rescued from the sea at about 4 a.m., having capsized a pedalo, that the proverbial really hit the fan.

Perhaps in earlier eras that sort of behaviour was expected, but with more money and more public interest in the game, there was no way the media were going to let us off this particular faux pas. If we had been winning, we might just have got away with it, but we weren't. Cricket was on the front page of the newspapers for the wrong reasons, and the player in the eye of the storm was none other than the guy who four months previously had been proudly leading the team out to Australia full of hope and expectation, Andrew Flintoff.

The negative publicity that surrounded the team that week, with cameraphone pictures being sold to newspapers and Andrew Flintoff being dropped for disciplinary reasons, sounded the final death knell for what was an already futile bid to win the World Cup. We performed pitifully in every respect throughout the tournament, failing to beat any mainstream opponent, before a consolation win against the West Indies in our last 'dead rubber' game. I had my first taste of being left out of the side, with Ed Joyce being preferred to me for the first half of the tournament, but my disappointment was as nothing compared to that of Duncan Fletcher. After a torrid winter, it was clear that heads were going to roll and, having given his all to the side for seven years, Duncan knew his time was up. He resigned on the eve of our final game in an emotional team meeting and in doing so brought an end to an era.

It felt extremely unfair to me that Duncan Fletcher left England cricket on those terms. In effect, he was paying the price for a winter in which the players were simply not good enough or lost form at just the wrong time. He had given so much to the team, which we should never forget was languishing at the bottom of the world rankings when he was brought in, as a relatively unheard-of replacement for David 'Bumble' Lloyd. To have overseen the transition of the team from those particularly humble beginnings into the side that overpowered the mighty Australians in 2005 was an incredible achievement.

He had to fight tooth and nail for many of the advances that we see as routine now. In the days just after the introduction of central contracts, the counties still felt a huge amount of ownership over the players, as well as an unhealthy cynicism about what happened to them while they were on England duty. Fletcher was bloody-minded enough to lock horns with the counties and effectively bypass them when it came to picking and working with England players.

His belligerent attitude to the counties made him few friends but was sorely needed. Anyone looking at the players that county cricket was producing could see that there were some fundamental flaws in the system. People weren't being prepared to play international cricket; they were being prepared to face a barrage of 70 mph bowling if they were batsmen, and simply to last through an interminable season if they were bowlers. Neither bore any relation to cricket at the highest level.

Where Fletcher made his greatest impact, in my opinion, was with the relatively small number of players that he worked with on a day-to-day basis. Players like Michael Vaughan and Marcus Trescothick are often cited as great examples of his coaching ability at work. Plucked from relative obscurity, they were transformed into high-quality international players under his tutelage. I would argue, though, that his methods rubbed off on many others too. Mark Butcher and Graham Thorpe significantly improved their play against spin under Fletcher, and I will always be grateful for the help he gave me in gaining a better understanding of the game of cricket.

His methods were all based on logic. He wasn't into new fads or ideas. He took the concepts of batting, bowling and fielding back to first principles, treating cricket as a game of angles. By doing so, he was able to debunk some of the myths.

For example, he would always argue that playing with the spin was a flawed method of dealing with spin bowling. At times it was far safer to be meeting a spinning ball with the full face of the bat, which in effect was playing against the spin. That technique definitely helped me against Shane Warne in 2005.

His reliance on using angles gave him a really good insight into opposition players' strengths and weaknesses. In an era when the statistical data on players was not as complete as it is today, he was streets ahead of any other coach I encountered in terms of dissecting a player's technique and compiling plans to make life difficult for them. He would notice things that no one else would.

For example, I remember sitting in a team meeting in 2004 discussing Herschelle Gibbs. Herschelle was a particularly talented player, seemingly with the ability to hit the ball to all parts of the ground. We were all debating where we should be trying to bowl at him when Fletcher intervened.

'Guys, it is pretty clear where we need to be bowling at him. Look at his bottom-hand grip. With a grip like that he is going to find it very difficult to hit the ball straight back at the bowler. If we can angle the ball in to hit middle and off stump, he is likely to get bowled.'

We all started studying Herschelle's bottom-hand grip in great detail, having never noticed anything unusual about it before. Needless to say he got out bowled more than once in that series.

In so many ways, Duncan Fletcher had the ability to surprise and inform us with his theories on the game. Whether it was the 'forward press' against spin, or using the theory of aerodynamics to help us understand reverse swing better, he was a treasure trove of cricketing information of the type you will never find in an instruction manual. Having, with notable exceptions, listened to coaches throughout my career up to that point largely spouting clichés and half-truths that weren't really relevant to my game, it was all a huge eye-opener for me.

His greatest achievement, in my opinion, finally led to his downfall. What English cricket was crying out for when he came into the job was an identity. Too many players either followed their own agendas, making sure that they kept their place in the team, or felt uncomfortable in a largely foreign environment. In conjunction with Nasser Hussain and then Michael Vaughan, Fletcher was able to create a feeling of togetherness amongst the England players. He loved nothing more than to let everyone know how different the approach of the England side was from that of the counties, and by being constantly reminded of how far ahead we were, we largely bought into the concept of 'Team England'. Also, because he was loath to talk to the media in any capacity, he created an aura about the set-up. The media were intrigued to know what was going on behind the scenes, especially when players started talking about what a profound effect he was having, but they could never put their finger on it. It all helped us to feel that we were part of a special bubble and in doing so created genuine team spirit in the side.

In the end, he probably created too many enemies for himself. Over the years he had taken on the ECB, the counties and the media, and there were a few people queuing up to see him go when the England team eventually fell from their pedestal. It is probably also true that some of the players in the team found him hard to communicate with. He was essentially a quiet, introverted leader and communication was not his strong point.

Undoubtedly, though, he dragged English cricket from the Dark Ages and I am absolutely certain that the team would never have enjoyed the many successes of recent years without his contribution. I was not the only one to shed a tear when he walked away.

DISGRACE

England in Australia 2006–07 – The Ashes

1st Test. BCG, Brisbane. 23–27 November 2006
Australia 602–9 dec (R.T. Ponting 196, M.E.K. Hussey 86, J.L. Langer 82;
A. Flintoff 4–99) and 202–1 dec (J.L. Langer 100*, R.T. Ponting 60*)
England 157 (I.R. Bell 50, **A.J. Strauss 12**; G.D. McGrath 6–50) and 370
(P.D. Collingwood 96, K.P. Pietersen 92, **A.J. Strauss 11**; S.R. Clark 4–72,
S.K. Warne 4–124)
Australia won by 277 runs.

2nd Test. Adelaide Oval, Adelaide. 1–5 December 2006
England 551–6 dec (P.D. Collingwood 206, K.P. Pietersen 158, I.R. Bell
60, **A.J. Strauss 14**) and 129 (**A.J. Strauss 34**; S.K. Warne 4–49)
Australia 513 (R.T. Ponting 142, M.J. Clarke 124, M.E.K. Hussey 91,
A.C. Gilchrist 64; M.J. Hoggard 7–109) and 168–4 (M.E.K. Hussey 61*,
R.T. Ponting 49)
Australia won by 6 wickets.

3rd Test. WACA, Perth. 14–18 December 2006
Australia 244 (M.E.K. Hussey 74*; M.S. Panesar 5–92, S.J. Harmison 4–48)
and 527–5 dec (M.J. Clarke 135*, M.E.K. Hussey 103, A.C. Gilchrist
102*, M.L. Hayden 92, R.T. Ponting 75)
England 215 (K.P. Pietersen 70, **A.J. Strauss 42**) and 350 (A.N. Cook 116,
I.R. Bell 87, K.P. Pietersen 60, A. Flintoff 51, **A.J. Strauss 0**; S.K. Warne
4–115)
Australia won by 206 runs.

4th Test. MCG, Melbourne. 26–28 December 2006
England 159 (**A.J. Strauss 50**; S.K. Warne 5–39) and 161 (**A.J. Strauss
31**; B. Lee 4–47)
Australia 419 (A. Symonds 156, M.L. Hayden 153; S.I. Mahmood 4–100)
Australia won by an innings and 99 runs.

5th Test. SCG, Sydney. 2–5 January 2007
England 291 (A. Flintoff 89, I.R. Bell 71, **A.J. Strauss 29**) and 147 (**A.J.
Strauss 24**)
Australia 393 (S.K. Warne 71, A.C. Gilchrist 62) and 46–0
Australia won by 10 wickets.

Australia won the series 5–0.

8

DROPPED LIKE A STONE

No one enjoys being humiliated. All confidence drains from your body and it becomes difficult to look people in the eye. Everywhere you go, it feels as if you are walking around naked, with people pointing and giggling at you. We have all been through it at some stage. The joke that goes down like a lead balloon; the speech where you can't get your words out; plucking up the courage to ask a girl out, only to be rejected; losing your job – the list goes on and on. I defy anyone to claim they haven't been humiliated at some point in their lives.

Humiliation is even more painful, however, when it is played out in public. Think for a moment about the politician caught with his trousers around his ankles, or the film star whose latest movie is a complete flop. It is one thing having your world come crashing down around you; it is quite another having the whole world know about it.

Getting dropped from the England cricket team feels very much like that. Aside from the immense pain of having the honour of representing your country taken away, along with your aspirations and dreams, you also feel a little like the Elephant Man. Suddenly the phone goes silent, people don't know what to say to you and even those close to you cannot ease the pain.

It happened to me at the beginning of September 2007. My

phone rang, I looked at the number and I knew at once that I was in trouble. The chairman of selectors, David Graveney, did not ring if he had good news.

'Straussy, we are leaving you out of the squad for Sri Lanka. We think we have better options against their spin bowlers. This is not the end for you, but you must take some measures to get yourself back in form . . .'

I stopped listening. I couldn't believe it. My world had come crashing down. What about all those match-winning performances over the three years I had been in the side? Did they count for nothing? What about all the work I had put into my game? What about the fact that I had captained the team in four Test matches? I felt bereft, I felt bitter and above all I felt completely lost. What was my future going to look like without international cricket? It was like a drug, and the thought of going back to county cricket without my regular fix held little appeal.

Although I didn't like to admit it, I knew it was coming, and in many ways I had brought it on myself. Throughout the 2007 season I had felt all at sea. Under the new regime of Peter Moores, who started as head coach in May 2007, past performances were cast aside. It was a new start for everyone and Moores seemed keen to break up some of the hierarchy that was in place under Duncan Fletcher. The ODI team, in particular, was overhauled after the end of the World Cup. There was no place for Michael Vaughan, myself and a few others who had flopped during the tournament. It was clear that Moores wanted to have a look at some of those who had not been considered for international duty during the Fletcher years.

Players like Owais Shah and Ryan Sidebottom came into the mix after years in the wilderness, which gave everyone involved in the side the clear message that no one's place was assured.

I don't know whether being dropped from the ODI team had affected me more than I thought or if I was going through a mid-career crisis, but that summer I just couldn't focus properly during the Test matches – first against the West Indies in May and June, and then against India in July and August. I was increasingly distracted by the thought of being dropped and was therefore trying to avoid it at all costs. The problem is that trying to play Test cricket with that sort of negative mindset is nothing short of purgatory. It is no fun doing something just to avoid something bad happening. There is a hint of desperation and it is all but impossible to play the game naturally, trusting in your instincts. I was walking around with a cloud over my head that summer and every score I got merely brought a temporary reprieve.

I knew I was really in trouble when I battled my way to 96 in the first Test of the three-match series against India, only for the media to pick over the moment of madness that led to my dismissal, suggesting that I hadn't done enough to justify my place in the team for the next series, in Sri Lanka. According to them, I needed more runs. I did, in fact, get more runs, with a half-century in the second Test, before finishing disappointingly at The Oval with scores of 6 and 32. It was impossible to keep them happy, though, and my place in the side was a hot topic, discussed both in the newspapers and in breaks in play on television.

No matter how hard players try not to read the media at

these times, it is impossible to get away from it completely. Just when you really need to focus on getting the process right, watching the ball and keeping it simple, your mind is awash with what people in the media are saying about you, as well as the various bits of advice that come your way from all sorts of different sources. It is a truly horrendous feeling. You know that your career is on the line, you know that you are not playing well, but you also know that there is only one way to get yourself out of this mess – and that is to get a century. A fifty is not enough. To put all the chatter to bed, nothing short of scoring a hundred runs will do.

The main problem with this is that scoring an international century is incredibly hard to do. You are very fortunate if you have twenty days in a career when you go to bed at night with the warm afterglow of scoring an international hundred. Now, when you are completely out of form, not sleeping and haunted by the thought of losing everything you have worked so hard for, you have no choice but to pull the proverbial rabbit out of the hat. As you prepare for what might be the last match you will ever play, nothing seems less likely. How could you possibly perform under those circumstances?

The amazing thing is that many England cricketers have gone to the precipice, looked over the edge and somehow managed to put in the performance necessary to keep the hounds at bay. When the pressure is at its greatest, they find a way to perform. It is quite amazing, and it is often indicative of a player who will go on to have a long and successful England career. In my time, I witnessed Paul Collingwood do it against South Africa in 2008, Ian Bell against the same opposition in 2009 and Alastair Cook against Pakistan in 2010. I also went through it against New Zealand in 2008.

With my career now comfortably wrapped up and finished, it is a little easier to look at the effect that the media have on a sports team from a more objective point of view. When you are in the thick of it, it is difficult not to feel victimised by the constant interest and intrusion by the travelling press corps.

I think that it is fair to say that the way the media in this country works makes it more difficult for professional players to perform. The problem does not lie so much with the criticism players have to contend with when they fail. Instead, I think that too often unrealistic expectations are thrust upon performers that bear little or no relation to logic. When the England football team enters a World Cup ranked as the eighth-best team in the world, the likelihood is that they will go out of the tournament in the quarter-finals. If they go out before then, they have under-achieved; if they stay in longer, they have over-achieved. When the team duly gets knocked out at the quarter-final stage, the country goes into mourning, careers are ended and managers are sacked. All for performing to the level they could be expected to reach.

On the other hand, the attention of the media can also have a beneficial effect. It spurs teams on to keep improving, it makes players superstars and it maintains interest in sports throughout the country. At a time when so much televised sport is only on satellite TV, many people in the country get their news and opinion about sport second-hand. If the media showed no interest, the population's attention would also start to wane. A few players having to go through a little mental anguish along the way is probably a small price to pay.

What gets my goat a little is the media's fascination with personalities and also its reluctance to give credit when it is due. For example, take a player like Jonathan Trott. His averages in both Test and ODI cricket place him in the very highest echelons of international cricketers. He will never get the credit he deserves, though, because he is not a 'sexy' player. He is too robotic. In fact, it is almost too predictable that he is going to go out and score runs.

The media are far more interested in the flawed genius who may or may not perform. With such a player, there is so much more for them to talk about, so many more chances for superlatives to be used, one way or the other. From a team's point of view, however, the steady performer is like gold dust. When you are trying to win a cricket series, you want to be as sure as possible that your players are going to perform when necessary. Steady is good.

I can't really blame the media for this. Clearly it is more interesting to write a story about a Kevin Pietersen or a Chris Gayle than it is about a Jonathan Trott. Unfortunately, focusing so much on personality and celebrity can have the unfortunate effect of encouraging players to separate themselves from their team-mates in order to gain attention, and that can be very difficult and divisive in a team sport.

In my case, the media interest and pressure served merely to remind me that I really wasn't playing well. The days when I could turn up to practice calm and assured, with a large reservoir of confidence to draw on, had long gone. In my mind, I was no longer living the dream. Nothing about international cricket was new any more. The travel was no longer so intoxicating; the daily ritual of focusing on the job at hand, steeling yourself for the travails of international sport, was beginning to wear me down. It was also getting increasingly difficult to leave Ruth and my son Sam, who was eighteen months old, full of energy and in need of a father. Three and a half years into my England career, I was definitely going through some sort of crisis, and if your mind is not clear off the pitch, then it is unlikely to be on the pitch.

I can see now that I definitely needed to be dropped at that stage of my career. As soon as I received that call from David Graveney in September 2007, my mindset changed. OK, I had to go through the humiliation stage, but that in itself made me sure that I never wanted to go through the turmoil of being dropped from the team again.

What really changed about me, though, was that my focus immediately shifted from being worried about being dropped to concentrating on what I had to do in order to get back into the side. My attitude became positive once again and straight away I felt better about myself and my prospects. One thing was obvious, though: I needed to do some work on my game. Throughout the summer, I had committed what I believe to be one of the cardinal sins when it comes to batting. I had tried to change my technique while I was out of form.

Possibly the greatest misconception purveyed by television

commentators is that if a player has a weakness exposed by a particular bowler, it is quite simple to make the necessary adjustments to counteract that weakness. For instance, I can imagine Ian Botham or Mike Atherton talking about a player who gets out lbw too often: 'Well, it is simple,' they may say. 'All he has to do is get a bigger stride in. That will get him outside the line of the ball and he can't be out lbw.' Or perhaps they might focus on him getting his front foot too far across instead. The clever people at Sky will then come up with all sorts of graphics to demonstrate what the commentators are talking about and how that will allow the player to 'correct' his problem.

There are, however, two difficulties the player will have to contend with. Firstly, making that adjustment is likely to be extremely difficult to achieve. Imagine a golfer trying to change their swing. It can take years before they finally get all the parts moving in sync to produce the perfect shot. In cricket, you have to coordinate the bat swing with foot movement, either back or forward, while judging whether to play or leave the ball. All that needs to be done in less than half a second. To make a fundamental change to how far you move your feet will take hundreds of practice hours to perfect. It can be done, but it is not something to be undertaken lightly.

Secondly, and far more importantly in my mind, while making that adjustment may fix one particular problem, what others is it going to create instead? Getting further forward may make it harder for you to play back-foot shots and also make you far more vulnerable to getting out to the short ball. You may find it harder to judge which balls to play, as they will be reaching you a split second earlier. There is no point in getting over your lbw problem if you have just created a number of other problems in its place.

Throughout my career, my biggest weakness was probably my driving. I was never a strong driver of the ball, partly because of a low(ish) backlift and partly because my short stride into the ball meant that my weight shifted backwards when trying to drive the ball hard. Throughout that 2007 season, Peter Moores and Andy Flower, then the batting coach, had been trying to encourage me to expand my driving skills, primarily by experimenting with a higher backlift. Their concern, which was entirely correct, was that international bowlers had worked out my game. They were no longer feeding me with back-of-a-length balls that I could either cut or pull away. They were instead bowling fuller and wider, knowing that I was unlikely to hurt them in that area and they were far more likely to get me out.

I practised hitting literally thousands of drives. I was focusing on getting my weight into the ball more and using a higher backlift in order to get more momentum. All of which sounds great, doesn't it? It had the potential to transform me from a one-trick pony into a far more complete and rounded international cricketer. I have to admit that despite being initially sceptical about the idea of making significant changes to my game, I began to allow myself to get excited at the thought of whacking opening bowlers through the covers or down the ground.

What was the result of all this well-thought-out graft? That summer I got out far more often driving the ball and I scored hardly any runs off the back foot.

The concentration on hitting front-foot shots in the nets had subconsciously made me look for scoring opportunities off the front foot. When they came along, I would be trying to put my new technique into practice, but ended up going after balls that were far more dangerous to play, with shots that, even though they had improved a little, were still my weakness. When you are trying to do this against high-quality international bowlers, the odds are more often than not in their favour. My far more productive back-foot game had been neglected and so my bread-and-butter shots were not coming off as often. No wonder I didn't score many runs that season.

In the latter part of my career I got far better at accepting my limitations. It didn't matter if I wasn't crashing the ball through the covers, as long as I wasn't getting out. If I was patient enough, the bowler would eventually feed me a ball to my strengths, which I would put away. In short, I started concentrating on my strengths and not my weaknesses.

If a player came to me for advice about altering their game, I would always counsel against rushing into making wholesale changes to their technique. Certainly, if you have reached international level, your technique, which has evolved over a long number of years, has got you to where you are. You have learnt to evaluate the low- and high-risk shots that come with your own individual technique. Your problem would have to be very serious indeed to throw away all that evolved know-ledge. More often than not, your issues will lie with shot-selection, despite what the commentators might say. That is something that is controlled by your head, not your technique.

Instead, I would probably get players to look first at things that are easier to control. Can they make slight adjustments to their stance or where they take their guard in order to help alleviate their problem? Keeping it simple is never a bad way to go.

There is obviously still a time and a place for technical adjustments. Early in a career, it would be foolish for any player to think that they didn't have to make any changes to their technique. Certainly, schoolboy cricketers should be constantly trying to drill in the correct fundamentals in order to progress up the levels as they get older. On the other hand, you only have to look at the wide array of techniques in world cricket to realise that there is no such thing as one perfect technique. Would anyone coach Shivnarine Chanderpaul to bat the way he does? What about Virender Sehwag, who hardly ever moves his feet? What both those players know, however, is what shots to play in what circumstances. That comes from the bitter experience of learning from their mistakes.

Looking back on my career, it still frustrates me that I tinkered with my technique as much as I did. Perhaps it is inevitable, if you are practising for thousands of hours every year, that you will try different things in practice in the constant search to become a better player. When I think about it, though, how much did all my tinkering really help me? I arguably became a better player against spin as I got older by experimenting with different ideas in the nets, but I am not sure I helped myself against the quicker bowlers. I think I would probably have scored more runs if I'd constantly honed my own technique, rather than searching for a magical cure.

Mind you, I probably did that far less than many of my contemporaries . . .

As I approached the winter of 2007–08, at home for the first time since I had started playing cricket for England, my task was fairly straightforward. I had to sit back and reflect on where I had gone wrong in the lead-up to my axing as a player and reconnect with what had worked well for me in the past. My experiment of trying to become a powerful driver of the ball, à la Matthew Hayden, had clearly not worked, so it was back to the nets for me and also back to basics.

I gave myself three months to refresh mentally, get myself into tip-top shape physically and regroove my technique to something resembling the way I had played in my early days for England. Given that England were going to follow their tour to Sri Lanka in December with a visit to New Zealand in March, it also made perfect sense for me to go and play some winter cricket there, to get back in form and be ready and waiting if the call came to come back into the side.

It was incredible how good it felt to be chasing my dream of playing for England once again.

India in England 2007 – The Pataudi Trophy

1st Test. Lord's, London. 19–23 July 2007
England 298 (**A.J. Strauss 96**, M.P. Vaughan 79) and 282 (K.P. Pietersen
134, **A.J. Strauss 18**; R.P. Singh 5–59)
India 201 (W. Jaffer 58; J.M. Anderson 5–42, R.J. Sidebottom 4–65) and
282–9 (M.S. Dhoni 76*, K.D. Karthik 60)
Match drawn.

2nd Test. Trent Bridge, Nottingham. 27–31 July 2007
England 198 (A.N. Cook 43, **A.J. Strauss 4**; Z. Khan 4–59) and 355 (M.P.
Vaughan 124, P.D. Collingwood 63, **A.J. Strauss 55**; Z. Khan 5–75)
India 481 (S.R. Tendulkar 91, S.C. Ganguly 79, K.D. Karthik 77; M.S.
Panesar 4–101) and 73–3 (C.T. Tremlett 3–12)
India won by 7 wickets.

3rd Test. The Oval, London. 9–13 August 2007
India 664 (A. Kumble 110*, M.S. Dhoni 92, K.D. Karthik 91, S.R. Tendulkar
82) and 180–6 dec (S.C. Ganguly 57)
England 345 (I.R. Bell 63, P.D. Collingwood 62, A.N. Cook 61, **A.J. Strauss
6**) and 369–6 (K.P. Pietersen 101, I.R. Bell 67, **A.J. Strauss 32**)
Match drawn.

India won the series 1–0.

One glorious day in May. New Zealand's Chris Martin (*left*) was the first bowler I faced in my debut Test at Lord's in 2004.

On the balcony of the dressing room at Lord's, my team-mates and an injured Michael Vaughan (*centre*) applaud as I make a century in my first Test innings.

Above: Happy to get back to my South African roots on my first Test tour in 2004–05.

Above right: A team visit to a game reserve. As far as tours are concerned, there are few better locations.

Right: Enjoying the series win at Centurion with Michael Vaughan – a fantastic captain, with a particularly natural feel for the game.

Below: The runs keep coming. Leaving the field with Graham Thorpe after scoring 126 and 94 in the 1st Test at Port Elizabeth.

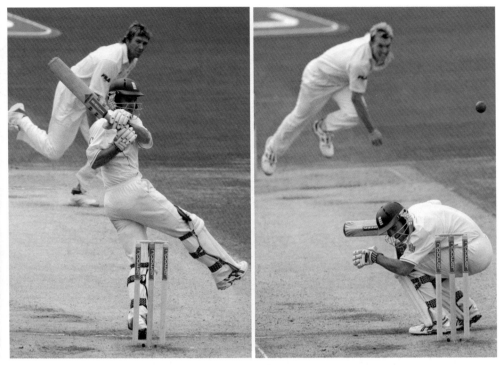

Welcome to Ashes cricket! Hitting a four off Glenn McGrath (*left*) and avoiding a bouncer from Brett Lee (*right*) during the 1st Test at Lord's in 2005 – the start of a memorable series.

With my partner in that match, Marcus Trescothick, one of the great England openers. Unfortunately we lost the Test by 239 runs and were sent off to lick our wounds.

Above: With Peter Moores on the New Zealand tour of 2007–08. When he took over as coach, he decided to shake things up.

Right: Daniel Vettori bowling at Napier in the 3rd Test: my last chance to re-establish my England place after being dropped in 2007.

Below: Life is good again. On my way to a career-saving 177 in the second innings at Napier.

A great start to the summer of 2008: a series victory against New Zealand for England and a Man of the Series award for me.

Two months later, despite 135 from Paul Collingwood (*above*), South Africa won the 3rd Test and the series at Edgbaston, ending the career of Michael Vaughan.

With Peter Moores and new captain Kevin Pietersen (*right*). The early days of KP's regime were encouraging, with victory in the final Test at The Oval and the subsequent ODI series.

Left: Smoke billows from the Taj Mahal Hotel in Mumbai during the terror attacks in November 2008.

Above: The Indian government subsequently promised us 'presidential levels of security' – even at a nets session in Chennai.

Below left: Celebrating after scoring two centuries in the 1st Test at Chennai in December 2008. It was an absolute pleasure to be on the pitch for that match.

Below right: My feats were immediately overshadowed by Sachin Tendulkar, whose monumental unbeaten century on a crumbling pitch took India to victory. What a player.

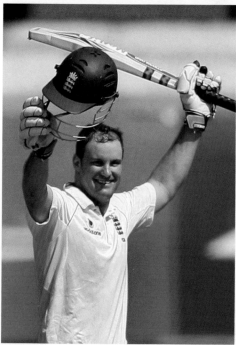

9

LETTING GO

I am sitting in a plastic chair alongside the cricket pitch in Napier, New Zealand, in March 2008. This is not a glitzy cricket stadium, but actually a rugby ground that has been hurriedly transformed in order to host a cricket match. I have all my batting equipment on, apart from my helmet and gloves, which sit on the ground beside me.

God, I feel tired. I am weary to the bone. 'I am not sure how much longer I can take this,' I say to myself, before quickly banishing the thought from my mind.

In truth, I don't think I have had one full night's sleep for the last three weeks. As soon as my head hits the pillow, thoughts about the fate of my career come flooding into my mind. Even when I do manage to drop off, I am frequently woken by the same recurring dream. In it, I am frantically trying to get my pads on in time to get out to the middle to bat, but I can never manage to do up the straps quickly enough. Also, my thigh pad seems to be hidden from view, and in my panic to get to the crease before being timed out by the umpire, I am too flustered to find it. Just when all hope is lost, and I am resigning myself to not getting out there in time, I wake up. The team psychologist tells me that it is a classic anxiety dream.

I hate having to wait to bat. All my career I have opened the batting. Although you have to go through the serious challenge of facing the opposition's best bowlers armed with the new ball, you at least have the certainty of knowing when you have to go through the ordeal. For this series, I am occupying the jinxed No. 3 position. Michael Vaughan, the captain, has elevated himself back up to opening after a prolonged slump at No. 3, so I am having to contend with waiting around, unsure of when my time is going to come.

I am fully aware that the innings in front of me, whenever the first wicket falls, has every chance of being my last in an England shirt. Having been brought back into the side on a hunch for the New Zealand series, I have so far not repaid the faith of the captain in the slightest. Scores of 43, 2, 8 and 44 in the first two Tests and a duck in the first innings of this one have not been good enough to silence the doubters. The media are wondering what I have done to deserve getting back into the team. My team-mates have been supportive, but they too know the score. If I fail in this innings, there is no easy way back for me.

Of all the situations in which to bat for your career, this one feels a long way down the list. Having been 4–3 in our first innings, we had recovered well to make 253 on the back of a Kevin Pietersen century. A fine bowling performance by Ryan Sidebottom wrested the initiative back in our favour, skittling them out for 168, but we are now batting in the final session of day two on a wicket that has yielded twenty dismissals in less than two days, knowing that this innings is likely to dictate the direction in which the series goes. Also, I am on a pair. No cricketer likes facing the prospect of getting two ducks in the same *game, and I am having to contend with that prospect on top of the far more serious task of saving my international career. If only I wasn't feeling so tired.*

I don't really know what to do with myself. I am too nervous to sit still and relax, but I am too tired to be jumping around and psyching myself up. Besides, I have no idea how long I am going to have to wait. I watch Michael Vaughan taking strike against Chris Martin. We are sitting side-on to the action, so I can't see how much he is swinging it. All I can see is that he is getting it through to the keeper pretty well.

He bowls a short-of-a-length ball. Vaughan spots it early and unfurls one of his trademark pull shots. It bounces a little more than he expects and catches the edge of his bat on the way through to the keeper, Brendon McCullum. The noise in the ground increases as the New Zealanders launch into the tell-tale confident appeal and wild celebrations that precede the raising of the umpire's finger. Vaughan looks forlornly at his bat and begins to make his way back to the pavilion.

I place my helmet on my head, strap each glove on my hands, pick up my bat and start making my way out to the middle. I have this one innings to save my career.

My route back into the England team was created far more by England's failings in the subcontinent before Christmas than by my stellar form for my team in New Zealand, Northern Districts. Ravi Bopara, in particular, had struggled in the difficult and draining conditions in Sri Lanka, finishing the series with the dreaded pair in the final Test. It was enough for the selectors to wield the axe, only three games after he'd come into the side as my replacement. From the outside, it looked pretty harsh on him, given that I had endured a fruitless twelve months leading up to my own axing from the side, but in many ways it came about as a result of the manner of his dismissals, which some regarded as 'soft', rather than the lack of runs.

For my part, I was absolutely delighted but also a little unnerved by my speedy return. By the time the side was picked, I had not played any first-class cricket since the end of the miserable summer of 2007, and even though I was about to play some one-dayers and Twenty20 cricket in New Zealand, my reserves of confidence were hardly brimming over. Fortunately, I did feel fresh and in a far better place mentally for the challenges that lay ahead.

By the time I met up with my England team-mates at the conclusion of the ODI series in February 2008, I was genuinely relieved to be back in the fold. My time with Northern Districts had not been a complete success. The cricketing diet of Twenty20s and one-dayers had really not been the ideal preparation for a Test series. Most of my practice sessions had revolved around clearing my front leg and mowing the ball over midwicket in order to take advantage of the fielding restrictions in the Twenty20s, which was just about the direct opposite of how I wanted to play in the Test matches.

I had found the month with the young New Zealand players fascinating but ultimately very trying. It was immediately noticeable that professional cricket in New Zealand stood somewhere between club and first-class cricket in England. In a rugby-mad country, it was not hard to see that this English sport played second fiddle. There wasn't a lot of money going around, many of the facilities were basic and if players had not made it into the New Zealand side by their late twenties, they were usually looking for a new form of employment. There was no room in the budget for old, experienced heads in provincial sides.

I greatly admired the attitude of both the players and the administrators of Northern Districts. There was far less cynicism than is prevalent in English county cricket, probably owing to the absence of bitter and twisted old pros, and it was clear that players were intent on following their dreams. The lack of money in the game meant that you either made it up a step to international cricket, or you didn't have very much to pay the mortgage with. Provincial cricket was not an end in itself, as county cricket is for so many players in England, but rather a means to an end.

The players were fit, dedicated and willing to learn, but the standard, also because of the lack of experienced players, was definitely lower than back in England. I suppose that, with a far smaller population than the UK, there are just fewer good players to go around, and the lack of resources did not help either.

All of this meant that I really should have stood out in the team. I was older, more experienced and highly motivated to get runs under my belt before the Test series. My consequent lack of success, therefore, was acutely embarrassing. Up to my final game for the side, my highest score was a paltry 39 in my first game, and I really couldn't get to grips with the twenty-over game at all. Knowing that I didn't have the power to clear the ropes in the middle overs put me under a lot of pressure to get off to a flyer. I was never able to simply wait for a ball in the right area like so many of the really good Twenty20 players, confident that it would definitely go for a boundary. I found myself going harder and harder at every ball I faced, and as a result losing timing and rhythm.

I know that many people probably see Twenty20 cricket as a bit of a slogathon, but it is a difficult game for batsmen. With the lack of time in the innings, you have to worry about not getting out but also make sure that you score quickly enough to keep the scoreboard ticking over. It is horrible to see a cricket game slip away due to you using up too many balls. I would have preferred a low score every time to that degrading feeling of coming back to the dressing room having effectively lost the game for the team.

Probably because it was not an easy game for me to play, I was both fascinated by and more than a little jealous of the players who made it look easy. The Northern Districts wicketkeeper, Peter McGlashan, was a particularly clever exponent of the various unorthodox shots that have become so prevalent in the game today, but the player I have most admired in that format actually plays for England, Eoin Morgan. I always found it phenomenal just how much power he was able to extract from his relatively small stature. Also, his calmness at the crease, combined with great confidence in his ability to pull out the big shots when they mattered, set him apart from many other big hitters in world cricket. Partly because of limited availability, he has only shown glimpses of what he is capable of in the IPL, but if I were running a franchise, he would be one of the first names on my team sheet.

Thankfully my time with Northern Districts ended on something of a high, with a century in my last fifty-over game on the back of some outrageous fortune. Early in my innings, an attempted pull shot ballooned up to mid on, offering the simplest of catches to the fielder. There was no way he could drop it. As soon as I saw it going towards him, I started the long, shameful walk to the pavilion and my partner, a talented young player called BJ Watling, gently jogged down the wicket in a sympathetic pretence to run a single. Quite amazingly, the fielder managed to lose his composure completely and drop the ball, before regaining it and running out BJ, who was now stranded in the middle of the wicket. Lady luck deserted my young partner that day and shone instead on me. Who knows what would have happened if I had re-entered the England ranks completely devoid of form, rather than feeling relatively perky after registering my century later in the day.

As soon as I met up with the team in Christchurch, it was immediately apparent just how much I had missed being involved. There is no doubt about it, international cricket is a drug. It is intoxicating, exhilarating and, having been denied my regular fix for so long, I was relishing everything about it. I loved catching up on the gossip with Michael Vaughan and Matthew Hoggard, the other two Test specialists training with me prior to the arrival of the rest of the squad, who were involved with the ODI series. When you are out of the side, you are out of the loop completely. Everything that goes on during a cricket tour passes you by. It's not that the players are deliberately trying to exclude you, but they are caught up with what they are doing and focused on playing cricket for England. Their attention is on the matches themselves, the politics, the day-to-day rigmarole of touring and the other players alongside them, not the players who used to play with them. Nothing demonstrates to a player more starkly the fickle nature of cricket at the highest level than a spell out of the side. The bandwagon simply rolls on without you.

I have to say that the gossip I was hearing was slightly disconcerting. There was a growing feeling in the camp that the team was not operating on all cylinders. I got the distinct impression that Michael Vaughan, in particular, was struggling with Peter Moores's new regime. Moores has never been a person to take a back seat, and Vaughan, who had been used to getting a fair amount of leeway when Fletcher was coach, seemed uncomfortable with the increasingly hands-on role of the coach and his support staff.

One of the biggest quandaries for any coach is how much to push and challenge players and how much to encourage and support them. At times the two are mutually exclusive. Peter Moores had earned an excellent reputation at Sussex and with the England Academy by challenging players to get better. He is one of those people who can never sit still, always coming up with new ideas. The sheer energy he gives off is catching and in the county cricket environment his methods had proved very successful. Pushing and cajoling county players to keep going while the mental and physical demands of a never-ending season take their toll is a fantastic way of separating your team from your competitors, especially when the county cricket culture doesn't really encourage players to push themselves too hard. His repeated success with Sussex showed that his methods worked, and he brought a very similar philosophy into his new role with the national team.

After the initial honeymoon period of his first summer in charge, it had become apparent that those methods were working less well within the England cricketing environment. It may just be that the job of following Fletcher was a particularly difficult one, given that most of the senior players were very much wedded to his ideas and philosophies. However, international cricket differs from county cricket in the sense that players need far less pushing and prodding in order to get themselves up for a game of cricket. Every time they go out there to play, they are playing for their careers. They are bound to be up for it. What is required at the highest level is a coach who is able to calm players down, allowing them to play to their strengths and instilling confidence in their methods. People may think that an England dressing room during the days of a Test match is a hive of energy and activity, but it has always been very relaxed and chilled out when we have been playing our best. Energy conservation, both mental and physical, is very much the order of the day for the players not out there in the middle. Moores's philosophy that 'energy cannot be saved, it can only be created' ran very much contrary to that.

It was clear by the start of the New Zealand tour that some of the senior players were getting mildly irritated by the constant nannying of the support staff. No batting, bowling or fielding practice was complete without the coaches getting involved in some capacity, telling players how they should be doing things differently or better. For players who were fiercely protective about their games, it was unsurprising this made their hackles rise.

By the time I arrived in New Zealand, many of the ODI players were particularly irked at having had to do a fitness session minutes after a tense tied ODI against New Zealand, in order to 'show them how strong and committed' the side was. The camp was not happy and Michael Vaughan and Paul Collingwood, the captains of the Test and one-day sides, had the difficult jobs of bridging the gap between the players and the management.

Although I never had the close relationship with Moores that I had with Duncan Fletcher, I did, and still do, admire him greatly. He chose the difficult option when he started working with the England side. He could easily have come in, not changed things very much, cosied up to the senior players and kept the status quo. Instead, he decided to shake things up and try to take the England team forward. It is clear that his methods did not work as well as he would have wanted them to, but perhaps the team did need to move in a different direction. Perhaps we had all become too stuck in our ways. I am sure that if he had his time again, he would do things differently, and he probably learnt a huge amount through his time as England coach. I am certain that he will be a very fine international coach again one day.

* * *

Having been out of the side for the Sri Lanka tour, I found myself playing the therapist's role of listening to players talk through their grievances with the new regime. Clearly, a few of the lads wanted to get things off their chests and I was the perfect sounding board for that. In truth, though, I was in no real position to be making judgements on Peter Moores and the rest of his staff at that stage. My focus for the tour had to be on getting myself back into the side and into form. If neither of those happened, then I would be reading about the ups and downs of the England team in the newspapers like everyone else, far from the inner sanctum of the dressing room.

I knew as well as anyone that this series was going to be make or break for me. I had been lucky enough to get a second chance. A lean time with the bat now would mean a possibly permanent return to county cricket. If I am honest, I was petrified at the thought of my international career coming to a premature and painful end, and it was this thought that kept me awake at night.

Sleeping has never really been difficult for me. I have always managed to drift off peacefully at the drop of a hat, a habit that frequently exasperates my wife when we settle down for a video or take a trip to the cinema. In the first few years of my career, I might have had the odd night when it would take a bit of tossing and turning before finally settling down. In New Zealand, though, it became a problem. On the nights when I knew I wouldn't be batting the next day, I would usually get to sleep all right, but when there was a chance that I might have to perform, most of the night would be spent staring at the ceiling. The early hours, when the rest of the world is eerily quiet, pass by with the pace of a funeral procession. A lonely hotel room, thousands of miles from your support network, is the perfect environment for your mind to run amok. Thoughts you would never countenance in the daylight hours take root and start to multiply. By the time morning comes around you have been on a mental ghost train, terrified by all the things that could possibly go wrong.

I remember Marcus Trescothick coming down to breakfast in the early stages of the 2006–07 Ashes tour. He looked absolutely shot to pieces, ashen-faced, having visibly aged overnight. As he sat down beside me, I asked him what the matter was, expecting him to say that something terrible had happened back at home.

'I'm fine,' he said. 'I'm just having a little trouble sleeping.'

Having never experienced depression, I have very little appreciation of what sufferers go through, but I am led to believe that the times when you are on your own at night are particularly difficult to endure. With Marcus, the warning sirens were loud and clear and, despite my offer to provide company if he felt he needed some at any time, it was unsurprising that a few days later he was on a plane back to the UK.

Although I never felt I was depressed, I found myself desperately trying to show everyone, the management and my team-mates, that I was fine, fully in control of myself and relaxed about the prospect of going out to bat, when I was actually in a state of near panic. Tired beyond measure, under pressure, searching for form and feeling very alone – it is no surprise that my returns in the first two Tests were so meagre.

My mood was greatly improved by the arrival of Ruth and Sam, who at least allowed me to get away from my own predicament on days off or after play, but by the time the final Test started, even their distraction was having no effect. I was being consumed by my fears. My six-ball duck in the first innings reflected my own disorientation as much as the quality of the bowling. I could sense my England dreams slipping from my fingers, never to return.

It was then, at my lowest ebb, that I decided to let go.

I let go of all my fears, all that negative emotion, all my worries and dreams. There was no point in beating myself up any more. If the worst came to the worst and I never played for England again, I would still have my health, my wonderful family and a career that most people would give an arm and a leg for, playing professional cricket. I had also been lucky enough to experience a few of English cricket's greatest moments. Life would go on.

The night before my second innings, I slept the best I had for some time. I felt as if a load had been taken off my mind, although it was only because mentally I had stopped fighting. The odds were just too great: one innings to ensure your international future, when you are in poor form, exhausted and completely lacking in confidence. Perhaps other people still had some faith in me, but I didn't. I was just determined to try to enjoy and appreciate every moment of that innings. What would be would be.

As I take my guard and look around the field, I feel surprisingly calm. The New Zealanders, who are full of beans at getting our captain out so early in the innings, are swarming around me, reminding me that I am facing the prospect of getting my second duck in the game.

Chris Martin, an excellent bowler to left-handers, keeps bowling wide of my off stump. There is no way I can have a go at one of those balls. With it swinging away from me quite dramatically, the chances are that I would be giving catching practice to the slip fielders. I have to be patient.

Finally he bowls a ball on middle and leg stump, I feel the reassuring vibrations of the ball hitting the middle of the bat and watch it race away to the square-leg boundary. There is going to be no pair for me in my last Test.

As the innings progresses, I find myself enjoying it more and more. I have no idea where it has come from, but I am feeling unusually stubborn. I have no interest in scoring quickly. I have no interest in relieving the pressure that is being applied by the two New Zealand spinners, Daniel Vettori and Jeetan Patel. I am just batting. If they want to get me out, they are going to have to bowl me a damn good ball, because I am not going to help them.

Even the close of play and a night stranded in no-man's-land on 42 does little to break my concentration. For one of the only times in my career, I am completely in the zone. No thoughts of what might happen in the future or what has happened in the past enter my head. I am just cruising along, watching the ball and playing the correct shot. If only I could get myself into this frame of mind more often.

New Zealand v England
(3rd Test)

Played at McLean Park, Napier, on 22–26 March 2008

Umpires: DJ Harper & RE Koertzen (TV: GAV Baxter)
Referee: J Srinath
Toss: England

ENGLAND

AN Cook	b Martin	2	c McCullum b Patel		37
MP Vaughan*	lbw b Southee	2	c McCullum b Martin		4
AJ Strauss	c How b Southee	0	c Bell b Patel		177
KP Pietersen	c How b Southee	129	c Taylor b Vettori		34
IR Bell	c and b Elliott	9	c Sinclair b Vettori		110
PD Collingwood	c Elliott b Patel	30	c and b Vettori		22
TR Ambrose†	c Taylor b Patel	11	c and b Vettori		31
SCJ Broad	c McCullum b Southee	42	not out		31
RJ Sidebottom	c Bell b Southee	14	not out		12
MS Panesar	b Martin	1			
JM Anderson	not out	0			
Extras	(lb 9, w 3, nb 1)	13	(lb 3, w 1, nb 5)		9
Total	(96.1 overs)	253	(for 7 wkts dec)	(131.5 overs)	467

NEW ZEALAND

JM How	c Strauss b Sidebottom	44	lbw b Panesar		11
MD Bell	lbw b Sidebottom	0	c Broad b Panesar		69
SP Fleming	c Collingwood b Sidebottom	59	c Ambrose b Panesar		66
MS Sinclair	c Broad b Sidebottom	7	c Ambrose b Broad		6
LRPL Taylor	c Ambrose b Broad	2	c Collingwood b Panesar		74
GD Elliott	c Ambrose b Sidebottom	6	c Bell b Broad		4
BB McCullum†	b Sidebottom	9	b Panesar		42
DL Vettori*	c Cook b Sidebottom	14	c Ambrose b Anderson		43
TG Southee	c Pietersen b Broad	5	(10) not out		77
JS Patel	c Panesar b Broad	4	(9) c Broad b Panesar		18
CS Martin	not out	4	b Sidebottom		5
Extras	(lb 13, w 1)	14	(b 6, lb 5, w 4, nb 1)		16
Total	(48.4 overs)	168	(118.5 overs)		431

NEW ZEALAND	O	M	R	W		O	M	R	W
Martin	26	6	74	2		18	2	60	1
Southee	23.1	8	55	5		24	5	84	0
Elliott	10	2	27	1		14	1	58	0
Vettori	19	6	51	0	(5)	45	6	158	4
Patel	18	3	37	2	(4)	30.5	4	104	2

ENGLAND	O	M	R	W		O	M	R	W
Sidebottom	21.4	6	47	7		19.5	3	83	1
Anderson	7	1	54	0		17	2	99	1
Broad	17	3	54	3		32	10	78	2
Panesar	1	1	0	0		46	17	126	6
Collingwood	2	2	0	0		2	0	20	0
Pietersen						2	0	14	0

Fall of wickets:

	Eng	NZ	Eng	NZ
1st	4	1	5	48
2nd	4	103	77	147
3rd	4	116	140	156
4th	36	119	327	160
5th	125	119	361	172
6th	147	137	424	276
7th	208	138	425	281
8th	240	152	–	329
9th	253	164	–	347
10th	253	168	–	431

Close of play:
Day 1: Eng (1) 240–7 (Broad 42*, Sidebottom 3*, 92 overs)
Day 2: Eng (2) 91–2 (Strauss 42*, Pietersen 7*, 32 overs)
Day 3: Eng (2) 416–5 (Strauss 173*, Ambrose 28*, 122 overs)
Day 4: NZ (2) 222–5 (Taylor 34*, McCullum 24*, 82 overs)

Man of the match: RJ Sidebottom
Result: **England won by 121 runs**

I reach 50 and hardly notice. A quick raise of my bat to my team-mates, who are all applauding warmly. I am not finished yet. I take my guard again and face up to the next ball. Shortly afterwards, Kevin Pietersen departs and I am joined at the crease by Ian Bell, who seems to be intent on hitting the New Zealand bowling to all parts. Often in those circumstances I have to fight not to try and score at the same tempo. Not today, though. I am in my bubble. Nothing can take me out of it.

I reach the nervous nineties and for the first time I am aware that the career-saving century is around the corner. This time, though, I am not having to fight myself. I am more than prepared to be patient, even though the new ball is a few overs away, and with its arrival my chances of getting out are bound to increase. I wait.

New Zealand take the new ball while I am on 97. Chris Martin comes steaming in, as if re-energised by the new bit of leather in his hand. He lets it go. It pitches on middle and off stump, evades my attempted defensive shot and goes through to the keeper. A close shave.

A few balls later, I see my opportunity when he overpitches and I launch a cover drive. Ironically, it is the same shot that I spent so much time working on over the previous twelve months. The ball hits the middle of the bat and races to the boundary. I have done it, I have saved my career. I have found myself on the edge of a cliff and have managed to cling on with my fingertips. All my worries, concerns and fears have evaporated in the space of a few minutes. I have passed the greatest test I have faced in my life. I will be part of the side for the summer of 2008. Life is good, I am happy.

I take my guard and prepare to face the next ball.

England in New Zealand 2007–08

1st Test. Seddon Park, Hamilton. 5–9 March 2008
New Zealand 470 (L.R.P.L. Taylor 120, J.M. How 92, D.L. Vettori 88; R.J. Sidebottom 4–90) and 177–9 dec (S.P. Fleming 66; R.J. Sidebottom 6–49)
England 348 (M.P. Vaughan 63, P.D. Collingwood 66, T.R. Ambrose 55, **A.J. Strauss 43**) and 110 (I.R. Bell 54*, **A.J. Strauss 2**; K.D. Mills 4–16)
New Zealand won by 189 runs.

2nd Test. Basin Reserve, Wellington. 13–17 March 2008
England 342 (T.R. Ambrose 102, P.D. Collingwood 65, **A.J. Strauss 8**; M.R. Gillespie 4–79) and 293 (A.N. Cook 60, P.D. Collingwood 59, **A.J. Strauss 44**)
New Zealand 198 (L.R.P.L. Taylor 53, D.L. Vettori 50*; J.M. Anderson 5–73) and 311 (B.B. McCullum 85, L.R.P.L. Taylor 55; R.J. Sidebottom 5–105)
England won by 126 runs.

3rd Test. McLean Park, Napier. 22–26 March 2008
England 253 (K.P. Pietersen 129, **A.J. Strauss 0**; T.J. Southee 5–55) and 467–7 dec (**A.J. Strauss 177**, I.R. Bell 110; D.L. Vettori 4–158)
New Zealand 168 (S.P. Fleming 59; R.J. Sidebottom 7–47) and 431 (T.G. Southee 77*, L.R.P.L. Taylor 74, M.D. Bell 69, S.P. Fleming 66; M.S. Panesar 6–126)
England won by 121 runs.

England won the series 2–1.

10

EVERYTHING CHANGES

Bangalore is one of my favourite cities in India. The centre of the country's rapidly developing IT sector, it has transformed itself in the last decade into a first-world, fast-paced, thriving metropolis. Nowhere demonstrates this rapid expansion more than the Karnataka Golf Association golf course. Built in 1989, in wasteland to the east of the city, it is now surrounded on all sides by brand-new offices housing some of the world's most recognisable technology brands. It is not uncommon for the caddies at the club to say, 'Aim at the Microsoft building in the distance, with a bit of fade, and you will end up in the middle of the fairway.' Bangalore is a city in a hurry. New five-star hotels are going up at a frightening pace, catering for the increasing numbers of IT executives who are arriving to oversee their company's operations.

Amongst the ever-developing city landscape lies the M. Chinnaswamy cricket stadium, housing one of the best batting wickets in India and also the Indian National Cricket Academy. It is late November 2008, two weeks before England's Test tour to India gets under way, and I have travelled here to spend a little time with the Performance Squad (which is a fancy name for England A – a group of aspiring young England cricketers). This is the acclimatisation period that cricketers who are in either the Test squad or the ODI squad but not both tend to go through on overseas tours these days. While I am getting used to the humidity alongside my young colleagues, the ODI team is in the midst of a particularly dispiriting thrashing by the Indians. England have always struggled to play one-day cricket in this part of the world, never managing to match the power and audacity of the Indian players in their home conditions, especially when it comes to playing spin. This latest beating, however, is one of the worst. When I turned off the television last evening, India had just knocked off the winning runs with plenty of overs to spare to take a 5–0 lead in the seven-match series.

Although I still yearn to be part of the ODI squad again, I confess I am not missing being a part of this particular series. From bitter past experience, I know what the dressing-room atmosphere can be like once a team gets caught in a rut. This losing run, with a Test series to follow, is likely to be a tough one to get out of. Instead, I am making use of the excellent cricket facilities at the cricket ground in Bangalore, mixing three hours of batting a day with some fitness sessions – and the odd nine holes of golf to provide a little respite.

My accommodation in the ground itself is simple but spacious. One of the privileges of being part of the England Test team is that I do not have to live in the dormitory with the other Performance Squad members. Dave Parsons, the coach, wants them to realise that perks only come when you reach the top. Although I protested to him about receiving this preferential treatment, my protests were not particularly loud or forceful. I am more than happy to be sitting in the relative comfort of my single room, complete with my own television.

In India, hours can be wasted very easily by flicking through the hundreds of satellite TV channels. There seems to be very little rhyme or reason as to where they are situated, so in the midst of twenty or so channels showing Bollywood classics, you can stumble across the National Geographic channel or an English movie channel. You can never be sure what is going to be revealed next. It is like a huge game of roulette.

For a cricket lover, though, there is always a feast of cricketing action to choose from, whether it be current matches or games stretching right back to the 1980s. I think it is fair to say that the only World Series Cricket I have ever watched has been on one of the sports channels in India. I suspect the late Kerry Packer would be quietly satisfied to know that nearly forty years on from the inception of WSC, hundreds of millions of people are still watching the likes of Viv Richards and Michael Holding in his made-for-TV tournament.

While flicking through the channels this morning, looking for a few cricket highlights to inspire me for what is likely to be a busy day's training, I come across one of the many Indian news channels. It is clear straight away from the dramatic footage in front of me that something terrible has happened overnight. Pictures of the train station in Mumbai being sprayed with bullets are being looped continuously alongside reports of bombs, indiscriminate killings and a large number of hostages being held in the Taj, probably India's most iconic hotel. This is being played out in front of millions of television viewers. I watch the scenes in complete horror. There is no editing of the footage here. It is all happening too quickly. Shots ring out from around the Taj Hotel. Bodies are being dragged out of one of the side entrances. It looks like a movie, but this is real. People are dying and the terrorists who are perpetrating these heinous acts are doing it in a chillingly cold and calculated manner.

What I was witnessing was the Mumbai terror attacks in which 166 people were killed and more than 600 injured. Although I was sitting safely in my room, hundreds of miles from the scene of this terrible tragedy, I suddenly felt very vulnerable and a long way from home. India was under siege, speculation was rife that further attacks were imminent and everyone was nervous and jumpy.

In the hours that followed, all the cricketers staying at the academy, including myself, were of the opinion that we needed to get out of the country as soon as possible. Looking back, it seems very much an emotional and illogical response. There was no reason to think that Bangalore was likely to be targeted, but there was something about the scenes of families being ripped apart that made us all desperate to be with our loved ones.

Nearly 1000 miles away, there were similar conversations among the members of the ODI squad in Cuttack, the venue for the previous night's one-day loss. It did not seem to be a time for playing cricket. India needed to mourn its dead and come to terms with what had happened. After consultation with Reg Dickason, the England team's security expert, the decision was made for both the members of the ODI squad and the players involved in the Performance Squad in Bangalore to go home and let things settle down.

As I sat on the plane heading home the next morning, my head was buzzing with thoughts about what I had just witnessed. Of course, I was still heavily affected by what I had seen on television. The scenes of fathers, mothers, sons and daughters being murdered, families ripped apart, seemed more poignant when you had children of your own. The Taj, in particular, seemed very close to home. I had stayed there many times, and the Middlesex team, full of my friends and colleagues, were due to be staying there less than forty-eight hours later in preparation for a newly formed Twenty20 competition, the Champions League, bringing together teams from around the world who had won their domestic Twenty20 competitions. If the timings had been a little different, cricketers from Finchley, Southgate and Ealing could have been among the dead.

I wondered what this would mean for the game in India. Pakistan had ceased to hold international cricket at all because of safety concerns regarding terrorist activity. Could the same happen to India? If so, how would the game survive without all the income generated there? It was clear that in the space of a few hours, everything in the world of cricket had changed.

Earlier in 2008, all those involved with the England cricket team had been through a difficult summer. It had started uneventfully with a relatively straightforward 2–0 series victory over New Zealand, with us chasing down a challenging 294 in the second Test at Old Trafford. I was once again at peace with myself and my game. All the worries, soul-searching and distractions had gone, to be replaced with a Zenlike state in the middle. I was relishing my return to form and determined to make the most of it. Two fifties and a century in the series were enough for me to take home the Man of the Series award, less than two months after being convinced that I was playing my last game for my country.

Behind the scenes, though, things were becoming increasingly fraught. An ODI series defeat against the same opposition brought with it the spotlight of media interest and some searching questions for Peter Moores and Paul Collingwood, the ODI captain. There was a growing feeling, both inside and outside the squad, that something wasn't quite right. With the arrival of South Africa's extremely talented squad just around the corner, the omens were not good.

One player who was finding himself under increasing pressure was our Test captain, Michael Vaughan. The consistency he had shown en route to becoming the number-one player in the world in 2003 had deserted him, and although he was still getting the odd big score, they were coming along less frequently. Also, with hindsight, it was apparent that he was beginning to suffer from the effects of being England captain for a long period of time.

I remember the gaunt expression on Nasser Hussain's face when he resigned from the England captaincy in 2003. He had the exhausted look of a man who had simply run out of steam, worn down by the constant demands of players, administrators, media and, of course, his own worries and expectations. Although Michael Vaughan was still very much in control of himself and the team, the fault lines were beginning to appear. He desperately needed a strong series against South Africa in order to release the pressure that was simmering below the surface.

The final two months of his career must have been, by some distance, the most painful. The four-match series against South Africa proved to be a stark reminder to our team that we were some way behind the best in the world. To some extent, we all struggled with the potent combination of sheer pace demonstrated by Morne Morkel and Dale Steyn and the nagging accuracy of Makhaya Ntini and André Nel. Their batsmen, meanwhile, demonstrated huge reserves of patience and discipline that our bowlers were unable to match. Even though we took the series by the scruff of the neck in the early skirmishes at Lord's, they were able to bat out the last two days of the game to secure a draw and in doing so wrest the initiative away from us permanently.

A shocking performance at Headingley, where we lost six wickets before lunch on the first day, was overshadowed by the left-field selection of Darren Pattinson, an Australian with an English passport who had been taking plenty of wickets for Nottinghamshire. It was an unaccountably strange stab in the dark by the selectors, especially as his hit-the-deck type of bowling was not what was required in the swing-friendly conditions in Leeds, but his selection had no bearing whatsoever on the result of the game. The batsmen were to blame.

The final nail in our coffin was delivered with ruthless efficiency by Graeme Smith in the third Test at Edgbaston, with one of the best innings I witnessed as an England player. His 154 not out in the fourth innings on a turning wicket was leading from the front in its truest form. It also brought the end of Michael Vaughan's England career. In a series in which he desperately needed to score runs, he had struggled against Dale Steyn, in particular, and a return of 40 runs in three Tests was enough to tip him over the edge.

Less than twenty-four hours after the end of the game, he was tearfully announcing his resignation. Even though all of those around him had seen how hard cricket was becoming for him, it was still a major shock and represented a seismic shift in the England cricket team. For me, it was a very emotional moment to see him step down. He was my first captain, the guy who had given me my chance, and also someone who had shown great loyalty towards me when I was going through my own struggles. He was, in my opinion, a fantastic captain, with a particularly natural feel for the game.

For me, Michael Vaughan had two very strong assets as a captain. Firstly, he was able to achieve the deceptively difficult task of putting players at ease when they were involved in the pressure-cooker environment of international cricket. He never gave the impression that he took it too seriously, which is probably why he was so popular with the players when he followed Nasser Hussain's more combative leadership. There was a calmness about him, an ability to take all the pressure on his shoulders and spare the rest of the team from its effects. Never was this more in evidence than during the famous Ashes victory in 2005, when the public attention and the fiercely contested nature of the games meant that the captains found themselves in the spotlight as never before. One thing I greatly admired about him was that he was always prepared to make difficult decisions out in the middle. He was not hesitant, he did not need a committee of players to support him and he was ready to gamble in order to achieve victory. His sporting declaration against South Africa at the Wanderers in 2004 was a great example.

His other great strength was that he read the game particularly well. He rarely let matches drift for extended periods and was always thinking of ways to force errors out of batsmen. He was very instinctive, rarely relying on facts and figures to back up his intuition, and he was as good as any captain I played with or against in this facet of the game.

I always had the impression that he enjoyed the politics of being England cricket captain. He would drop the odd comment in a press conference or have a quiet word to players, administrators or journalists to ensure that his agenda was being met. Perhaps he was forced to play politics a little too much in the final months of his career, with all the difficulties of managing the transition from the Duncan Fletcher regime to the very different set-up under Peter Moores, but he will quite rightly go down as one of England's best captains.

*　　*　　*

Michael Vaughan's resignation left a gaping hole in terms of leadership. One obvious candidate to replace him was Paul Collingwood, who was already leading the limited-overs team. However, he had endured a harrowing time against New Zealand in the recent ODI series, including getting embroiled in a nasty incident when Ryan Sidebottom prevented one of the New Zealand players running through for a single and Paul refused to withdraw England's appeal for a run-out. He had attracted heat from all sides as the woolly expression 'spirit of cricket' was bandied about.

I think that having to defend himself and his cricketing morals to such a degree meant that he completely lost his appetite for leading the England cricket team. He saw his opportunity to take a back seat when Vaughan resigned and promptly followed suit with his own resignation as captain. It was a shame because Paul had been one of the great servants of English cricket. Without the huge reservoirs of natural talent possessed by some of his team-mates, he turned himself, through sheer bloody-mindedness and hard work, into a high-quality Test match cricketer. Throughout my time with the team, he was the ultimate team man, selfless to the core, and he believed passionately in the need for the team to come first. Most people probably felt that he wouldn't be missed significantly when he retired from playing at the end of the Ashes series in 2010, but his boots were incredibly hard to fill, as much for his off-field influence as anything else. I am not sure if he was ever truly comfortable leading the ODI team, but he did a good job in trying circumstances and he was probably the best candidate at the time to take over the captaincy of the Test side.

*   *   *

After losing the ODI series to New Zealand and the Test series to South Africa, and suddenly finding themselves without a captain for either form of the game, the selectors were no doubt feeling under serious pressure. At no time since Nasser Hussain took over the captaincy had English cricket been in such a precarious situation. After judging, wrongly in my opinion, that the experiment of two separate captains, in Vaughan and Collingwood, had not worked, they decided to unify the jobs once again and therefore needed the new captain to be playing all forms of the game for England. If those were the requirements, there was only one possible candidate for the job and that was Kevin Pietersen.

On the surface, at least, there was some appeal in Kevin being given the job. He was undoubtedly one of the best players in the world and his place in the side would never be in jeopardy. He was also a natural risk-taker and would therefore be prepared to make decisions in the middle that most captains would not. He is a maverick and you can never be sure what he is going to do next. That is potentially unsettling for opposition players.

There were two obvious drawbacks to his becoming captain, however. First, it was already obvious to everybody that he and Peter Moores did not get on at all. They were barely on speaking terms. The precedent of a captain and coach not gelling had already been set, spectacularly unsuccessfully, by Fletcher and Flintoff, so if it was going to work out, some hasty patching-up of their relationship was required. Secondly, KP would have to convince the players that he genuinely cared for the team and his team-mates, and that he wasn't doing the job purely for his own advancement. Although we had all appreciated his precocious talents and his ability to turn a match on its head, there were still question marks about his commitment to the team. He was very much the superstar, and superstars often like to separate themselves from the mere mortals around them.

At this stage my name was not in the mix. I was not in the ODI team and had only recently re-established myself in the Test side. If the selectors had decided to stick with separate captains, then perhaps my name might have been mentioned for the Test captaincy, but that was not the preferred route. I understood the situation and in any case I was still feeling grateful just to be in the team after the struggles of the previous two years. My captaincy ambitions had dimmed somewhat, but I was certainly interested to see how Pietersen would fare. It was going to be an entertaining ride, one way or another.

The early signs of Kevin Pietersen's regime were encouraging. He showed plenty of energy and seemed determined to take his chance to shape the way that English cricket teams played the game. A win in the final dead-rubber Test against South Africa was followed by an impressive ODI whitewash against the same opposition. His new tactic of using Flintoff, Harmison, Broad and Anderson as a four-pronged attacking force had clearly unsettled the South Africans and boded well for a far more attacking style of one-day cricket.

From that moment, however, things became far more difficult for both him and the England cricket team as the result of a couple of events that were difficult to foresee. One was the Mumbai bombings. The other was the Allen Stanford fiasco.

Most cricket fans remember the arrival of Allen Stanford on Lord's cricket ground, courtesy of his own private helicopter. They probably also recall him posing next to a perspex case loaded with cash to publicise a new deal forged with the ECB, in which it was agreed that his Stanford XI would play a series of games against England over a five-year period, with each game being played for 20 million dollars. This kind of money was unheard of. Each player in the team would stand to earn one million dollars for one day's work. There was one catch, however: it was winner takes all. The loser would end up with nothing.

It goes without saying that the players were pretty excited by the arrival of this new revenue stream. We were talking about life-changing amounts of money as the game of cricket entered a new era in which the glitzy nature of Twenty20 cricket was breaking down long-established boundaries. Suddenly cricket was sexy and its new-found popularity brought with it the money men, not only in India, in the form of the IPL, but also from other parts of the world.

The ECB, who were keen not to be held to ransom by the BCCI (the Board of Control for Cricket in India), had actively sought to find ways of exploiting Twenty20's incredible potential and that is how they had crossed paths with Allen Stanford. What both the ECB and the players found difficult to dispel, however, was the perception that this association was purely mercenary. In effect, the England team were being hired out. They were not playing another international team and there was an air of moral corruption about the whole thing. The media certainly saw it that way and kept posing awkward questions to Giles Clarke and David Collier, the chairman and chief executive of the ECB.

Similar questions were being asked within the England cricket team. There was a fair amount of debate about how the booty should be split up. If it was just going to the eleven players who were selected for the game, then it would be unfair on those in the squad who were left out. What about the player who was selected for the vast majority of England Twenty20 games but was left out for this particular game because of the conditions on the day? Was it fair to say 'Tough luck, you may get your chance next year'?

Also, was it fair on those players who toured around the world constantly on Test and ODI tours, enduring months away from home, to miss out completely on this new-found wealth while Twenty20 specialists walked away with all the spoils? And wouldn't giving the money simply to the Twenty20 players create a major incentive for players to specialise in Twenty20 cricket at the expense of Test cricket? Was that something the ECB wanted to encourage?

With all these questions flying around, it was unsurprising that division lines were beginning to form within the wider England squad. When a game of that nature is staged, with money the sole motivator, players follow human nature and look only at the dollar signs. I can't imagine for one moment that any player had serious thoughts about the pride of wearing the three lions or the potential to entertain millions of people. This was about money, pure and simple, and everything else was window-dressing. The final decision was made to split most of the money between the eleven players, with a lesser amount going to members of the Twenty20 squad who missed out on the game and the support staff. This, of course, was dependent on England winning the game.

Very few people paused to ask where all the money was coming from. Allen Stanford was a businessman and so it was fair to assume that there must have been good financial reasons for him to invest 100 million dollars into the concept over five years. The players might not have been interested in how he planned to recoup that investment, but the ECB should have been. Perhaps there was a sound economic model, but it always had the whiff of being too good to be true. In light of his subsequent conviction for fraud on a massive scale, a lot of people, including the ECB and some of the West Indian former greats who were by his side throughout the tournament, have cause to shuffle around uncomfortably whenever his name is mentioned.

After months of meetings and squabbles, the game finally took place in November 2008 in Antigua in front of a large and enthusiastic crowd. I was over there playing for Middlesex in a far less important domestic version of the main event and I was surprised by the electricity in the ground on the day of the game. In under three hours, people's lives were going to be changed for ever.

The atmosphere, however, did not serve to inspire the England cricket team. Players who had seemed particularly uncomfortable throughout the week did not turn up to perform and the game was won at a canter by the Stanford Superstars. It is an understatement to say that it was a damp squib.

Ironically, after months of deliberations about money, the

England team walked away with nothing but damaged pride, regrets and an unhealthy dressing-room atmosphere. Kevin Pietersen, the captain, sat in the middle of it all and was under pressure, less than two months into the job, to heal the divisions before a traditionally arduous and energy-sapping tour of India.

I didn't envy the task that Pietersen had on his hands. A seven-match ODI series against India, who are near to unbeatable at home, was next on the England cricket team's agenda, in November and December 2008. They would have to contest that series with a group of players who, if they weren't in shock after letting a million dollars slip through their fingers, were inwardly bitter at not being given the opportunity to play in the game. It was hardly a recipe for success.

The tour progressed largely the way many people expected it to. India were too strong for an England side who were struggling once again with subcontinental conditions. A 5–0 scoreline was a fair reflection of the gulf between the two teams. Having played no part in the proceedings, it is difficult for me to know exactly what the dressing-room environment was like during those difficult weeks, but I suspect that the combination of the Allen Stanford affair and the dispiriting losses to India brought many of the fault lines within the side to the surface. The England cricket team was not a happy ship.

South Africa in England 2008 – The Basil D'Oliveira Trophy

1st Test. Lord's, London. 10–14 July 2008
England 593–8 dec (I.R. Bell 199, K.P. Pietersen 152, S.C.J. Broad 76,
A.N. Cook 60, **A.J. Strauss 44**; M. Morkel 4–121)
South Africa 247 (A.G. Prince 101; M.S. Panesar 4–74) and 393–3 dec
(f/o) (N.D. McKenzie 138, G.C. Smith 107, H.M. Amla 104*)
Match drawn.

2nd Test. Headingley, Leeds. 18–21 July 2008
England 203 (K.P. Pietersen 45, **A.J. Strauss 27**; M. Morkel 4–52, D.W.
Steyn 4–76) and 327 (S.C.J. Broad 67*, A.N. Cook 60, **A.J. Strauss 0**)
South Africa 522 (A.B. de Villiers 174, A.G. Prince 149) and 9–0
South Africa won by 10 wickets.

3rd Test. Edgbaston, Birmingham. 30 July – 2 August 2008
England 231 (A.N. Cook 76, I.R. Bell 50, **A.J. Strauss 20**) and 363 (P.D.
Collingwood 135, K.P. Pietersen 94, **A.J. Strauss 25**; M. Morkel 4–97)
South Africa 314 (N.D. McKenzie 72, J.H. Kallis 64; A. Flintoff 4–89) and
283–5 (G.C. Smith 154)
South Africa won by 5 wickets.

4th Test. The Oval, London. 7–11 August 2008
South Africa 194 (G.C. Smith 46) and 318 (A.B. de Villiers 97, H.M. Amla
76)
England 316 (K.P. Pietersen 100, P.D. Collingwood 61, **A.J. Strauss 6**)
and 198–4 (A.N. Cook 67, **A.J. Strauss 58**)
England won by 6 wickets.

South Africa won the series 2–1.

11

MY TURN

Little over a week after the final shots from the Mumbai attacks had rung out, the England cricket team made its way back into the country. The process of getting players to agree to continue with the tour had been a particularly onerous one for Hugh Morris, the managing director of England cricket, who tended to be thrust into the limelight only when things were going wrong, and Reg Dickason, our security consultant.

In the hours and days immediately after our return, the idea of going back into the country that had just witnessed such terrible acts sounded absurd to most of the players. It seemed perverse to escape from potential danger, only to return to it again so soon. It could also be argued that, although cricketers often think of themselves as being more important than they actually are, the combination of an English cricket team and India, where cricketers are deified, represented a tempting target for any other terrorists who might have entered the country and been lying low.

My own mind on the subject changed once I heard Reg Dickason's assessment that, from a safety point of view, the tour could proceed. The Indian government, in a desperate attempt to show the world that they were in control of the situation, had promised 'presidential levels of security', with specialist soldiers on call to ensure that the team was looked after at all times. India badly needed the tour to go ahead.

If our security consultant reckoned that it was all right to go, then I really couldn't think of a compelling reason not to. If players did not believe him, or were prepared to follow their own ideas about potential safety, then it was pointless employing him in the first place. We had to trust him and get back to doing our jobs. In any case, it increasingly felt like the right thing to do. The world had to get back to normal and the show had to go on, otherwise in some small way the terrorists would have won. Other players were less inclined to go back than I was, but after some rather fraught discussions, we were all persuaded that it was the right course of action.

Given the extraordinary circumstances surrounding our return, any hopes of a normal build-up to the two Test matches had been thrown out of the window. A three-day trip to Abu Dhabi was hastily arranged in order to prepare ourselves as much as possible for the first Test, which had been relocated to Chennai in order to provide more safety for both teams. Nonetheless, we would only fly into India two days before the start of the game.

Bizarrely, all the distractions and commotion meant that we approached the match in a far more relaxed frame of mind than usual. It was one of those occasions when the fact that it was being played at all was more important than who won. Certainly, I can't remember any other Test match in which I felt so completely at peace and at ease with myself throughout the game. It was an absolute pleasure to be on the cricket pitch, doing what we do best, after everything that had gone on over the previous fortnight.

It offers some sort of explanation for the two centuries that I struck during the game. Batting in India is never easy, especially without extensive practice in those conditions, but on this occasion I never really felt troubled, either by seam or spin. In fact, the biggest problem I faced was the stifling humidity, which made batting for hours more of a physical than a mental hurdle. At the end of the game, having batted for more than twelve hours, I was completely exhausted, but the twin hundreds, a rare feat on the subcontinent, were one of my proudest achievements.

Inevitably, given the circumstances in which the game was played, my feats were completely overshadowed by those of an Indian player, Sachin Tendulkar. His unbeaten century to take India to victory, on a pitch that was literally breaking apart, was the stuff of cricketing legend. If ever there was a moment when India needed its great idol to perform, it was there, when the whole country had been rocked by the events in Mumbai. As if answering their prayers, Sachin delivered.

Sachin Tendulkar took part in the first Test match I ever went to as a schoolboy, with my dad in 1990 at Lord's, watching Graham Gooch on the way to compiling 333. It is completely bewildering that Sachin is still playing today, after his fortieth birthday. He has performed all over the world, in all formats, with a consistency that has set him apart from all others that have played the game. His record is flabbergasting. Almost 16,000 Test runs have been scored in 198 Tests with 51 hundreds, alongside the not insignificant figures of over 18,000 ODI runs in an astonishing 463 games. We all know that he has now scored 100 international centuries. The figures are

India v England
(1st Test)

Played at Chepauk (Chidambaran Stadium), Chennai, on 11–15 December 2008

Umpires: BF Bowden & DJ Harper (TV: SL Shastri)
Referee: JJ Crowe
Toss: England

ENGLAND

Batsman	1st innings		2nd innings	
AJ Strauss	c and b Mishra	123	c Laxman b Harbhajan Singh	108
AN Cook	c Khan b Harbhajan Singh	52	c Dhoni b Sharma	9
IR Bell	lbw b Khan	17	c Gambhir b Mishra	7
KP Pietersen*	c and b Khan	4	lbw b Yuvraj Singh	1
PD Collingwood	c Gambhir b Harbhajan Singh	9	lbw b Khan	108
A Flintoff	c Gambhir b Mishra	18	c Dhoni b Sharma	4
JM Anderson	c Yuvraj Singh b Mishra	19	(10) not out	1
MJ Prior†	not out	53	(7) c Sehwag b Sharma	33
GP Swann	c Dravid b Harbhajan Singh	1	(8) b Khan	7
SJ Harmison	c Dhoni b Yuvraj Singh	6	(9) b Khan	1
MS Panesar	lbw b Sharma	6		
Extras	(lb 7, nb 1)	8	(b 10, lb 13, w 2, nb 7)	32
Total	(128.4 overs)	**316**	(for 9 wkts dec) (105.5 overs)	**311**

INDIA

Batsman	1st innings		2nd innings	
G Gambhir	lbw b Swann	19	c Collingwood b Anderson	66
V Sehwag	b Anderson	9	lbw b Swann	83
RS Dravid	lbw b Swann	3	c Prior b Flintoff	4
SR Tendulkar	c and b Flintoff	37	not out	103
VVS Laxman	c and b Panesar	24	c Bell b Swann	26
Yuvraj Singh	c Flintoff b Harmison	14	not out	85
MS Dhoni*†	c Pietersen b Panesar	53		
Harbhajan Singh	c Bell b Panesar	40		
Z Khan	lbw b Flintoff	1		
A Mishra	b Flintoff	12		
I Sharma	not out	8		
Extras	(b 4, lb 11, nb 6)	21	(b 5, lb 11, nb 4)	20
Total	(69.4 overs)	**241**	(for 4 wkts) (98.3 overs)	**387**

INDIA	O	M	R	W		O	M	R	W
Khan	21	9	41	2		27	7	40	3
Sharma	19.4	4	32	1		22.5	1	57	3
Harbhajan Singh	38	2	96	3	(5)	30	3	91	1
Mishra	34	6	99	3	(3)	17	1	66	1
Yuvraj Singh	15	2	33	1	(4)	3	1	12	1
Sehwag	1	0	8	0		6	0	22	0

ENGLAND	O	M	R	W		O	M	R	W
Harmison	11	1	42	1		10	0	48	0
Anderson	11	3	28	1		11	1	51	1
Flintoff	18.4	2	49	3	(4)	22	1	64	1
Swann	10	0	42	2	(5)	28.3	2	103	2
Panesar	19	4	65	3	(3)	27	4	105	0

Fall of wickets:

	Eng	Ind	Eng	Ind
1st	118	16	28	117
2nd	164	34	42	141
3rd	180	37	43	183
4th	195	98	257	224
5th	221	102	262	–
6th	229	137	277	–
7th	271	212	297	–
8th	277	217	301	–
9th	304	219	311	–
10th	316	241	–	–

Close of play: Day 1:   Eng (1) 229–5 (Flintoff 18*, Anderson 2*, 90 overs)
                    Day 2:   Ind (1) 155–6 (Dhoni 24*, Harbhajan Singh 13*, 45 overs)
                    Day 3:   Eng (2) 172–3 (Strauss 73*, Collingwood 60*, 54 overs)
                    Day 4:   Ind (2) 131–1 (Gambhir 41*, Dravid 2*, 29 overs)

Man of the match: V Sehwag
Result: **India won by 6 wickets**

absolutely extraordinary. Having played international cricket for nearly ten years, I know something of the stresses and strains that go with playing the game at the highest level, but to do it for twenty-four years, in all the different forms of the game, is a feat just as impressive as his immense performances in those games.

When I was playing, he was one of the very few opponents that I couldn't help admiring on the cricket field. Of course I was desperate to get him out, but I always felt that I was in the presence of greatness. There was a nimbleness of footwork and a deftness of touch that separated him from mere mortals, but what impressed me most was his ability to get into a mental zone. Nothing flustered him. He never seemed to run out of patience. He just watched the ball and selected the requisite shot from his huge armoury. In that sense, bearing in mind the pressure and expectation heaped on his shoulders every time he went out to bat, he was unique.

I remember going into the Indian dressing room after his monumental innings in Chennai, ostensibly to get a few bats signed by him for charity, and marvelling at his calm, unaffected state. Most players would have been bouncing around the room and swinging from the rafters after such an extraordinary performance. He was just sitting there surrounded by his kit as if nothing had happened.

'Well played, Sachin, that was an unbelievable innings on a wicket that was turning so much,' I said, trying not to sound too sycophantic.

'Thanks. The wicket was very slow at the end,' he countered, modest to the last.

Perhaps it is the combination of his extraordinary consistency, meticulous preparation and calm, contained manner that means that some people preferred to watch the likes of Lara or Ponting or even Sehwag in their prime. Those batsmen were far less predictable, but were touched by a genius that most people couldn't get close to. Tendulkar, though, is the only player I played against that has the full package. He has the genius, a technique that defines perfection and a mental fortitude that defies belief. What a player.

If Tendulkar's match-winning century knocked the wind out of our sails on our return to India, there were some far more menacing clouds on the horizon. It was quite a shock to me, having not been involved in the ODI series, to see just how far the relationship between Peter Moores and Kevin Pietersen had deteriorated. In team meetings they went through the motions, saying the right things, but the body language between them told a different story. There was no rapport, and away from the formal settings I didn't see them speaking at all, which is an unusual situation in an international environment, with so many decisions to be made on a daily basis.

By now, the issues between them had become an open topic of discussion amongst the team and support staff. In such circumstances, the players feel particularly exposed and vulnerable. It was clear that some manoeuvring was going on. Pietersen was talking to senior players about what he thought was wrong with the set-up, while Moores was also trying to seek advice about how to move forward. The players were caught in the middle, either feeling pressure to take sides in the underlying dispute or denying that anything was going on at all.

From my perspective, it was one battle I really didn't want anything to do with. I understood and agreed with some of Pietersen's issues and concerns with Peter Moores's methods, but my instinct was always to work *with* someone rather than *against* him. I couldn't see how forcing the issue, which was apparently what Pietersen was trying to do, was going to help things. Driving wedges between players and support staff, who were fiercely loyal to Moores, was never going to have the desired effect. The only way out of the situation was for Moores and Pietersen to get in a room together and thrash out their differences, but the testy relationship they had shared prior to Kevin becoming captain did not allow them to do that. There was no way out.

As we headed home for Christmas, after a tame, fog-affected draw in the second Test match in Mohali, we did so with an uneasy feeling about the future. It was quite clear that the ECB, and Hugh Morris in particular, were going to have to get involved to sort out the situation between Moores and Pietersen before we set off again for the West Indies, shortly after New Year. How he was going to do that was anyone's guess, but it looked likely that one or the other would be losing their job in the near future.

One of the more unfortunate elements of the whole saga was that word started leaking to the press that Kevin was trying to get rid of Peter Moores. If it had all been played out behind closed doors, then there might have been a chance to work things out amicably, but with the media speculating about divisions in the camp and Pietersen's political manoeuvring, the ECB was effectively pushed into a corner. If they decided to support Pietersen, then Peter Moores and his support staff would have every reason to feel completely betrayed. In effect, the ECB would be yielding to the captain's heavy-handed demands. If, however, they decided to keep the coach in place, then they faced the prospect of losing their newly appointed captain, and they would be ignoring some of the discontentment in the squad. Once the prospect of any sort of rapprochement had been ruled out, they effectively had only one course of action left, and that was essentially to get rid of both of them.

I can only assume that Peter Moores felt pretty bitter about being dismissed in this fashion, but he has always kept a dignified silence on the subject, to his great credit.

It is also fair to assume that Kevin Pietersen felt betrayed by the ECB, especially because of the leaks to the press that forced the issue into the open. It was a significant breakdown in the relationship between Pietersen and the ECB, from which neither side has ever fully recovered. I am sure that some of the later issues between him and the ECB over the IPL had their genesis during the first week of January 2009.

Apart from the odd casual conversation with Hugh Morris about how everyone was feeling in the camp, I really didn't have anything to do with the matter until a couple of days before Moores was dismissed and Pietersen announced his resignation. Over the New Year period, I was reading what was going on in the newspapers like everyone else, increasingly disturbed by the direction of events.

I was not surprised, therefore, to receive a phone call from Hugh Morris on 6 January. I assumed that he would be ringing around the whole team to give us some sort of insight into what had been going on behind the scenes. The call started off pretty much as I had expected. He gave me a little of the background and told me where the ECB stood on the issue. He had that cautious tone of voice, though, that you hear when people are trying to be careful with their words. He didn't want to give too much away.

Pretty soon the topic of conversation turned to potential candidates for the captaincy, if the ECB felt that it had to look elsewhere. My first instinct was to push the case for Alastair Cook taking over. I felt that perhaps there was too much baggage carried by the senior figures in the side, the likes of myself, Collingwood, Flintoff, Harmison and, of course, Pietersen. Maybe this was the time to pass the baton on to the younger generation in order to achieve a fresh start.

'Straussy, I hear what you are saying,' Hugh Morris said, 'but would you consider doing the job yourself if it were offered to you?'

In a way I was quite surprised and a little shocked that he asked me the question. The conversation had turned very quickly from one in which hypotheticals were being discussed into a far more direct line of enquiry. Given my level of surprise, and having not thought about it in any great length, I replied that I would have to get back to him.

As soon as I put the phone down, I knew what my answer

was likely to be. Of course I wanted to do the job. I felt that I had unfinished business in the role, and actually the more I thought about it, the more I believed that I might just be able to bring a team that was clearly in a state of chaos back together again. There was one issue, however, that needed to be addressed before I replied in the affirmative.

I had to speak to my wife, Ruth, about it. On paper, it sounds like the best job in the world, but anyone who had witnessed what Pietersen had gone through could see that it was not a job for the faint-hearted. It would require complete commitment, long hours, many months away from home and far more scrutiny on me and us as a family. If I was going to take the job, then I wanted both of us to go into it with our eyes firmly open.

'Andy, this is your dream job. Of course you should take it. We will be there to support you all the way,' she said, as soon as I asked her about her thoughts.

I spoke to Hugh an hour or so later. 'Hugh, I have had a think about doing the job and I have decided that I would like to do it if offered.'

That was the end of it. Earlier that day I had gone to my local café in Ealing for a coffee and a bit of breakfast, curious about how the situation between Moores and Pietersen was going to be resolved. Now, as I tucked into my dinner, with a glass of wine in my hand, it looked as if I was going to take over as England captain. What a difference a day makes.

England in India 2008–09

1st Test. MA Chidambaram Stadium, Chennai. 11–15 December 2008
England 316 (**A.J. Strauss 123**, M.J. Prior 53*, A.N. Cook 52) and 311–9
  dec (**A.J. Strauss 108**, P.D. Collingwood 108)
India 241 (M.S. Dhoni 53) and 387–4 (S.R. Tendulkar 103*, Yuvraj Singh
  85*, V. Sehwag 83, G. Gambhir 66)
India won by 6 wickets.

2nd Test. Punjab CA Stadium, Mohali. 19–23 December 2008
India 453 (G. Gambhir 179, R. Dravid 136) and 251–7 dec (G. Gambhir
  97, Yuvraj Singh 86)
England 302 (K.P. Pietersen 144, A. Flintoff 62, A.N. Cook 50, **A.J. Strauss
  0**; Harbhajan Singh 4–68) and 64–1 (**A.J. Strauss 21***)
Match drawn.

India won the series 1–0.

12

CHANGING THE
CULTURE

As excited as I was to be given the opportunity, I was under no illusions about how difficult the task of captaining England was likely to be. On the surface, at least, everything was in chaos. I was inheriting a team with no coach, with a support staff appointed by the previous regime, with players who were divided and dispirited by what had been going on. Oh, and we had also lost our two previous series. The situation on the ground demanded action, fast.

I was particularly pleased that Andy Flower had been given the role of acting coach for the West Indies tour that was due to start at the end of January 2009. I had always held him in very high esteem, both for his performances as a batsman and for the way he carried himself. I had enjoyed working with him as a batting coach, in which role he had avoided the obvious traps of telling everyone to do it the way he had once done it. I also felt that he would be able to gel the management and support staff together, which was not going to be easy, given their close relationships with the previous coach. He seemed to be the perfect man for the job, but the ECB, quite wisely after everything that had gone on, decided that they would wait until after the West Indies tour to appoint the position full-time.

Before meeting with Flower to discuss plans for the future, I wanted to be clear in my mind exactly what grievances the players had, either with the coaching staff or with the way the operation was being run. It was important at this stage that I didn't assume I knew what everyone else was thinking. It would be impossible for me to provide a way forward without first knowing exactly what was wrong.

The message I got back from the players was remarkably consistent. While they generally felt that they had been bombarded with information, statistics and directions from the coaching staff, above all they just wanted the dressing room to be a harmonious place, without in-fighting, agendas and egos ruling the roost.

Once I had finished my conversations with the players, I immediately felt far more reassured about the way ahead. The dressing room was not as divided as everyone said it was. All Andy Flower and I had to do was provide a direction and keep everyone together. It was obvious that we couldn't forge a completely new direction forward for the England cricket team in the week or so that we had available to us before leaving for the West Indies. What we did, though, was concentrate on the areas that needed addressing most urgently.

After everything that had happened, it was clear that the focus had to be on bringing the team back together. We both had ideas about how to do this, but we also understood that there might be better-qualified people to help us in this regard. Andy knew a guy called Alan Stevens, whose company specialised in healing conflicts in the corporate environment. We went to see him and listen to his advice.

'What is your culture?' he asked. 'How do you operate as a team? Do you, for instance, have a "charter", where the players buy into a way of operating?'

He seemed more than a little surprised when I replied that we had never gone down that route. Cricketers tend to be a little sceptical, to say the least, of corporate speak, and the idea of everyone sitting in a room, talking about things like 'values' and 'behaviours' had been viewed as too much of a hard sell by previous regimes.

As I sat there, it started to dawn on me that this element might be crucial to our development as a team. If we wanted players to genuinely commit to being a team, rather than just talking a good game about it, then they had to be involved in the process of deciding what our team was about. This was not something that could be dictated to them by management. They had to believe in it. They had to sign up to it. It had to be *their* team.

Fortunately, all of this fitted quite easily with another area that I had strong views on: personal responsibility. In fact, I didn't really like to call it that, as it sounded suspiciously close to the corporate speak that the players were so resistant to. I preferred to call it 'allowing players to think for themselves'.

When I looked back on it, the main issue with the regime of Peter Moores was that the management and support staff were just too hands-on. As I said earlier, I don't blame them for it. They were trying their best to make a difference and were incredibly energetic in challenging players to get better.

There was one crucial element missing, though, which was that the players did not have enough control in the process. Too often it felt like a teacher/pupil relationship between the support staff and the players. Coaches told the players what to do and they, in turn, either nodded their heads obediently or silently resented the fact that they were being told what to do when they were already world-class performers in their own right.

It obviously caused more than a little friction, but it also didn't make sense. When I considered the great Australians of the early 2000s, it was immediately clear that the team was made up of strong, self-reliant cricketers, who knew their own games well and were able to make good decisions in the cauldron of a pressurised match situation. If players were never allowed to make decisions off the pitch, why should anyone expect them to make good decisions on the pitch?

To me, what was really needed was an adjustment of the relationship between the players and the support staff. I wanted the likes of Bell or Pietersen or Anderson to use the various experts that we had at our disposal as consultants, be they psychologists, fitness experts or coaches. In other words, the players had to be in control of the situation. If they were going to work on an aspect of their game, it had to be at their instigation.

I know that some members of our coaching staff shuffled about very uncomfortably when I first proposed this. They were worried either that the players weren't ready to be given that responsibility or that it would give them an excuse to be lazy or set in their ways. I saw it completely differently. To me, it took away excuses from the players. They would be unable to sit in a corner and moan about what the coach was telling them to do, or complain that they didn't agree with the training methods. With more responsibility came accountability. In other words, they would be given enough leeway to prepare the way that they saw fit, but ultimately they would be accountable for their own performances. If they didn't perform, then they could expect a knock on the door.

In the long term, I imagined that the best type of environment was one in which the coaches and players operated on a similar level. That is to say that sometimes the coaches could push players and sometimes the players could be left alone to do their own thing. In order to get there, though, the teacher/ pupil relationship had to go. For that reason, we decided that, for the West Indies tour at least, the training session on the day before a game would be completely optional. Players could chill out, relax and not train at all if they felt they were ready. Conversely, they could spend hours going through meticulous preparation if they thought they needed it. The crucial aspect, though, was that the players were in control of their own destinies, and this was an excellent way of demonstrating that they were to be trusted.

Having informed the players that they were going to have a greater say in their own preparation, it was also easier for everyone to get in a room and start thinking about how the team should operate. The players could see that the idea of putting together a charter was now less likely to be a box-ticking exercise and actually had the potential to put them at the forefront of everything we did.

Alongside Alan Stevens, we spent a few hours thinking about

how we wanted the team to work. Looking at it now, our first draft was fairly simplistic and rudimentary, but to me it marked a significant shift. For the very first time since I had been involved in the team, every player, from Andrew Flintoff all the way down to the youngest debutant, had the ability to have a say in how they prepared themselves and how the team operated on a day-to-day basis. From there, player 'buy-in' to whatever we were doing was going to be far more realistic.

In trying to build an environment where the team came first, I also felt that we really had to try to bring the families more into the fold. For too long, the wives and children of the players were expected to play the silent and thankless role of providing encouragement and support, often from the other side of the world, while never really being welcomed into the bosom of the team. Celebrations tended to be boys-only affairs and too little thought was given to those who had to deal with the realities of being married to an international sportsman.

So after every win, when the girls were around, we would have a family celebration together, where they too could bask a little in the success of the team. Also, the PCA and Medha Laud of the ECB did a fantastic job in being available to help families cope with the very trying circumstances of being alone for months on end.

It always immensely frustrated me when the media would start talking about the arrival of families on a tour being a distraction for the players. If anything, the truth was the complete opposite, and I still believe that more should be done in the future to make sure that the England cricket team caters for the needs of the players' families.

The final difficulty to be addressed was our relationship with the media. It was clear to anyone who had watched England play ODI cricket that we were far too fearful of getting out. Opposition teams would take more risks and attempt to put pressure on our bowlers, rather than be reactive and hesitant. Our players found that difficult to do, partly because they were concerned about their place in the team, but also because they were worried about the media reaction to their dismissal.

It was obvious that this situation was unhealthy. If we wanted to be the best team in the world, then we needed to readjust our attitude towards the media. The truth was that they were not there for our benefit. Their job was to write or talk about interesting topics. If a player was out of form, then it was an interesting topic that might sell newspapers. The fact that the media talked about it did not mean that there was a vendetta against that particular player. Everyone in the team had to stop worrying about the media and start focusing on the stuff that we could control.

With that in mind, I suggested banning newspapers from the dressing room. This was not some sort of draconian reaction to what the papers said about us, but far more about making sure that our place of work, the dressing room, was free from distractions. If a player was going through a hard time, the last thing he needed was to have a room full of newspapers all talking about the pressure he was under for his place in the side.

It was also a physical demonstration of a more general idea, which was not to let anything take our attention away from our job. If we just concentrated on what we had to do, then we were going to give ourselves the best chance of performing well. Everything else, from the media to opposition players and cricket politics, was not important. The only thing that mattered was us.

Those tenets – personal responsibility, the team coming first and focusing on ourselves – stayed with the team all the way through my captaincy. I believed in them strongly. So did Andy Flower, and I think that the vast majority of the team bought into the ideas. Of course, nothing is as simple as that. Getting the environment right is only one element in the giant jigsaw of getting a team to perform to a high level. Just as important is the need to improve the skill levels.

You only had to take a look at the world rankings in January 2009 to see that we weren't really that good. We were fifth in the world in Test cricket, sixth in ODI cricket. We had one player (Pietersen) in the top-ten batsmen in the world and no bowlers in the top-ten bowlers. Even with the best environment in the world, we simply weren't good enough to win consistently.

Although there wasn't much time before the start of the West Indies tour, as throughout my time as captain, Andy Flower never ceased to look for ways of improving us as players. The two areas in which our old methods were radically altered were in practising and analysis.

Through spending some time looking at other sports, Andy

had come to the conclusion that our own practice methods were far too laborious and unstructured. For example, he found that in American football, every drill is measured and there is a set time limit. The focus is on short, sharp, intensive drills, followed by a down time. He introduced this into the way we went about our business. When the support staff were in charge of practice, everything was extremely well organised. Richard Halsall, our assistant coach, was always at the ground early, alongside the likes of Graham Gooch, David Saker and Mushtaq Ahmed, to make sure that cones and other equipment were put in place well before the players arrived. In turn, when the players were on duty, we were expected to be fully focused. Our reward was that the drills wouldn't go on for very long.

Also, right from the start of the West Indies tour, practices were designed to be far more match-specific. General net sessions, where players went through the motions, were replaced by practices without the confines of nets, replicating specific match situations, where bowlers pitted their skills against the batsmen, with an element of competition thrown into the mix. Nothing puts you on the spot more than having to perform in front of your peers. Some of my most nervous moments were during specific-practice sessions when we were going at it hammer and tongs, well aware of our team-mates' strengths and weaknesses. In short, it was good practice, preparing us properly for the rigours of an international cricket match.

As for statistics, around 2006 I had read the book *Moneyball* by Michael Lewis, which told the story of Billy Beane, the Oakland A's and their efforts to keep pace with far wealthier teams in Major League Baseball. Beane's methods centred on using statistics in a new way. He was interested in what really won games of baseball, rather than the statistics that were traditionally used to reflect a player's relative worth. By spending time looking at the statistics of baseball in a completely different way, he was able to assemble a team of unfashionable, cheap players who did not fit the traditional mould yet actually delivered match-winning performances. The book struck a chord with me straight away. I had always had a feeling that the way that some of the statistics in cricket were put together was spurious to say the least. The game exalted a player's ability to execute a pleasant-looking cover drive or hit the ball for six over consistent productivity. Too often 'sexy' players were given precedence over less glamorous but more effective alternatives. Even when statistics were used to justify a selection, it was often to back up an argument rather than as the basis for selection.

In a game in which one per cent gains were beginning to be harder to find, statistics seemed to be one area where a big difference could be made. The problem was that in order to make those gains, you needed a statistician (or analyst) who understood both cricket and the complex mathematics that underlie statistics. The England team was fortunate to find someone who qualified on both counts when Nathan Leamon was appointed as England team analyst in the summer of 2009. Although we weren't able to benefit from his excellent skills on that first tour to the West Indies, over the next few years he had a massive impact on the way we understood the game and all its variables. Ultimately, the better use of statistics helped us win a lot of games.

It is not my intention to give away trade secrets in this book, but the research that he undertook helped us on many levels. Team selection, the balance of the team (e.g. whether to play four bowlers or five), winning the toss, declarations and opposition analysis were all greatly aided. In fact, the more he delved, the more opportunities presented themselves for further research. This is one area of the game where the surface has only been scratched.

While writing this, I can picture cricket traditionalists shaking their heads, muttering that captaincy is all about intuition – no captain worth his salt should have to rely on a statistician to tell him what to do! All I can say is that it makes it far easier to commit to a decision when there is solid evidence to back up what your gut feeling tells you. It definitely helps you. If the statistics and your intuition do not match up, then it should give you a little pause for thought and reflection. Is the statistical evidence faulty, or is your gut reaction based on biased experience? Either way, it is worth spending a little time thinking about the right course of action.

I should stress that I have never been a slave to statistics, and on many occasions Andy Flower and I decided to put our cricketing experience ahead of the statistical research, but it was always reassuring to know that we had done our homework before every game.

All in all, that was the philosophy that Andy and I cobbled together before heading out to the West Indies. Really simple concepts such as allowing players to think for themselves, the team coming first, concentrating on us and constantly trying to improve were the central tenets of the master plan. None of this was rocket science, but I think what made it appealing to both the players and the management, who were still smarting from the Moores/Pietersen debacle, was that it all sounded like common sense. On that, at least, everyone seemed to agree.

13

A YEAR TO REMEMBER

I have been feeling irritable all day long. It doesn't make sense. Waking up this morning, I knew that this is likely to be the most satisfying day I have had in an England shirt. Opening the curtains in my hotel suite, I surveyed some of the landmarks and sights that make London such an enticing tourist destination. Straight in front of me was the commanding presence of Tower Bridge, with the Tower of London providing a stark reminder of the history of the city. Further along the Thames, I could see the Millennium Wheel glistening with the reflection of the early-morning sun. In the distance, I could just make out Big Ben and the astounding architecture of the Houses of Parliament. Also, being a Sunday, there were none of the hordes of commuters rushing to get to work. The city was at peace, showing off her virtues when no one was looking.

I have every reason to feel on top of the world. It is 23 August 2009, day four of the final Ashes Test match, and Australia need a highly improbable 466 runs to win. With the series locked at 1–1, a victory for either side is going to be decisive. As it stands, all bets are off. There is only one side that can win this Test – and it is England.

As the day has worn on, though, things have not gone to plan, to say the least. What we thought would be a procession of wickets on a tired and worn track has turned into a great rearguard defence from an Australian team that refuses to go down without a fight. Mike Hussey, who has not made a run in the series, has suddenly found form at the very last moment and probably kept his place in the team as a result. Ricky Ponting, being the incredibly proud and competitive captain that he is, is unwilling to let go.

None of our ideas seem to be working. Either the bowlers are trying too hard to take wickets or the fielders are slightly out of position or the rub of the green seems to have deserted us. I am finding it difficult to keep calm and relaxed. Little things are annoying me. A scolding look and a word from one of our bowlers to a fielder when a ball is misfielded really gets me going. This is the time for us all to get stuck in together and find a way through the Australian batting line-up. We do not need in-fighting and petulance. A ball from Graeme Swann spins past the edge of Mike Hussey's bat once again. Surely our luck has to change at some point.

Midway through the afternoon session, all thoughts of holding up the Ashes urn and celebrating the night away have well and truly gone. At 217–2, a few members of the Australian dressing room are looking far too relaxed for my liking. They are starting to have hope again and that is a dangerous emotion for an opposing captain to deal with.

Hussey pushes a ball from Steve Harmison towards mid on and sets off for a risky single. In a flash, Andrew Flintoff belies his huge frame, swoops down on the ball, picks it up and hurls it towards the stumps at the wicketkeeper's end. He has a powerful throw and the ball hits the off stump an instant before Ponting gets his bat over the crease. We have our breakthrough and the burly all-rounder, in his last Test match for England, has delivered one final time.

The new man at the crease, Michael Clarke, is almost immediately run out in strange circumstances as I manage to deflect a ball that hits me at leg slip back onto his stumps. Two run-outs in ten minutes. It looks as if our luck is changing. Before long Marcus North is stumped by Matt Prior after dozily dragging his foot out of his crease while attempting a sweep. We are on a roll, momentum is with us and the Australian lower order are unable to stem the tide.

Shortly before the scheduled close of play, Mike Hussey prods forward to a delivery from Graeme Swann that catches the edge of his bat before hitting his pads and ballooning to Alastair Cook at short leg. The Ashes series is over. That precious little urn is coming back to England two and a half years after the most almighty walloping in Australia. It is also less than eight months since English cricket was on its knees following the Moores/ Pietersen saga.

I am about to go on stage to collect the smallest but most important trophy that an England captain can ever hold.

I can still scarcely believe that we won the 2009 Ashes series. How can you explain winning when the opposition had four out of the five top run scorers, the three leading wicket-takers, more hundreds and more five-wicket hauls? Statisticians around the country could put together a very interesting study into the probability of this happening, but I doubt it is very high.

In my opinion, however, nothing was more important for our later development as a side than winning that series in such unlikely circumstances. After so much time and effort had been spent trying to change the environment within the team, our lack of early success had given ammunition to the naysayers and doubters, who felt that cricket was merely a game in which teams flourished on the back of outstanding individual performances. Certainly, when we were bowled out for 51 in my first Test match in charge in Jamaica in February 2009, everyone could see just what a precarious position the team was in. Any illusions that a few meetings and some encouraging words could change a team's performance overnight were shattered on that day.

To the players' great credit, no one let the result affect their enthusiasm to do things differently. In fact, the humiliating nature of the defeat led Andy Flower to decide that enough was enough and he called a meeting to thrash out any lingering issues within the team. The two hours that followed, in which Flower skilfully and considerately forced all the underlying baggage between players to the surface, cemented everyone's opinion that he was the man for the coach's job full-time. His performance in that meeting room in Antigua, the venue for the next Test, demonstrated many of his great skills as a coach and a leader.

He wasn't afraid to go into uncomfortable territory. In fact, he seemed to revel in saying the difficult thing, much as inhospitable conditions brought the best out of him as a player. Moreover, he was able to do it in a manner that didn't get the players' hackles up. It was respectful, balanced, unbiased and constructive. He was not interested in anyone settling scores but merely focused on what was best for the team.

We all walked out of that meeting room feeling as if a great weight had been lifted. Issues concerning personal agendas, lack of dedication, lack of trust and poor decision-making had been aired and thrashed out, and it had been done in a way that didn't leave the players concerned feeling victimised. It was also clear to me that Andy and I had the potential to forge a very close relationship.

The truth is that I admired him greatly, both as a cricketer and as a person. It takes guts to stand up in a World Cup and make a heartfelt political protest about the state of your country, when you and your family could be in danger as a result, as he did in 2003. He had also made the very best of himself as a player and was admired around the world for his tenacity in the middle. After turning to coaching, he never for one moment assumed that he knew more than everyone else. He was inquisitive, impassioned and driven to succeed in this new venture.

Most importantly, as far as I was concerned, he was challenging. He never got sucked into the trap of uttering platitudes and clichés. Throughout our time as captain and coach, I could never be quite sure where he would stand on any given subject, but I knew that whatever view he had would be considered and well thought out. I loved nothing more than when we were debating, arguing and challenging each other on cricketing issues. It was great fun and extremely constructive.

Nothing demonstrated his communication skills better than what happened during a team-bonding session in Germany before the Ashes series in 2010–11. We had to take part in a variety of debates and he was given the unenviable task of defending Adolf Hitler's virtues as a leader. By the end of his five-minute speech, Hitler could have been confused for a latter-day saint who had sympathetically and single-handedly brought Germany out of the doldrums. As you can imagine, it was sometimes difficult to win arguments with a person as skilled as he was.

Largely thanks to that clear-the-air meeting, our performances in the West Indies picked up a little in the remaining games, but a combination of flat wickets and obdurate batting from the likes of Shivnarine Chanderpaul resulted in three draws to go with our defeat in the first Test. Thankfully, we had more success in the ODI series that followed, winning our first games of cricket of the whole winter, en route to a 3–2 series victory.

Despite a 2–0 Test series win against the same opposition in England at the beginning of the summer of 2009, in frigid conditions that were never likely to see the West Indies at their strongest, we approached the Ashes series that followed with more hope than expectation. There was a growing feeling that, while we might be on the right track as a side, this particular challenge might be coming a little too early.

By the time the Ashes series was about to start, I had become familiar with the increased interest and attention that is heaped upon an England captain whenever the old enemy are in town.

My turn. Facing my first press conference as England captain in January 2009, just before the West Indies tour.

Talking things through with acting coach Andy Flower at Port of Spain. He seemed to be the perfect man for the job.

The crowd at the 5th ODI against the West Indies in St Lucia. After losing the Test series, we regained some momentum by winning the game and the one-day series.

Relishing the responsibility. This century in the 3rd Test at Antigua was one of three in my first series as full-time captain.

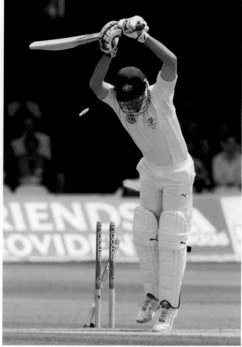

Andrew Flintoff strains every sinew at Lord's in the 2nd Test of the 2009 Ashes. He had just announced it would be his final series.

Nathan Hauritz shoulders arms to give Flintoff his fourth wicket in the second innings at Lord's.

His team-mates stand by as Flintoff bathes in the admiration of the crowd after taking his fifth wicket. We went on to win the game by 115 runs.

Stuart Broad in the middle of another purple patch in the final Test at The Oval. He took five top-order wickets in the first innings.

Jonathan Trott's selection for the Oval Test had raised some eyebrows, but his 119 in the second innings proved crucial – a truly stunning debut.

The celebrations begin as Graeme Swann finally ends Mike Hussey's rearguard stand of 121 at The Oval. I can still scarcely believe that we won the 2009 Ashes.

In the 2nd Test at Adelaide in 2010–11, James Anderson takes the prized wicket of Michael Clarke, leaving Australia three wickets down after only thirteen balls.

I won the toss at the 4th Test at Melbourne, but my instinctive decision to bowl first was met with groans from England supporters.

The Barmy Army were soon cheering as the nagging accuracy of England's seam attack, including Chris Tremlett (*left*) and James Anderson (*right*), skittled Australia for just 98.

Tim Bresnan celebrates one of his four key wickets in Australia's second innings at Melbourne, trapping Shane Watson lbw for 54.

Graeme Swann leads the 'sprinkler dance' after our win in the 4th Test in 2010–11 had ensured that the Ashes were not going to be prised from our grasp.

The Holy Grail: receiving the replica urn from Michael Vaughan. Victory at Sydney in the final Test capped off a resounding Ashes series win – the first Down Under since 1986–87.

As players, you have to deal with the phoney war, when ex-cricketers are all sticking in their twopenn'orth about the relative strengths of the sides. As captain, you are thrust into the limelight as never before. Anything you say about your side or the opposition is suddenly big news. On the one hand, it makes you feel pretty powerful, as if the full reach of your position is apparent for the first time; on the other, it makes you realise that there is a very fine line to be trodden. Playing the media game is a dangerous gamble. Partly because of our philosophy as a team, I tried to stay away from it as much as possible.

What I couldn't get away from were the newspaper reports about Andrew Flintoff oversleeping and missing the bus during a pre-series bonding trip to visit Flanders Field in Belgium. It was just the sort of off-field distraction that we didn't need when building up to an important series. The media loved it, especially as it bore some resemblance to the famous pedalo incident in the West Indies, and they were keen to get as much mileage out of it as possible. For the captain and the players, though, the last thing you want is to be justifying the team environment, as well as protocols on time-keeping and alcohol, especially when the new-found camaraderie in the ranks is still on shaky foundations.

Welcome to an Ashes series.

Although the off-field distractions were reaching fever pitch in the run-up to the series, I was at least comforted by my own form with the bat. In the six Tests that I had been in charge,

I had managed to score three hundreds against the West Indies, as well as an ODI century on my return to the side after an absence of nearly two years. It was apparent that the captaincy was having a dramatic effect. Gone were the doubts about my place in the side, replaced by a new-found responsibility and determination to lead from the front. With more of my time focused on team issues, there was far less opportunity for introspection. There were more important fish to fry. There is no doubt that your mindset determines your performances far more than your technique or talent. The trick is in finding a way to control it, and somewhat fortuitously, the call to captain the side had transformed my game.

It was not enough, though, to prevent us finding ourselves in real danger in the first game of the Ashes series, held for the very first time in Cardiff, in July. After four days in which we were largely dominated by an Australian side that was renowned for starting strongly, we were in a precarious position on the final day. With two wickets down overnight, still 220 runs off making Australia bat again, our only hope of salvation lay in batting out the day to secure a draw. By the time we got to lunch, however, we were five wickets down, and with James Anderson and Monty Panesar as our last two batsmen, hardly renowned as batting superstars, Australia were realistically only three wickets away from victory.

Their progress was obstructed by Paul Collingwood's brilliant six-hour vigil, with some vital assistance from Flintoff, Broad and Swann, but as the game entered its final hour, Australia only needed the wicket of either Anderson or Panesar to win the game.

Needless to say, in the dressing room confidence in our final pair was not sky-high. Andy Flower and I found a quiet area on the balcony to start discussing our reaction to the defeat and our path back into the series. Tired players were beginning to pack up their kit and think about getting home to loved ones. Whatever attention that remained on the game was more out of a completely irrational optimism than anything else.

Slowly, however, Panesar and Anderson started looking a little more certain at the wicket. The Australians were clearly getting rattled at their inability to finish things off, and as the time ticked by, a genuine sense of hope started to permeate the dressing room. No one was packing up kit now. In fact, everyone was rooted to their seats, unwilling and unable to move in case of tempting fate. Still the last pair held on.

With only a few minutes to go before the scheduled close, a buzz of excitement started to run through the lads. Someone suggested that we should try and waste as much time as possible to make sure that Australia couldn't get in more overs than their allotted number. Although a little concerned that we might be complicating things a little unnecessarily, I asked our physio, Steve McCaig, to take out another pair of gloves for Anderson and pretend that he was needed to check out a mystery injury. At the end of the over, out he trotted to the middle, coming to the aid of two completely bemused batsmen, only to be told where to go in no uncertain terms by Ricky Ponting and the umpires. The whole incident caused a bit of a stir at the end of the game, and big Steve McCaig's picture was all over the media the next day. Although he was no doubt a little embarrassed at being described as 'portly' and 'hefty' in the papers, he had done his bit for the team. Ironically, he is Australian.

As the clock ticked down to six o'clock and the conclusion of the game, the Australians were surrounding Anderson and Panesar, throwing everything they could muster in order to dismiss them. However, it was too late, and the final over, delivered by Nathan Hauritz, was beautifully negotiated by James Anderson. We had held out, but more importantly, we had done so with the sort of grit and determination that is only displayed by a true team. No disparate group of individuals could have managed to prevent a defeat in those circumstances.

If that wasn't encouraging enough, I had heard that during practice on the day before the game, Matt Prior had stopped his net and walked over to admonish a supporter who was getting stuck into Monty Panesar's batting ability. That was exactly what I was looking for from my team-mates: people who genuinely cared about each other and the team environ-ment. I bet that particular supporter was feeling more than a little foolish on that Monday evening.

As has so often been the case in Test series I played in, if one team dominates a Test match yet doesn't go on to win it, the momentum bizarrely sways towards the team that got out of jail. It doesn't really make sense, as the side who made all the running in the match should be satisfied with the way they played. It seems, however, that the relief of getting away with it is a stronger emotion.

Certainly, in the build-up to the second Test at Lord's, I could sense a greater hunger and urgency amongst the lads. There was a real determination to grab the series by the scruff of the neck, which was also helped by Andrew Flintoff's announcement that he was going to retire from Test cricket at the end of the series. He desperately wanted to end his career on a high and it was always a bonus when Flintoff was straining every sinew to win a match for England. He could buoy the spirits like very few others.

In fact, the whole of the second Test match marked a clear turnaround in the confidence and belief of the two sides. Guided by my sense of responsibility and a determination to set the tone, I went out on the first morning and played the most assured innings of my England career. The 161 I scored that day, aided by some early wayward bowling from Mitchell Johnson, was one of those very rare occasions when I felt as if I was completely in the zone. There is nothing in cricket quite like scoring a century at Lord's in an Ashes Test match. When you combine the unique atmosphere of the home of cricket with the equally special feeling you get playing in an Ashes Test match, you are left with a sporting environment that is without compare. Players, media, spectators, viewers and listeners are all captivated by the drama, and to be the central figure in that drama, feeling as though you have the opposition in the palm of your hand, is an experience that is genuinely like no other. I will be regaling my grandchildren with memories of that innings in years to come, but most importantly it shifted the momentum of the series back in our favour. Two solid bowling performances, including an epic spell from Flintoff on the last morning, were enough to complete a victory that no one would have anticipated a few days earlier, when we were hanging on by our fingertips in Cardiff.

England v Australia
(2nd Test)

Played at Lord's Cricket Ground, London, on 16–20 July 2009

Umpires: BR Doctrove & RE Koertzen (TV: NJ Llong)
Referee: JJ Crowe
Toss: England

ENGLAND

AJ Strauss*	b Hilfenhaus	161	c Clarke b Hauritz		32
AN Cook	lbw b Johnson	95	lbw b Hauritz		32
RS Bopara	lbw b Hilfenhaus	18	c Katich b Hauritz		27
KP Pietersen	c Haddin b Siddle	32	c Haddin b Siddle		44
PD Collingwood	c Siddle b Clarke	16	c Haddin b Siddle		54
MJ Prior†	b Johnson	8	run out (North)		61
A Flintoff	c Ponting b Hilfenhaus	4	not out		30
SCJ Broad	b Hilfenhaus	16	not out		0
GP Swann	c Ponting b Siddle	4			
JM Anderson	c Hussey b Johnson	29			
G Onions	not out	17			
Extras	(b 15, lb 2, nb 8)	25	(b 16, lb 9, w 1, nb 5)		31
Total	(101.4 overs)	**425**	(for 6 wkts dec) (71.2 overs)		**311**

AUSTRALIA

PJ Hughes	c Prior b Anderson	4	c Strauss b Flintoff		17
SM Katich	c Broad b Onions	48	c Pietersen b Flintoff		6
RT Ponting*	c Strauss b Anderson	2	b Broad		38
MEK Hussey	b Flintoff	51	c Collingwood b Swann		27
MJ Clarke	c Cook b Anderson	1	b Swann		136
MJ North	b Anderson	0	b Swann		6
BJ Haddin†	c Cook b Broad	28	c Collingwood b Flintoff		80
MG Johnson	c Cook b Broad	4	b Swann		63
NM Hauritz	c Collingwood b Onions	24	b Flintoff		1
PM Siddle	c Strauss b Onions	35	b Flintoff		7
BW Hilfenhaus	not out	6	not out		4
Extras	(b 4, lb 6, nb 2)	12	(b 5, lb 8, nb 8)		21
Total	(63 overs)	**215**	(107 overs)		**406**

AUSTRALIA	O	M	R	W		O	M	R	W
Hilfenhaus	31	12	103	4		19	5	59	0
Johnson	21.4	2	132	3		17	2	68	0
Siddle	20	1	76	2		15.2	4	64	2
Hauritz	8.3	1	26	0		16	1	80	3
North	16.3	2	59	0					
Clarke	4	1	12	1	(5)	4	0	15	0

ENGLAND	O	M	R	W		O	M	R	W
Anderson	21	5	55	4		21	4	86	0
Flintoff	12	4	27	1		27	4	92	5
Broad	18	1	78	2	(4)	16	3	49	1
Onions	11	1	41	3	(3)	9	0	50	0
Swann	1	0	4	0		28	3	87	4
Collingwood						6	1	29	0

Fall of wickets:

	Eng	Aus	Eng	Aus
1st	196	4	61	17
2nd	222	10	74	34
3rd	267	103	147	78
4th	302	111	174	120
5th	317	111	260	128
6th	333	139	311	313
7th	364	148	–	356
8th	370	152	–	363
9th	378	196	–	388
10th	425	215	–	406

Close of play: Day 1:   Eng (1) 364–6 (Strauss 161*, Broad 7*, 90 overs)
    Day 2:   Aus (1) 156–8 (Hauritz 3*, Siddle 3*, 49 overs)
    Day 3:   Eng (2) 311–6 (Flintoff 30*, Broad 0*, 71.2 overs)
    Day 4:   Aus (2) 313–5 (Clarke 125*, Haddin 80*, 86 overs)

Man of the match: A Flintoff
Result: **England won by 115 runs**

To me, one of the things that demonstrate the hold the Ashes series has on our country is the importance attached to it by the many cricket-mad celebrities out there. For some reason, people who are famous in their own right in different fields, from politics to music and acting, work themselves into a frenzy around an Ashes series. There have been plenty of stories over the years about stars like Elton John following the England cricket team on tour and throwing lavish parties after Test wins. My own experiences with cricketing celebrities centre on two equally bizarre events.

During the 2005 series, when we were giving our all against the mighty Australian side including Shane Warne, Daniel Radcliffe, aka Harry Potter, was interviewed on television about the Ashes. He let the world know that he was having a recurring dream that I, Andrew Strauss, was chasing him with a cricket bat. Now, it is strange enough to be told that someone you don't know is dreaming about you, but when the person in question is Harry Potter, the most famous wizard of modern times, it is all too much to compute. I suppose in some strange way I felt flattered.

The second event happened at Edgbaston before the third Test match of the 2009 Ashes series. During the pre-match press conference, I was asked by a particularly wily journalist whether I thought that the Australian cricket team had lost its aura – a hospital pass of a question for any England captain. To say no would be an admission that the Aussies still had a mental stranglehold over the English. That was not an option. To reply yes, though, would make it look as if I was arrogantly predicting the demise of Australian cricket, which was certain to be a fantastic motivator for a team that had inexplicably been defeated in the previous Test match. Struggling, I opted to say that they were still a very good team, but that there was no aura. Needless to say, the papers the next morning, the first of the Test match, were filled with 'Strauss slams Aussie no-hopers/They have no aura'-type headlines.

During one of the many breaks in play during that rain-affected game, Kevin Pietersen invited Piers Morgan into the dressing room to have a chat with the team. He'd clearly seen the headlines.

'I love what you are doing to the Aussie side, getting stuck into them like that,' he said when introduced to me. 'They hate it. They can give it but they can't take it. I should know. I have worked with them all my life.'

I nodded in agreement, pretending that my comments had all been part of a great masterplan to combat the Australian psyche, rather than a pretty lame attempt to get myself out of a difficult line of questioning, and he seemed satisfied. Off went the *Britain's Got Talent* judge, famed for his ability to say harsh comments to aspiring performers, impressed by my efforts to rile the opposition. If only he had known.

Regardless of 'aura-gate', we managed to continue our hold over Australia for the majority of that third Test match, but were unable to force a result because of the amount of time lost to rain. We headed to Leeds, therefore, in a particularly buoyant mood, knowing that we were only one victory away from winning the series and bringing the Ashes back home.

* * *

I made many mistakes as England captain, but two of my largest blunders occurred during the Headingley Test in 2009. Firstly, and most importantly, I encouraged the players during the preparation phase of the game to start thinking about the idea of lifting the little urn. My thinking was that having a tantalising goal at the end of the game would motivate the players to such an extent that it would elevate our performance. Phrases like 'This is the time to realise our dreams' were coming out of our pre-game team meeting and I was more than happy to go along with it. The first inkling that something might be wrong with this tactic came from Andy Flower on the afternoon before the game.

'I don't like the language that is being used in the dressing room,' he commented with a worried expression on his face. 'It feels like we are looking too far ahead, and not concentrating enough on the hard work that it is going to take for us to get there.'

I light-heartedly admonished him for being so negative, but deep down I was beginning to have my concerns as well. You hear stories all the time about golfers or athletes slipping up after allowing themselves to think about the result rather than the process. I was starting to hope rather than expect that the players would not fall into the trap.

Secondly, Matt Prior, so often the lynchpin in our side, went down with a back spasm with about forty-five minutes to go before the start of the game. He was writhing about in agony and it was clear that his participation in the game was in serious doubt. With only fifteen minutes left until the toss, Andy and I were rushing around everywhere, trying to locate Steve

Davies, the back-up wicketkeeper, who was playing for Worcestershire somewhere, as well as trying to get our medical staff to sort out Prior's back. By the time 10.30 came along, we still weren't in a position to name a side and I had to ask Ricky Ponting if we could delay the toss. Thankfully, we had allowed the Australians to change their team after the toss at Edgbaston when Brad Haddin broke his finger in the warm-up, so Ponting was happy to agree.

After putting Prior on the spot, saying that he could only play if he guaranteed that he would be ready to keep wicket by lunchtime, we decided to select him and I went out for the delayed toss. Having had little time to think about what to do if we won, and mindful that we might be without a wicketkeeper for the first hour or two of the match, I elected to bat first on a wicket that tended to help the bowlers on the first morning. Shortly after lunch we were bowled out for 102 and the match was as good as over. By the end of the third day, we had succumbed to a humiliating innings and 80-run defeat. I was kicking myself for at least a week after that game for making such a hasty and poorly thought-out decision. At least the players had stopped thinking about holding the Ashes urn aloft and realised we had a real scrap on our hands at The Oval.

After we'd fallen to the Australian all-seam attack at Headingley, hurried instructions were sent to The Oval that the groundsman, Bill Gordon, should prepare a wicket that encouraged spin bowling. Some might say that preparing wickets to suit your bowling attack is against the spirit of the game, but to me that is what home advantage is all about. You don't expect to see a seaming wicket in India, so why prepare a wicket in England to suit the opposition? In fact, for too long individual counties have been over-protective about the pitches their groundsmen produce for Test matches. Polite requests by the England set-up for a certain type of wicket have often been met with a frosty reception, or, as if to prove a point, a wicket specifically different from the one requested. More recently, though, the counties have recognised that their own fates are inextricably linked to the performance of the England cricket team and, with one or two exceptions, have been more willing to help.

In this instance, Surrey did us a huge favour by producing what looked like an old-fashioned 'bunsen burner' – a proper turning wicket. A second favour was delivered to us by Ricky Ponting when he chose not to select a front-line spinner in the Australian team, opting instead to stick with his four-pronged pace attack from Headingley, with the part-time spin of Marcus North to back them up. I was absolutely staggered when I read their team sheet, and after winning one of the most important tosses of my career, we set about making up for our mistakes in Headingley.

We were helped in that regard by one very important change to our side. Ravi Bopara was dropped after a number of failures during the series, to be replaced by Jonathan Trott. Trott, who was brought up in South Africa and had done a long stint in county cricket, was a bit of a risky choice for the deciding Test match in an Ashes series. At the time, there were far more calls to bring back Marcus Trescothick or Mark Ramprakash than to select Trott. He had impressed, though, both in the manner in which he scored runs for Warwickshire and in his great consistency with the bat. One look at him playing Flintoff and Harmison in the nets was enough for me. This was a guy who could seriously play.

What only became apparent during the Test match was that he had incredible concentration to go along with his excellent technique. In the most important game that most of us were ever likely to play in, he got into his little bubble of concentration, scratched out his guard constantly and in the second innings produced a hundred of the very highest quality. It was a truly stunning debut.

I managed to get two fifties in the game and Stuart Broad, who had been under some media pressure, produced an inspired spell to blow away the Australians in the first innings, to leave us tantalisingly on the verge of victory on the final morning of the game.

'I would like to ask the England captain, winner of the Compton-Miller medal for Man of the Series, to come forward and receive the Ashes urn.'

I walk up to the ceremonial stage and look at the most famous trophy in cricket. Behind me are my team-mates, who have overcome considerable odds to bring home the Ashes. It seems scarcely believable that we find ourselves in this position after everything that has happened with the team over the previous year. I swell with pride as I make my way to pick up the urn. I have managed to captain the side to Ashes glory while being named Man of the Series at the same time, but more than anything, I feel very fortunate to be sharing a stage with some unbelievable cricketers, all of whom have made massive sacrifices in time, effort and ego to get us here.

I reach forward and take hold of the delicate little trophy and thrust it up into the air. Immediately fireworks, music, champagne and pandemonium fill the air. We have just won the Ashes.

England in the West Indies 2008–09 – The Wisden Trophy

1st Test. Sabina Park, Kingston, Jamaica. 4–7 February 2009
England 318 (K.P. Pietersen 97, M.J. Prior 64, **A.J. Strauss 7**; S.J. Benn
4–77) and 51 (**A.J. Strauss 9**, J.E. Taylor 5–11, S.J. Benn 4–31)
West Indies 392 (R.R. Sarwan 107, C.H. Gayle 104; S.C.J. Broad 5–85)
West Indies won by an innings and 23 runs.

2nd Test. Sir Vivian Richards Stadium, Antigua. 13 February 2009
England 7–0
Match abandoned after 10 balls because of dangerous outfield.

3rd Test. Antigua Recreation Ground, St John's. 15–19 February 2009
England 566–9 dec (**A.J. Strauss 169**, P.D. Collingwood 113) and 221–8
dec (A.N. Cook 58, **A.J. Strauss 14**)
West Indies 285 (R.R. Sarwan 94; G.P. Swann 5–57) and 370–9 (R.R.
Sarwan 106; S.C.J. Broad 3–69)
Match drawn.

4th Test. Kensington Oval, Barbados. 26 February – 2 March 2009
England 600–6 dec (**A.J. Strauss 142**, R.S. Bopara 104, P.D. Collingwood
96) and 279–2 dec (A.N. Cook 139*, K.P. Pietersen 72*, **A.J. Strauss 38**)
West Indies 749–9 dec (R.R. Sarwan 291, D. Ramdin 166, S. Chanderpaul
70, D.S. Smith 55; G.P. Swann 5–165)
Match drawn.

5th Test. Queen's Park Oval, Port of Spain, Trinidad. 6–10 March 2009
England 546–6 dec (P.D. Collingwood 161, **A.J. Strauss 142**, M.J. Prior
131*) and 237–6 dec (K.P. Pietersen 102, M.J. Prior 61, **A.J. Strauss 14**)
West Indies 544 (S. Chanderpaul 147*, B.P. Nash 109, C.H. Gayle 102)
and 114–8 (G.P. Swann 3–13, J.M. Anderson 3–24)
Match drawn.

West Indies won the series 1–0.

Australia in England 2009 – The Ashes

1st Test. SWALEC Stadium, Cardiff. 8–12 July 2009
England 435 (K.P. Pietersen 69, **A.J. Strauss 30**) and 252–9 (P.D.
Collingwood 74, **A.J. Strauss 17**)
Australia 674–6 dec (R.T. Ponting 150, M.J. North 125, S.M. Katich 122,
B.J. Haddin 121, M.J. Clarke 83)
Match drawn.

2nd Test. Lord's, London. 16–20 July 2009
England 425 (**A.J. Strauss 161**, A.N. Cook 95; B.W. Hilfenhaus 4–103)
and 311–6 dec (M.J. Prior 61, P.D. Collingwood 54, **A.J. Strauss 32**)
Australia 215 (M.E.K. Hussey 51; J.M. Anderson 4–55) and 406 (M.J.
Clarke 136, B.J. Haddin 80; A. Flintoff 5–92)
England won by 115 runs.

3rd Test. Edgbaston, Birmingham. 30 July – 3 August 2009
Australia 263 (S.R. Watson 62; J.M. Anderson 5–80, G. Onions 4–58) and
375–5 (M.J. Clarke 103*, M.J. North 96, M.E.K. Hussey 64)
England 376 (A. Flintoff 74, **A.J. Strauss 69**, S.C.J. Broad 55, I.R. Bell 53;
B.W. Hilfenhaus 4–109)
Match drawn.

4th Test. Headingley, Leeds. 7–9 August 2009
England 102 (M.J. Prior 37*, **A.J. Strauss 3**; P.M. Siddle 5–21) and 263
(G.P. Swann 62, S.C.J. Broad 61, **A.J. Strauss 32**; M.G. Johnson 5–69,
B.W. Hilfenhaus 4–60)
Australia 445 (M.J. North 110, M.J. Clarke 93, R.T. Ponting 78, S.R. Watson
51; S.C.J. Broad 6–91)
Australia won by an innings and 80 runs.

5th Test. The Oval, London. 20–23 August 2009
England 332 (I.R. Bell 72, **A.J. Strauss 55**; P.M. Siddle 4–75) and 373–9
dec (I.J.L. Trott 119, **A.J. Strauss 75**, G.P. Swann 63; M.J. North 4–98)
Australia 160 (S.M. Katich 50; S.C.J. Broad 5–37, G.P. Swann 4–38) and
348 (M.E.K. Hussey 121, R.T. Ponting 66; G.P. Swann 4–120)
England won by 197 runs.

England won the series 2–1.

14

STEPPING OVER
THE LINE

I am sitting on my sofa, enjoying a rare opportunity during a Test match to spend the night at home. It is a Saturday evening in August 2010, and the knowledge that the traffic into London in the morning is likely to be light has tempted me to risk the forty-five-minute journey to Lord's cricket ground from my house in Marlow. Besides, after a see-sawing first three days of the Test match, during which we were put under enormous pressure by the excellent Pakistan fast bowlers, a monumental stand between Jonathan Trott and Stuart Broad of 332 has seen us wrest the initiative away from Pakistan. There is no way I will be needed to bat tomorrow, and with Pakistan reeling at 41–4, there is every chance that a follow-on might be on the cards.

Having flicked through the TV channels for a while, looking for anything that might take my mind off the cricket, I turn to Sky News to have a quick check of what's going on in the world before heading up to bed. I listen half-heartedly to the headlines, but suddenly I sit bolt upright. 'The Pakistan cricket team has been implicated in a match-fixing controversy by the News of the World *newspaper' is the headline that grabs my attention.*

Immediately, I download the online version of the News of

the World *and start reading in complete disbelief about Mazhar Majeed, the secret video footage and the no-balls delivered by Mohammad Asif and Mohammad Amir on the first day of the game I'm playing in. Straight away I feel as if I have been punched in the stomach. I can't honestly believe that this is happening. Pretty soon my disbelief turns to frustration and anger. All the hours of practice, all the team meetings, all the stress and mental turmoil that the team has gone through over the preceding weeks – it suddenly feels as if it was for nothing. The opposition were actually trying to give us runs. In fact, who knows if they were trying to win the game at all? I stop reading and brace myself for a particularly gruelling day tomorrow.*

Over the years I have played cricket, I have heard plenty of rumours about match-fixing. It was supposedly rife in the 1990s and many of the past England cricketers had stories to tell about potentially rigged matches and implicated players. The Hansie Cronje affair, which broke during a Middlesex preseason tour to South Africa, blew the whole shady world into the open for a time. I can't think of anyone in the game who wasn't completely shocked that someone like Cronje had taken money to underperform in matches. He just didn't seem the type of character to do it. The investigation that followed went some way to explaining how Cronje and his team-mates had got involved but did little to uncover what was happening in other parts of the world, particularly in the subcontinent.

Later, Mohammad Azharuddin, the Indian captain, was banned from cricket and it became apparent that this was bigger than anyone imagined. The problem was that the game's authorities still faced a devilishly difficult task in trying to unearth actual evidence implicating corrupt cricketers and officials. The ICC Anti-Corruption and Security Unit (ACSU) was established in 2000 to keep tabs on illegal betting and suspicious behaviour, but in truth they had neither the resources nor the powers to make any real progress. They weren't able to tap phones, gain access to bank accounts or take part in sting operations. All they could do was make it more difficult for players to contact their fixers by banning mobile phones in the dressing room and wait for a whistleblower to appear. It was hardly the stuff to make the hardened underworld figures making fortunes out of illegal betting shake in their boots.

As for whistleblowing, one major difficulty is that once a player has taken money from these people, he is forever under their control. It takes a brave man to give evidence against someone who has the motivation and means to hurt that person or his family.

So the game just meandered on, making optimistic statements about cleaning up the game and even finding a couple of low-profile players guilty of match-fixing. While everyone was congratulating each other on putting the problem of match-fixing to bed, persistent rumours remained about what was going on in some ODI tournaments.

Mind you, even with all this knowledge at our disposal, as far as I knew, none of the players in the England side had ever heard of any game in which we had played being affected. It seemed a very faraway problem, and just about the only time we had anything to do with the ACSU was when we grudgingly handed our mobile phones over to their representative before games. 'As if,' we all thought, 'taking away our mobiles is really going to stop it happening.'

All this goes some way to explaining our utter dismay and surprise when we turned up at Lord's on that Sunday morning. There were plenty of conversations in the dressing room about the no-balls and how suspicious they had looked, but overall we were in shock – not to mention baffled by the idea that the game might still go ahead. It seemed completely wrong to persist with the pretence that we were actually playing a proper game of cricket.

God knows how Jonathan Trott and Stuart Broad felt, after fighting so valiantly to register centuries, but it was all but impossible to look the Pakistan players in the eye as we made our way to and from the nets. With 20,000 supporters already in the ground, it became apparent pretty quickly that we would have to keep up the charade. We had an obligation to play, but no one was in the mood to continue the game.

Perhaps unsurprisingly, the Pakistan team were in a far worse state than we were. There was no way their batsmen could concentrate on the task at hand and we bowled them out twice in less than a day to finish off the game and take the series. No victory has given me less pleasure, and receiving the trophy in the Long Room, with rain pouring down outside, seemed somehow apt. No atmosphere, no celebration, just going through the motions. Players, administrators and media were all sharing the same feelings.

Unfortunately, however, this was far from the end of the story.

*   *   *

The England team had been through a great deal since winning the 2009 Ashes campaign. The never-ending treadmill of international fixtures meant that the euphoria of winning the Ashes was short-lived. Immediately afterwards, at the end of the 2009 summer, there was an interminable seven-match ODI series against Australia, followed by a Champions Trophy in South Africa, before the more traditional winter assignments: Test and ODI tours to South Africa and Bangladesh. Undoubtedly, the toughest and most enthralling assignment would be the Tests against South Africa, but the sheer amount of one-day cricket meant that we had to give our attention to the shorter form of the game.

Any illusions we had about our abilities were soon shattered by a 6–1 drubbing by Australia. Despite being in a fantastic position to take advantage of the confidence gained during the Ashes campaign, too many of us switched off, thinking that we had done our summer's work, while the Australians were hell-bent on retribution. The result spurred us to have a long think about England's ODI inadequacies over the years and how we might overcome them.

It was clear to anyone who had watched England for a long time that, although we could generally match sides in the more bowler-friendly English conditions, as soon as we went away from home, on flatter, more spin-friendly wickets, we were vulnerable. Other teams seemed to have far more attacking batsmen capable of taking the game away from the opposition, as well as more match-winning bowlers. In ODI cricket the ability to take wickets either early in the innings, with the new ball, or in the middle overs, when sides are generally accumulating singles, is absolutely crucial, and without either bowlers capable of bowling at over 90 mph or mystery spinners, we were at a distinct disadvantage.

After the series defeat to Australia, it was apparent that unless we changed our philosophy, we were likely to stay trapped in the same cycle as English sides for most of the last two decades. Somehow, we had to encourage our batsmen to play a more positive, expressive brand of cricket, while finding ways to attack with the ball.

After asking our analyst, Nathan Leamon, to do some background research into what wins one-day internationals, we decided to focus all our energy on dot-ball percentage. We wanted players to stop worrying so much about losing and to ignore all the criticism accompanying any poor performance. Somehow we had to encourage them to go out and play in a more uninhibited fashion. Focusing on dot-ball percentage seemed to be the answer. We discovered that generally the batting side that allows fewest dot-balls (i.e. balls that aren't scored off) wins one-day games. Our focus when batting, therefore, should be on making sure that we scored off between 50 and 60 per cent of the balls we faced. Everything was to be logged by computer and, whether we won or lost, that is what we should be aiming to achieve. Automatically it put players in a far more positive frame of mind.

On the bowling side, it was obvious that we couldn't suddenly turn our players into mystery bowlers, capable of blasting out opposition teams on flat wickets. Instead, we decided to play to our strengths and use accuracy to our advantage. If we could force other teams to use up a lot of balls without scoring (i.e. a lot of dot-balls), then we had a good chance of forcing mistakes. So out went overly attacking field settings and in came players capable of fielding exceptionally well in order to force dot-balls, while the bowlers concentrated on containment. It was a far from sexy game plan, but over the course of 2009–10 things started to work for us.

A journey to the semi-finals of the Champions Trophy in October was accompanied by ODI series victories against South Africa in November and Bangladesh in March 2010, quickly followed by another ODI victory against Bangladesh in the early part of the summer. Clearly we were on to something and it was incredible to feel that we were finally getting somewhere with ODI cricket.

Alongside the limited-overs improvement, our performances in Test cricket built on the encouraging results from the 2009 Ashes. An enthralling series was played in South Africa, where in Centurion and Cape Town we twice managed to hang on, nine wickets down, in much the way we had in Cardiff against Australia. In between those magnificent rearguard performances, we enjoyed an emphatic innings victory in Durban thanks to some breathtaking bowling from Graeme Swann. The final Test, in Johannesburg, was something of an aberration, when the effects of a long tour, a poor decision at the toss and some high-quality fast bowling by

South Africa proved too much for us. However, a 1–1 series draw against a very good side was no disgrace, and yet again I was heartened by our fighting spirit and togetherness. Without those qualities we would never have drawn the series.

Although many of the players had a good series with the bat, I struggled against a bowler who was rapidly becoming my bogeyman, Morne Morkel. Most players have one or two bowlers that they just can't seem to get on top of, and in my case it was Morkel. For a left-hander, his willingness to come around the wicket, angle the ball in and then get it to seam away towards the slips was particularly awkward. Also, his disturbing bounce made him very hard to handle. My technique, which was far more geared towards hitting the ball on the leg side, didn't fit well with his style of bowling. He gave me very few scoring opportunities.

Looking back, I can see that my struggles against him became far more mental than technical. Having succumbed to him a few times, I began searching for ways of adjusting my stance or backlift to counteract him. I am far from certain that any of these helped, as even in my final series as an England cricketer, in the summer of 2012, he had the better of me. I would have been far better, in hindsight, concentrating on watching the ball and leaving it well, rather than trying out technical changes, but that is easier said than done when you lose confidence in your technique. He is one man I will not miss facing in retirement.

*　*　*

One point of contention, in what was a very successful winter, was the decision that James Anderson and I should miss the Bangladesh tour in February and March 2010. The idea was to rest ahead of what was going to be a gruelling eighteen months, including a full summer schedule, an Ashes campaign away from home and a World Cup in India.

While Anderson slipped under the radar somewhat, there was plenty of attention focused on the captain missing a tour. To some people it seemed that I was abdicating my responsibility, opting not to travel to an inhospitable part of the world while my team-mates suffered. I can understand why people felt that, but the decision for me to rest was based entirely on what was in the best interests of the team. Strangely, I drew a bit of perverse pleasure from hearing ex-players and commentators criticising the decision. For me, it was a demonstration that we were willing to fly in the face of convention in order to achieve our goals, and this was a problem that needed to be addressed.

It had been clear for a long time that the sheer volume of international cricket was making it incredibly hard for players to perform consistently in all forms of the game. Either they were getting injured, and were therefore out of action for extended periods of time, or they were getting burnt out by the constant demands of time away from home, practice, mental application and pressure. Andy Flower and I decided that rather than run away from these uncomfortable truths, we should meet them head-on. If we were able to manage our players better than other teams, then hopefully we would be at an advantage.

After looking at the packed international schedule for the next eighteen months, it was clear that we had to be proactive if we wanted to protect ourselves against players burning out at exactly the wrong time – against Australia in the Ashes or during the World Cup. As soon as we looked at it that way, then the twin series against Bangladesh seemed to be the perfect opportunity to rest players who were likely to have busy schedules in the coming months. Anderson and I would miss the tour, while Collingwood and Broad would miss the Test series in England that followed. Other players, such as Pietersen, for instance, would be monitored on a match-by-match basis.

With hindsight, I am not sure we got the resting policy exactly right. By the end of the World Cup in India, we were all completely dead on our feet, rest or no rest. What I do know is that no international captain or coach can afford to stick their head in the sand and pretend that the schedule is not something that needs to be managed.

Of course, in an ideal world, the schedule would be less hectic and longer breaks would be found for players to rest, recuperate and prepare for upcoming series. In that regard, England, being the only nation that plays cricket throughout the English summer, is at a disadvantage, as there is no longer an off season for our international cricketers. However, I think players are all realistic enough to appreciate that you cannot have your cake and eat it. If we want to be paid more, then we have to play more. With the advent of the IPL and other domestic Twenty20 leagues, the schedule is being further squeezed. This is not a problem that is going away. Sensible management is required and players have to think about what their priorities are.

Recently, the decision by the ECB to split the coach's role, with Andy Flower doing the Test job and Ashley Giles coming into the limited-overs role, shows both the effects of the unremitting schedule, which forced a change to be made, and also some sensible foresight by the board. Increasingly cricketers and coaches will start specialising in one form of the game or another, especially where Twenty20 is concerned.

One of the real benefits of my missing the Bangladesh tour was that it provided the opportunity for Alastair Cook to take over the reins and get some important captaincy experience. From the moment I met him, Cook has always impressed me. I vividly remember him arriving at the very last minute on the India tour in 2006 after Marcus Trescothick's withdrawal. Here was a twenty-one-year-old, flying straight from the pacy wickets of the West Indies, where he had been playing for the A team, about to make his debut on the dust bowls of India, complete with the inevitable jet lag, and he looked supremely unaffected and confident.

He even had the cheek to inform Duncan Fletcher that he was comfortable taking over Trescothick's place at first slip, while I was forced to continue at second slip, having believed that I had earned the right to make my way up the pecking order.

From the moment he dismissively pulled the ball for four in his first over in Test cricket, he has always seemed likely to be one of English cricket's highest run-scorers. To go alongside his talents with the bat, he is one of those annoying people with no obvious flaws. His work ethic is extraordinary, he is the fittest in the squad, he goes out of his way to help others, and challenges bring out the best in him. He has always been immensely popular in the side, as well as respected for his fastidious manner. For those great qualities, in particular, he has always had the look of a future England captain.

His stint in charge in Bangladesh in 2010, when England won both the Test and ODI series convincingly, confirmed to everyone that he could cope with the dual demands of opening the batting and captaincy, as well as helping him get a far greater understanding of what the role entails. I am sure that it has stood him in good stead now that he has the job full-time.

The highlight of the 2010 summer was always going to be the matches against Pakistan. England has had a long and chequered cricketing history with Pakistan, with on- and off-field crises such as ball-tampering often overshadowing some excellent competitive cricket between the two sides. In many ways the two teams are the antithesis of each other. Traditionally England cricketers have tended to be measured, technically correct and organised. Pakistan, in contrast, have been inspired, unpredictable and capable of extraordinary flair. The battles between the sides have seemed to represent the clash of two different cricketing cultures, and that is what has made the cricket so captivating.

The 2010 Pakistan cricket team was something of an unknown quantity. Unable to play cricket at home because of security issues, their recent performances had ranged from the sublime, bowling Australia out for 88 en route to a victory in Headingley of all places, to the ridiculous, somehow managing to lose a Test match in Sydney after leading by over 200 runs in the first innings. We did know that their bowling attack, with Mohammad Asif being complemented by Umar Gul and the enormously talented left-armer Mohammad Amir, was going to cause real trouble in English conditions. Their challenge was likely to be how their batsmen would cope with the English conditions and our very skilful and confident bowlers.

The series played out more or less as expected. We blew their inexperienced batting line-up apart in Nottingham and Birmingham, before their bowling attack got the better of us at The Oval, to leave the result of the series still up in the air by the time the two sides met in the fourth and final Test at Lord's at the end of August. There had been some spellbinding periods of play in one of the few series where the ball completely dominated the bat. A fascinating conclusion looked to be in store at Lord's. Little did anyone know that three days later, the result of the series would be the last thing on anyone's mind.

The aftermath of the spot-fixing scandal was long, drawn out and particularly painful. A five-match ODI series was scheduled and I don't think that either side was at all comfortable about going ahead with the fixtures. The Pakistanis were understandably distracted by the ordeal and by all the speculation in the press about which other games might have been influenced. For us, everything just seemed too raw. Although the players involved in the no-ball saga at Lord's – Mohammad

Asif, Mohammad Amir and Salman Butt – were not going to take part, trust between the two sides had completely broken down.

As the one-day series began, there was a frosty atmosphere between the two sets of players, with tensions simmering away. Not surprisingly, it all came to the surface before the series finished. After a very professional start, when we won the first two games, including chasing down almost 300 at Headingley, we lost the third game at The Oval, where the Pakistanis outfoxed us with some excellent reverse-swing bowling. The problem came after that game, when the chairman of the Pakistani Cricket Board suggested in the media that the England team may have been match-fixing, so sudden and severe was our collapse.

To me, this was a step too far. Here we were, professionally continuing a series when many sides would have been unwilling to keep up the facade, only for the chairman of the PCB to question our integrity, rather than addressing the very serious problem that had been uncovered in his team. Maybe we were all just too emotional, but as far as I and the rest of the players were concerned, he had crossed the line. Imagine what sort of pandemonium would have broken loose if Giles Clarke, the ECB chairman, had accused Pakistan of match-fixing on a whim, without any evidence.

A meeting to discuss the matter was hastily arranged between the players and Angus Porter, the chief executive of the PCA, our union. Feelings were high and, as captain, I was particularly galled at our integrity being called into question in the circum-stances. As we discussed the possible responses, it was clear that none of us had any stomach left to play the fourth ODI, which was scheduled for the next day at Lord's. Obviously, the ECB, with all the financial ramifications of cancellation at the forefront of their minds, were keen to finish the series.

When I look back at it, I think this was one of the defining moments of my captaincy. A situation had developed very quickly in which the ECB and the players were sitting on different sides of the fence and the captain had to navigate a way through the mess. Nasser Hussain had his moment with the Zimbabwe situation during the 2003 World Cup. Kevin Pietersen had his with the Mumbai bombings. I believe that it is only in conflict that you are truly tested as a leader. Those under your charge are looking for you to take control and fight their corner; those that employ you are looking for you to restore order. All you have to guide you are your own values.

One thing I was absolutely certain about was that whatever we did, I wanted us to do it together, as a team. Nothing would destroy everything we had worked for over the previous eighteen months quicker than the team breaking up into rebel factions. I was determined not to let that happen. Although the overwhelming majority of the players felt that boycotting the game was the correct course of action, we invited Giles Clarke to come into the room and put forward the ECB's case for the game to continue.

There have been many things said about Giles Clarke over the years, and he certainly is a character who polarises opinion. He does, however, possess excellent powers of persuasion. He sat in the room talking about the dangerous precedent that we might set, the potential damage to the political relations between Pakistan and England, as well as the duty we had to the thousands of supporters who would be turning up at the ground the next day. When he left the room, the clock was ticking towards midnight and we, as a group of players, had a decision to make.

Having listened to his arguments, as well as having had a little time for my indignation to subside, I told the guys that my own views had changed somewhat. The more I thought about it, the more I realised that boycotting the game would make *us* the news story, with people questioning and discussing our motives, rather than concentrating on the serious issues within the Pakistani cricket team. Far better, to my mind, to put together a joint statement, written by us, the players, showing our displeasure at the chairman of the Pakistan Cricket Board in the strongest possible terms, and then get on with playing the cricket. In a lot of ways, it was the moral high ground.

After some time spent drafting a potential statement, we put it to a vote, with everyone committing beforehand that, whatever the majority decision was, we would all do it together. The majority voted for playing the game. The crisis was over.

Somehow, we got through the last two ODIs. Even though we had to consciously keep a lid on our emotions, it was clear that even the tiniest episode might start something off. Jonathan Trott, for instance, was disciplined before the Lord's game for hitting the Pakistani opening bowler Wahab Riaz with his pad after an altercation in the nets.

From our point of view, the excellent way that we finished the series, with a resounding win at the Rose Bowl to take the honours 3–2, boded extremely well for the future. We had been through some tough moments over the summer, but we had stuck together, shown plenty of resilience and managed to ignore the many distractions to win every series we played.

All those qualities would be needed in spades for our next assignment, an Ashes tour to Australia.

England in South Africa 2009–10 – The Basil D'Oliveira Trophy

1st Test. Centurion Park, Centurion. 16–20 December 2009
South Africa 418 (J.H. Kallis 120, J.P. Duminy 56; G.P. Swann 5–110) and
301–7 dec (H.M. Amla 100, A.B. de Villiers 64; J.M. Anderson 4–73)
England 356 (G.P. Swann 85, **A.J. Strauss 46**; P.L. Harris 5–123) and
228–9 (K.P. Pietersen 81, I.J.L. Trott 69, **A.J. Strauss 1**; F. de Wet 4–55)
Match drawn.

2nd Test. Kingsmead, Durban. 26–30 December 2009
South Africa 343 (G.C. Smith 75, J.H. Kallis 75, A.B. de Villiers 50;
G.P. Swann 4–110) and 133 (G.P. Swann 5–54, S.C.J. Broad 4–43)
England 574–9 dec (I.R. Bell 140, A.N. Cook 118, P.D. Collingwood 91,
M.J. Prior 60, **A.J. Strauss 54**)
England won by an innings and 98 runs.

3rd Test. Newlands, Cape Town. 3–7 January 2010
South Africa 291 (J.H. Kallis 108, M.V. Boucher 51; J.M. Anderson 5–63)
and 447–7 dec (G.C. Smith 183, H.M. Amla 95)
England 273 (M.J. Prior 76, A.N. Cook 65, **A.J. Strauss 2**; M. Morkel
5–75) and 296–9 (I.R. Bell 78, A.N. Cook 55, **A.J. Strauss 45**)
Match drawn.

4th Test. New Wanderers Stadium, Johannesburg. 14–17 January 2010
England 180 (P.D. Collingwood 47, **A.J. Strauss 0**; D.W. Steyn 5–51) and
169 (P.D. Collingwood 71, **A.J. Strauss 22**; M. Morkel 4–59)
South Africa 423–7 dec (G.C. Smith 105, M.V. Boucher 95, H.M. Amla 75)
South Africa won by an innings and 74 runs.

Series drawn 1–1.

Pakistan in England 2010

1st Test. Trent Bridge, Nottingham. 29 July – 1 August 2010
England 354 (E.J.G. Morgan 130, P.D. Collingwood 82, **A.J. Strauss 45**;
   M. Asif 5–77) and 262–9 dec (M.J. Prior 102*, **A.J. Strauss 0**; U. Gul 3–41)
Pakistan 182 (U. Gul 65*; J.M. Anderson 5–54) and 80 (J.M. Anderson
   6–17)
England won by 354 runs.

2nd Test. Edgbaston, Birmingham. 6–9 August 2010
Pakistan 72 (J.M. Anderson 4–20, S.C.J. Broad 4–38) and 296 (Z. Haider
   88; G.P. Swann 6–65)
England 251 (K.P. Pietersen 80, I.J.L. Trott 55, **A.J. Strauss 25**; S. Ajmal
   5–82) and 118–1 (I.J.L. Trott 53*, **A.J. Strauss 53***)
England won by 9 wickets.

3rd Test. The Oval, London. 18–21 August 2010
England 233 (M.J. Prior 84*, **A.J. Strauss 15**; W. Riaz 5–63) and 222
   (A.N. Cook 110, **A.J. Strauss 4**; M. Amir 5–52, S. Ajmal 4–71)
Pakistan 308 (A. Ali 92*, M. Yousuf 56; G.P. Swann 4–68) and 148–6
   (S. Butt 48; G.P Swann 3–50)
Pakistan won by 4 wickets.

4th Test. Lord's, London. 26–29 August 2010
England 446 (I.J.L Trott 184, S.C.J. Broad 169, **A.J. Strauss 13**; M. Amir
   6–84)
Pakistan 74 (G.P. Swann 4–12) and 147 (f/o) (Umar Akmal 79*;
   G.P. Swann 5–62)
England won by an innings and 225 runs.

England won the series 3–1.

15
THE HOLY GRAIL

Twenty-six people are gathered in a big circle on the outfield of the Sydney Cricket Ground. The sixteen players selected for the Ashes tour are there, alongside the large but invaluable backroom staff who have accompanied us. In the middle there are a couple of large coolboxes, filled mainly with ice, beer and white wine. Although the alcohol has been flowing freely for over four hours already, appetites are nowhere near sated. Even Jonathan Trott, who never drinks, has a beer in his hand as he surveys the scenery.

We are surrounded by the imposing stands of the SCG. Although it feels minuscule in comparison to the Melbourne Cricket Ground, with a seating capacity of over 40,000 people it dwarfs any cricket ground in England. The vast silence and emptiness of the place could not be in greater contrast to the scenes hours earlier, when English supporters were enjoying wild celebrations after witnessing an English Ashes victory in Australia for the first time in twenty-five years. Other than a couple of sprinklers that are quietly irrigating the square, there is no sign of life apart from the English cricketers sitting on the outfield.

The previous few hours had been mayhem. We all knew what to expect on that morning of 7 January 2011 as we came to the ground. Three Australian wickets were needed to wrap up an innings victory and complete a resounding Ashes series win. Although we had to put up with the inevitable lower-order resistance, Chris Tremlett, an unlikely Ashes hero, finally bowled Michael Beer, an unlikely Ashes participant, to finish the series and spark the massive celebrations from players and supporters alike.

The presentation started in comical fashion, when a producer from Channel 9, the host broadcaster, informed me that, as the victorious captain, I was going to receive a crystal-glass replica of the Ashes urn. While it was about ten times the size of the original urn, and far more impressive visually, it just did not feel right to go onto the stage and pick up anything other than the little urn that embodies all the cricketing history and tradition between England and Australia. After I informed the producer that a 'real' Ashes urn was required, she went scurrying off to find a suitable replica from one of the vendors selling memorabilia around the ground. She came back with a life-sized urn, probably mass-produced in China and costing about ten dollars, but it proved a worthy substitute for the original urn, which is safely tucked away in the museum at Lord's.

After we had done the obligatory jumping up and down on the stage, as well as all the usual media duties, we embarked on a lap of honour to thank the many English cricket fans who had supported us all around the country over the previous seven weeks. Getting close to them, posing for photos, gave us all a very real and humbling impression of the passion on the supporters' faces. For many of them, this

was the highlight of their sporting lives, and they were determined to enjoy every moment of it. No group of people
deserved this day more than the large and disparate group of
supporters who follow us around the world all year long – the
Barmy Army. Their loyal support, humour and good spirits
had kept us going many times over the previous years when
the odds were against us, and finally they had their moment
in the sun.

The contrast between that day and the ghastly journey in
the lift with the disgruntled English cricket supporters in Perth
four years earlier could not have been greater. Today was
redemption for them and for us.

I was also immensely pleased that our families were there
with us to savour our victory. They deserved it as much as
any of us did. The support we received from them during a
very trying and arduous seven weeks was extraordinary. I
know that sports people tend to thank their families and
support networks in a slightly clichéd way when they are
successful, but the role they play can never be overestimated.
Besides, it was fantastic to be able to take my boys, Sam and
Luca, onto the outfield of the SCG at the end of the game.

From there, it was back to the dressing room for a whole-
hearted and impassioned rendition of the England team
song, led as always by Graeme Swann, before the festivities
began in earnest. This was one of those rare moments in
international cricket when players could let their hair down
completely, in the knowledge that they had achieved something that would live with them for ever. It also marked the
end of Paul Collingwood's England career. After 68 Tests

and over 4,000 runs, he had decided that it was time to call it a day. Any thoughts that it might be a solemn occasion, however, were immediately dispelled by the huge grin on his face and an undisguised appetite to enjoy his final moments.

My celebrations were briefly interrupted by a telephone call. I answered, expecting it to be a friend or a family member. Instead, I heard the following: 'Mr Strauss, this is the Prime Minister's office. He would like to offer you his congratulations in person. If this is OK with you, he will be ringing you shortly.'

I considered trying to freshen myself up a little and was concerned that it was going to be obvious that a few drinks had passed my lips, but in the end I really wasn't bothered. What else would the Prime Minister expect? He had surely heard about the visit to 10 Downing Street after the 2005 Ashes . . .

Finally the call came through, and I thought it was a fantastic gesture from David Cameron. He was enthusiastic, sincere and obviously really pleased that we had managed to vanquish the Aussies. I passed on his congratulations to the lads and got back to the serious business of enjoying the moment. A couple of hours later, we all found ourselves sitting together on the outfield of the SCG.

I take a look at the group of individuals around me. There are people from all walks of life. Some were born abroad, in faraway climes. Others had hardly set foot outside the UK until cricket came a-calling. Northerners and southerners, private schools and comprehensives, young and old, tweeters and non-tweeters – all sitting together. As well as the cricketers, there are the coaches, a physiotherapist, a doctor, a psychologist, an analyst, a media-relations expert and a masseur. Everyone has taken a very different path with their lives, only for us all to end up here together, on a cricket field in Australia, having been through an extraordinary shared experience.

One of the people who would have least expected to be sitting in the circle is Eoin Morgan. A prodigiously talented Irishman, he probably had dreams of playing rugby or some other sport for his country at a young age. Although he has played no part in the series, he has been a very popular member of the touring squad. The conversation in the huddle has stopped momentarily and, after a short period of silence, Morgan starts talking about his favourite moments of the tour. Once he has finished, David Saker, the bowling coach, follows with his memories and before long all the players and support staff are recounting what they remember about the remarkable seven weeks we have all been through. The combination of emotion and alcohol combine to make this moment particularly poignant. You can hear a pin drop as we go from person to person.

Perhaps a little caught up in all the nostalgia, and trying to nail my one abiding memory of the tour before my turn comes, I cast my mind back to what we have all been through, and immediately some incredibly vivid recollections come back to me, each one linked to an Australian city.

Hobart

I am sitting in the dressing room with Alastair Cook, Andy Flower and Paul Collingwood, beer in hand. It is not long after lunchtime and we have just completed a ten-wicket victory against Australia A. Our final warm-up game is now finished and tomorrow we will be making our way to Brisbane for the first Test. In fact, our main bowlers, Anderson, Broad and Finn, are already there, getting used to the stifling humidity that is so different from the more temperate conditions in Tasmania. Conversation turns to the match that we have just played.

So far, everything on the tour had gone exactly according to the long, elaborate and meticulous plan that we had put together as part of our preparations for the tour. In the months leading up to the 2010–11 Ashes, we had set ourselves the challenge of being the most thoroughly prepared English team ever to leave these shores in the quest to win the Ashes. Eighteen months of work had gone into the process, involving a number of different ECB departments, alongside myself, Andy Flower and the rest of the management team. Hugh Morris had been especially busy, making sure that the tour itinerary allowed us enough time to prepare properly for the start of the series, while, probably for the first time ever, we had also involved the players fully in the preparation process.

Under the excellent tutelage of Steve Bull, the previous psychologist to the England team and now a corporate consultant and leadership mentor, we had arranged a number of pre-Test dinners for the players during the summer of 2010. The idea was to create an informal environment for them to start thinking about the Ashes series, as well as getting their hugely important input about how best to prepare for the series. Over the course of those dinners, we covered a lot of ground. All sorts of issues were thrown around, from the relative strengths and weaknesses of the two sides, to what the unique challenges of an Ashes series were likely to be and our potential responses to those challenges.

Some of what we got back from those meetings we expected. However, there were issues and potential solutions that we would perhaps never have addressed if we hadn't involved the players. As a result, we gave a lot of thought to how best to get away from the pressure of the series between games, as well as how to approach the warm-up games and how to handle the Australian public. Suddenly, the prospect of touring Australia became much more real. An added benefit was that as the players had been part of the preparations, they were far more likely to buy into our methods. We all knew what lay in front of us and how we were going to deal with it.

One thing that was agreed on was for us to treat the warm-up games like a mini, three-match Test series. We decided to make sure that we won that series, so as not to fall into the trap of starting a tour on the wrong foot, something that had caused problems for so many England teams in the past. Now, that victory in Hobart against Australia A, following a thrilling run chase against Western Australia in Perth in the first match of the tour, had given us a 2–0 victory in the mini-series. It was just what we wanted. All the batsmen had got runs and the wickets had been shared evenly amongst the bowlers. We had no form worries.

What had also struck us all by then was just how negative the Australian public were being about their team's chances. Hours of planning had gone into how we should react to the Aussie supporters, who normally see it as their civic duty to get stuck into the Poms at every opportunity. However, our experience out and about in the early weeks of the tour seemed to confirm the growing suspicion that the Aussies did not rate their cricket team as they once did.

For the first time, they genuinely thought we had a chance.

Paul Collingwood takes a sip from his bottled beer. 'Lads, we have just thumped Australia's best young players by an innings,' he proclaims in his thick Geordie accent. 'You know what, we are 100 per cent ready for that first Test in Brisbane.'

I nod my head in agreement and feel a warm, comforting sensation in my stomach. We are ready.

Brisbane, Part 1

I feel the ball make contact with my bat. The vibrations immediately tell me that it hasn't come off the middle. In fact, the feedback tells me that, from my attempted cut shot, it has come off the top edge. I look up to see where the ball is going. There is a gap between the third slip and gully fielders and I desperately hope it has managed to find that opening. It is clear, though, that it is travelling straight towards the gully fielder, Mike Hussey, and I just have time for a frantic plea to the gods for him to drop it before the eruption of the crowd tells me all I need to know. I am out, caught Hussey, bowled Hilfenhaus for 0. It was the third ball of the Ashes series.

Our arrival in Brisbane for the first Test marked the end of the phoney war. Even in my time in the England cricket team, the pre-Ashes hype has increased dramatically, with news vans and interviewers now camping outside hotels, looking for any scrap of information to feed the voracious appetite of the twenty-four-hour news cycle. All of this makes it particularly hard for the players to keep their minds on the job.

The final hours before the start of the game were like purgatory. Although we were completely prepared for what was to come, the combination of adrenalin continually pumping through our veins and the importance of the match in Brisbane meant that everything, from eating to sleeping, was a struggle.

The bus ride from the hotel to the ground was quiet. Players were lost in thought about how they were going to fare on the day. I wasn't worried, though. It was entirely normal. Immediately on arrival at the ground, the vibrant atmosphere of the occasion lightened the mood. A lap around the ground as a planned part of the warm-up routine allowed us to take in the impressive spectacle. With more than an hour to go before the start of the game, the ground was close to full and the boos and whistles that came in our direction from every section of the crowd told us all we needed to know. We were on enemy territory.

Minutes later, I was in the middle, shaking the hand of Ricky Ponting, the Australian captain, and getting ready for the toss. This was definitely one I secretly would not mind losing. There was a tinge of green in the wicket, but with Nasser Hussain having made the fatal mistake of inserting Australia in 2002, only to see them rack up nearly 500 runs, I had made up my mind to bat first regardless. The coin came down in my favour. We were going to bat, and my attention had to change quickly from captain to opening batsman.

I felt in wonderful form going into the match. Two hundreds in the warm-up games, scored with great fluency, told me that my mind and technique were both in a good place. Also, as captain, I was determined to get out there and lead the guys on what is always the toughest day in an Ashes series. Setting the right tone, with so many nerves around, is very difficult, especially when you are batting. This was one of those moments when it was vital that the captain led the way. As Cook and I made our way to the middle, I experienced a feeling of grim determination. This was my moment.

For a second, I am completely shell-shocked. I cannot believe what has just happened. I look up towards the Australian fielders, who are all huddling together in celebration. Slowly I become aware of the severity of the situation. Four years after Steve Harmison bowled the first ball of the 2006–07 Ashes series straight to second slip, I have just set exactly the same tone. The captain has succumbed to the pressure and England are 0–1 in the first over of the series. I trudge back to the dressing room, knowing that I will have to rely on my team-mates to change the story. My part in the opening salvos is over.

Brisbane, Part 2

Again, I look up to see where the ball has gone. I have just played my favourite cut shot, this time off the spin of Xavier Doherty. It has gone fine of the backward-point fielder and immediately I know that it is going to race away for four runs. I let out a totally spontaneous guttural scream of relief, before punching the air. Alastair Cook makes his way towards me to offer his congratulations. I take off my helmet, raise my bat and just for a moment allow myself to wallow in the warm glow of an Ashes hundred away from home. All of this only three days after my first-innings duck.

The game in Brisbane did not follow our carefully planned script in any way. After my first-over dismissal, a semi-recovery was shattered by a hat-trick by Peter Siddle. Even though we were on the receiving end, it was pure cricketing theatre and it was a fitting way to justify the unbelievable hype that surrounded the fixture. At the end of play, we all knew that our eventual first-innings score of 260 was nowhere near enough. Fortunately spirits were still reasonably high. Along one bench in the subterranean dressing room sat Matt Prior, myself and Stuart Broad. All three of us had been dismissed for 0, and in total we had faced five balls between us. The fact that three ducks were sitting in a row was not lost on our team-mates, who seemed to enjoy our bad fortune in a way that only cricketers who have been through similar disasters can understand.

Australia went on to score 481, largely courtesy of Mike Hussey. Ironically, he came into the game under serious pressure for his place in the side and his first ball dropped agonisingly short of third slip. If the ball had carried a foot further, it may have spelled the end of his international career. Such are the small margins in cricket. However, it didn't, and he proved once again just what a fine player he is with his 195. I don't think there is anyone out there, with the possible exception of Rahul Dravid, who could concentrate for as long as Hussey. With our game plan largely based on suffocating opposition players, he was one of the few in world cricket whose patience consistently outlasted that of our bowlers.

With our backs suddenly against the wall, we knew it would take something very special for us to escape the game with anything other than a heavy defeat. The task facing us was to bat for almost two days, albeit on a wicket that was flattening out.

After an initial scare, when the first ball from Hilfenhaus came alarmingly close to completing the dreaded pair for me, Alastair Cook and I undertook the task with real gusto, knowing that simply trying to survive would not get us in the right mindset. After I departed, shortly after lunch on day four, having scored 110, Jonathan Trott and Cook then set about producing the sort of partnership that an English fan could only dream about. Australia tried everything to get them out, but to no avail. For over seven hours at the crease they could not be prised apart.

Australia v England
(1st Test)

Played at Woolloongabba, Brisbane, on 25–29 November 2010

Umpires:	Aleem Dar & BR Doctrove (TV: AL Hill)
Referee:	JJ Crowe
Toss:	England

ENGLAND

AJ Strauss*	c Hussey b Hilfenhaus	0	st Haddin b North		110
AN Cook	c Watson b Siddle	67	not out		235
IJL Trott	b Watson	29	not out		135
KP Pietersen	c Ponting b Siddle	43			
PD Collingwood	c North b Siddle	4			
IR Bell	c Watson b Doherty	76			
MJ Prior†	b Siddle	0			
SCJ Broad	lbw b Siddle	0			
GP Swann	lbw b Siddle	10			
JM Anderson	b Doherty	11			
ST Finn	not out	0			
Extras	(lb 8, w 7, nb 5)	20	(b 17, lb 4, w 10, nb 6)		37
Total	(76.5 overs) **260**		(for 1 wkt dec)	(152 overs)	**517**

AUSTRALIA

SR Watson	c Strauss b Anderson	36	not out		41
SM Katich	c and b Finn	50	c Strauss b Broad		4
RT Ponting*	c Prior b Anderson	10	not out		51
MJ Clarke	c Prior b Finn	9			
MEK Hussey	c Cook b Finn	195			
MJ North	c Collingwood b Swann	1			
BJ Haddin†	c Collingwood b Swann	136			
MG Johnson	b Finn	0			
XJ Doherty	c Cook b Finn	16			
PM Siddle	c Swann b Finn	6			
BW Hilfenhaus	not out	1			
Extras	(b 4, lb 12, w 4, nb 1)	21	(b 4, lb 1, w 1, p 5)		11
Total	(158.4 overs) **481**		(for 1 wkt)	(26 overs)	**107**

AUSTRALIA	O	M	R	W		O	M	R	W
Hilfenhaus	19	4	60	1		32	8	82	0
Siddle	16	3	54	6		24	4	90	0
Johnson	15	2	66	0	(4)	27	5	104	0
Watson	12	2	30	1	(6)	15	2	66	0
Doherty	13.5	3	41	2		35	5	107	0
North	1	0	1	0	(3)	19	3	47	1

ENGLAND	O	M	R	W		O	M	R	W
Anderson	37	13	99	2		5	2	15	0
Broad	33	7	72	0		7	1	18	1
Swann	43	5	128	2		8	0	33	0
Finn	33.4	1	125	6		4	0	25	0
Collingwood	12	1	41	0					
Pietersen					(5)	2	0	6	0

Fall of wickets:

	Eng	Aus	Eng	Aus
1st	0	78	188	5
2nd	41	96	–	–
3rd	117	100	–	–
4th	125	140	–	–
5th	197	143	–	–
6th	197	450	–	–
7th	197	458	–	–
8th	228	462	–	–
9th	254	472	–	–
10th	260	481	–	–

Close of play:	Day 1:	Aus (1) 25–0 (Watson 9*, Katich 15*, 7 overs)
	Day 2:	Aus (1) 220–5 (Hussey 81*, Haddin 22*, 80 overs)
	Day 3:	Eng (2) 19–0 (Strauss 11*, Cook 6*, 15 overs)
	Day 4:	Eng (2) 309–1 (Cook 132*, Trott 54*, 101 overs)

Man of the match:	AN Cook
Result:	**Match drawn**

The score of 517–1 will go down in folklore for anyone that was on that tour. Ever since, wherever we are around the world, a massive, blown-up picture of the scoreboard at Brisbane, with those figures, alongside the scores of 235 and 135, for Cook and Trott respectively, has pride of place in the dressing room.

We had managed the great escape.

Adelaide

We are all huddled together at the Adelaide Oval, celebrating the wicket of Michael Clarke. I don't think that any of us can quite believe the start we have had in the second Test match. In the space of the first thirteen balls of the game, we have dismissed Simon Katich, run out with a direct hit from Jonathan Trott, Ricky Ponting, caught first ball, and now Michael Clarke. This is the flattest wicket in Australia and we lost the toss. At last, James Anderson has got the rewards he deserves after bowling magnificently at Brisbane without much success. I am in the middle, urging the players to keep calm and not look too far ahead. Emotions can run away with you in these circumstances, and the last thing we need now is to give the Aussies a way back into the game. As the players sip on the isotonic drinks delivered by the twelfth men, we can all sense that this might be one of the pivotal moments of the Test series. Australia are on the ropes at home in an Ashes series for the first time in decades.

In a situation that echoed the feelings following the Cardiff Test match in 2009, we had taken all the momentum into the Adelaide Test match. The Australians' plight was not helped by having some very weary bowlers after their marathon second-innings stint in the field, as well as their selectors dropping Mitchell Johnson after an inconsistent display in Brisbane. Of all the contributors to the 2010–11 Ashes, the Australian selectors, in my opinion, performed the worst of everyone. You can never tell what is going on in an opposition dressing room, but by dropping Johnson after one Test, as well as jettisoning Nathan Hauritz before the series even started and constant chopping and changing throughout, their selectors did nothing to dispel the impression that there was panic in the Australian ranks. It reminded us of the worst days of English selection, decades earlier.

In the huddle before taking the field, I got James Anderson, the leader of the bowling attack, to speak to the players. He went on to stress the importance of staying patient, trying to go for less than three an over and building up pressure. We all knew that we had a long day ahead of us on a very flat wicket.

Our early breakthroughs, though, completely changed the complexion of the game. We had the Aussies by the jugular and we had to press home our advantage. Bowling them out for 245, despite another rearguard performance by Mike Hussey, represented a complete triumph for our bowling attack and set the game up perfectly for our batsmen to take advantage on day two of the Test match.

This time it was the turn of Kevin Pietersen to take centre stage, scoring a blistering 227 in the manner only he can.

Alongside him, Alastair Cook was looking as if the Aussies would never dismiss him. His hundred really took the sting out of the attack. We had the Australians by the scruff of the neck, and Bell and Prior added the final insult with a partnership of 52 in just 33 balls before I opted to declare, with a score of 620–5.

Only ten wickets and a forecast that warned of heavy rain on the last afternoon of the game stood in the way of a redeeming Ashes victory in Adelaide, and despite some excellent resistance from Michael Clarke, who was ironically dismissed by Kevin Pietersen in the last over of the fourth day, the Australians were unable to stem the tide. Graeme Swann took his fifth wicket of the innings to bring the game to an end shortly before lunch on day five. Within an hour, the ground was completely under water, drenched by the anticipated rain.

The ghost of Adelaide 2006 had been laid to rest.

Melbourne

I grab my England blazer and cap from their hooks above my seat in the dressing room and put them on. I walk through the great labyrinth of tunnels and roads underneath the enormous superstructure of the Melbourne Cricket Ground and make my way out to the ground for the toss. On my way, I am met by James Avery, our media-relations man, who gives me the two team sheets that he has printed for me to hand to Ricky Ponting and the match referee. As I step onto the outfield, it is bathed in sunlight, showing the splendour of the

MCG, with its 90,000 seating capacity, in all its glory. Briefly, the hairs at the back of my neck stand up as I appreciate the enormous size of the ground and the significance of the day's cricket ahead of us.

This is Boxing Day, the most important day in the Australian cricket calendar, and with a full house expected, we could be seeing one of the largest crowds ever for a game of cricket. In addition, after Australia's emphatic win in Perth, the series is locked at one a piece. With so much expectation, anticipation and emotion around, today has the potential to be absolutely pivotal in deciding the direction of the Ashes series. Quite simply, this is the most important day of cricket in my life.

After exchanging pleasantries with Ponting, the match referee, Ranjan Madugalle, and Mark Nicholas, the presenter for Channel 9, I wait for Ricky Ponting to toss the coin. It goes up. I call 'heads' and wait for it to fall. Finally it comes to rest. Heads it is.

'England have won the toss,' explains Mark Nicholas to the expectant crowd. A great cheer erupts from the section housing the Barmy Army. For once, though, they are completely outnumbered.

'Andrew, what are you going to do?' Mark continues.

'We are going to bowl first,' I reply.

A groan can be heard from the same fans who were cheering seconds earlier. It is clear that not many of them agree with my decision.

As I walk back to the dressing room, I mutter to myself, 'This had better work, or I am in serious trouble.'

Playing cricket on Boxing Day is always slightly surreal. For a start, Christmas Day is completely ruined. To me, Christmas lunch without alcohol is like a beach without water. It just doesn't work. When you throw into the mix that you are thousands of miles away from home, have had to do training in the morning and you are putting on your Christmas hat in an enormous hotel dining room, you get the gist. It's not fun.

This Christmas, in particular, there was plenty of tension around the dinner table. The loss of the third Test in Perth was both unexpected and confidence-sapping. An equally unexpected spell of devastating swing bowling from Mitchell Johnson had destroyed our middle order and turned the game on its head. We never recovered from the shock and subsided meekly to a 267-run defeat.

There was a strong argument doing the rounds that Australia had grabbed back the momentum in the series in time for the crucial stages. Also, both Andy Flower and I had been concerned enough by the quiet, energy-less practice session on Christmas Eve for us to call a halt and remind everyone of the importance of the next few days. We all knew that we couldn't afford to get stage fright as we had in the opening sessions in Brisbane.

It was for this reason that the toss was so crucial. Without doubt, it was the most significant toss of my career. Although players usually pay too much attention to the toss in the irrational search for omens from the cricketing gods, it is rarely as vital as it is made out to be. This time, though, with such a massive game ahead, in such a heated atmosphere, there was a good chance that the team who won the day's cricket on Boxing Day would go on to win the match.

The problem I was facing, as I looked at the wicket on the day before the game, was that the decision was as clear as mud. The statistics leant towards batting first. The wicket in Melbourne tends to deteriorate and get more inconsistent as the game moves on. On the other hand, it didn't look quite right. It was the type of wicket that Justin Langer, when he was Middlesex captain, used to describe as a 'baby eagle – it's ------- ugly'. It was next to impossible to know how it would play on day one, or for that matter later in the game.

On the morning of the game, I arrived early, still unsure of what I was going to do. David Saker, who had played most of his cricket at the MCG, edged towards bowling first. Andy Flower was not sure. The closer we got to the toss, the more my gut feeling told me that bowling first was the right call. It would only work, though, if I could convince the bowlers that it was the right idea.

I called Jimmy Anderson over to ask his opinion about the toss.

'I think there is going to be some movement in it,' he said.

That was enough for me.

'Jimmy, I'm glad you said that, because we're going to bowl first. Potentially we can put Australia out of the game if it offers us assistance. If not, we are still in the game. Are you OK with that?'

'Yes. We just need to make sure that we don't chase the game,' he replied.

With that, the decision was made.

What followed was the most extraordinary day of cricket I have ever played. A procession of Australian batsmen came and went. There was very little playing and missing. Our bowling attack, which by then included both Chris Tremlett and Tim Bresnan, relentlessly put the ball on a length on off stump and the Australians could not find a way to deal with it. Tremlett's delivery to Ricky Ponting seemed to encapsulate the one-sided nature of the contest perfectly. Pitched just short of a length, it bounced awkwardly, nipped away and Ponting had no answer as he was caught brilliantly by Graeme Swann at second slip.

Just after lunch, a glance at the scoreboard told spectators everything they needed to know. On Boxing Day, in front of 90,000 die-hard fans, the Aussies had been bowled out for 98. If we could somehow manage to negotiate the initial barrage from Australia with the ball, we were well on the way to winning the game.

To me, the way that the Australians bowled that afternoon showed the great difference between the sides in that series. Whereas our bowlers relied on nagging accuracy, pressure and the vagaries of the wicket to press the opposition into mistakes, the Aussie bowlers and Ponting, the captain, tried far more to make things happen, switching between different plans every few overs. Perhaps the Australian bowlers weren't able to deliver on the plans that Ponting was trying to carry out, and perhaps he was forced to chase the game as they had been bowled out for 98, but it demonstrated the dangers of setting attacking fields with radically different bowling plans. The opposition can get momentum, you cannot stem the tide of runs and any pressure you have built up can quickly dissipate.

I suppose any strategy relies on the bowlers' ability to carry it out, and in that regard we were very fortunate. We did, however, tailor our bowling attack to our method, dropping Steve Finn for the Melbourne Test because he was finding it difficult to apply the pressure we were looking for (despite taking the most wickets in the series up to that point).

What cannot be denied is that the Australian method did not work. By the end of the day, we had reached 157–0. If Carlsberg did days of cricket, this was it. Australia were out of the Test match and the result of the game was a formality.

Three days later, the players were doing the 'sprinkler dance' to 20,000 Barmy Army supporters on the boundary, safe in the knowledge that the Ashes were not going to be prised from our grasp. We had an unassailable 2–1 lead.

My attention is drawn back to the circle of players in front of me on the outfield at the SCG. One after another the guys have gone through a rich and varied array of brilliant memories from the tour and it is now my turn to add to the conversation. I think briefly once again about everything that has happened over the last two months and suddenly come to the realisation that my favourite memory is actually taking place right in front of me. A group of people who have all been through an incredible shared experience are sitting together with a beer in hand, enjoying the moment. Nothing demonstrates the unique camaraderie on this tour better than the previous forty minutes.

This, more than making centuries and taking five-wicket hauls, is why we play the glorious game of cricket.

England in Australia 2010–11 – The Ashes

1st Test. BCG, Brisbane. 25–29 November 2010
England 260 (I.R. Bell 76, A.N. Cook 67, **A.J. Strauss 0**; P.M. Siddle 6–54)
and 517–1 dec (A.N. Cook 235*, I.J.L. Trott 135*, **A.J. Strauss 110**)
Australia 481 (M.E.K. Hussey 195, B.J. Haddin 136, S.M. Katich 50; S.T.
Finn 6–125) and 107–1 (R.T. Ponting 51*)
Match drawn.

2nd Test. Adelaide Oval, Adelaide. 3–7 December 2010
Australia 245 (M.E.K. Hussey 93, B.J. Haddin 56, S.R. Watson 51;
J.M. Anderson 4–51) and 304 (M.J. Clarke 80, S.R. Watson 57,
M.E.K. Hussey 52; G.P. Swann 5–91)
England 620–5 dec (K.P. Pietersen 227, A.N. Cook 148, I.J.L. Trott 78,
I.R. Bell 68*, **A.J. Strauss 1**)
England won by an innings and 71 runs.

3rd Test. WACA, Perth. 16–19 December 2010
Australia 268 (M.G. Johnson 62, M.E.K. Hussey 61, B.J. Haddin 53) and
309 (M.E.K. Hussey 116, S.R. Watson 95; C.T. Tremlett 5–87)
England 187 (I.R. Bell 53, **A.J. Strauss 52**; M.G. Johnson 6–38) and 123
(**A.J. Strauss 15**; R.J. Harris 6–47)
Australia won by 267 runs.

4th Test. MCG, Melbourne. 26–29 December 2010
Australia 98 (J.M. Anderson 4–44, C.T. Tremlett 4–26) and 258 (B.J.
Haddin 55*, S.R. Watson 54; T.T. Bresnan 4–50)
England 513 (I.J.L. Trott 168*, M.J. Prior 85, A.N. Cook 82, **A.J. Strauss 69**, K.P. Pietersen 51; P.M. Siddle 6–75)
England won by an innings and 157 runs.

5th Test. SCG, Sydney. 3–7 January 2011
Australia 280 (M.G. Johnson 53; J.M. Anderson 4–66) and 281 (S.P.D.
Smith 54*, P.M. Siddle 43, M.J. Clarke 41)
England 644 (A.N. Cook 189, M.J. Prior 118, I.R. Bell 115, **A.J. Strauss 60**; M.G. Johnson 4–168)
England won by an innings and 83 runs.

England won the series 3–1.

16

THE ONE-DAY RIDDLE

Why have England never won a fifty-over World Cup? It is a question that has occupied the minds of English coaches, players, journalists and supporters time and time again, usually at the end of yet another miserable World Cup campaign.

I asked myself that question at the conclusion of the 2011 World Cup in India. We had just endured a particularly painful experience, so soon after our magnificent victory in Australia, and the contrast in emotions could not have been starker. After a brutal ten-wicket defeat to Sri Lanka in the quarter-final, my dreams of leading England to victory in a World Cup had been laid to rest.

Yet I couldn't help but feel riddled with regrets. We should have been one of the favourites to win the event, especially with our confidence so high after winning in Australia. Our recent form against any side other than Australia in the ODI format had been good, and we had come up with a method that seemed to work on most wickets around the world. How, then, had we managed to lose to both Ireland and Bangladesh in the course of a pitiful campaign?

It only takes a few seconds of reflection on the way I felt at the end of the Sri Lanka game to come up with the first reason. We were absolutely exhausted. I know that many people won't sympathise with this point of view, thinking that playing cricket for a living and travelling the world cannot really be all that tiring. However, since we had left home for Australia at the start of the Ashes tour, we had spent 145 days in hotel rooms and only five nights in our own beds at home. We had played cricket on fifty-six of those days, we had practised on another eighty and we had had to cope with all the emotions that accompany an Ashes tour to Australia and the build-up to a World Cup. We were dead on our feet, unable to think straight, at a time when logical, intelligent thinking was crucial.

Since the 2011 World Cup, the ECB has made the sensible decision to move the Ashes so that it no longer coincides with the World Cup. In one fell swoop it has eliminated one of the primary reasons why an England side has not won the competition before. Some people will say that the Ashes series has never prevented Australia winning the World Cup, but there is a big difference between playing a series at home, with the opportunity to get out of the bubble and enjoy time with friends and loved ones, and enduring a three-month tour, when you are all living in each other's pockets.

In an age when teams around the world move heaven and earth to make sure that they tailor their preparations perfectly to peak for the World Cup, we had been operating with both arms tied behind our backs. Even efforts to mitigate against the inevitable drop-off in performance, such as resting players for the previous year's Bangladesh home and away series, did not work as we would have wanted.

Mind you, I think that most observers would struggle to be convinced that tiredness is the only reason we haven't won a World Cup. One look at the history of the ODI rankings tells us all we need to know. Since 1999, England have spent most of their time occupying positions five, six, seven and eight in the rankings. So, over four World Cups, England could hardly have been expected to win. In fact, a quarter-final knockout was what the rankings suggested, and that, by and large, is what we got.

Although the ODI team has made a significant breakthrough since Alastair Cook took over the captaincy, rising to number one in 2012 for the first time in recent memory, it is quite clear that over the last fifteen years the England ODI team simply hasn't been good enough to win consistently. No one can run away from that fact. But why have we not been good enough and what can be done about it?

Well, I think it is fair to say that ODI cricket is simply not the priority in England that it is in other parts of the world. When it comes to assessing where we stand in the pecking order in the world game, our administrators, players and supporters tend to look at our form in Test cricket. As a result, everything from tour schedules to player-rotation strategy has been tailored towards peaking for Test series, often at the expense of ODI planning and preparation.

I am uncomfortable with this attitude for two reasons. Firstly, I think that it is a little too convenient simply to say that ODI cricket isn't as important. Would we be thinking that way if we had been number one in the world in that form of the game for a long period of time? I doubt it. We turn our back on ODI cricket too much, not because it isn't as important, but because we aren't very good at it.

I also think there is a flawed assumption that it's a question of either/or – that in order to be good at one form of the game, it is impossible to allot enough time, effort and resources to the other form of the game as well. Australia, over a decade or so, proved that this needn't be the case; it is more than possible to dominate all forms for a long period.

With that in mind, the decision by the ECB to appoint Ashley Giles as the specialist ODI coach is an excellent step in the right direction. Now there is no excuse for England one-day sides to be under-prepared for a series. Whereas it was impossible for Andy Flower to be concentrating on preparations for ODIs while in the middle of a Test series, Giles can be doing all the hard work as that Test series is going on. The two forms of the game clearly require different skills and methods, so a different style and emphasis from a coaching point of view seems logical. Would you expect the England rugby coach to oversee both the fifteen-a-side and the seven-a-side versions of the game? In fact, the decision to split the coaching makes so much sense that I wouldn't be surprised to see many other teams following in England's footsteps, finances permitting.

I do think, though, that England have a couple of obvious disadvantages that we still need to overcome to perform consistently in ODI cricket. Without doubt, our weather doesn't help. In most other parts of the world, one-day cricket is not played in the same way as in England. In other countries, flat, drier wickets encourage more expansive stroke play, as well as more variety and skill from the bowlers. Simply running up and putting the ball on the spot will not work. In England, however, more cautious batting against the new ball is a necessity on many of the wickets and bowlers are rewarded for accuracy, not variety. That is in direct contrast with other parts of the world. It is unsurprising to see that the England team is generally far more competitive at home than it is away from home.

I also don't think that the county system has helped the development of the right sort of one-day cricketers. County one-day matches are frequently played when players are close to exhaustion after strenuous four-day games, or straight after another one-day game. There is little or no time to prepare properly, analyse the opposition team, tailor your strategy in order to maximise your chances of winning and work on the specific shots required for that form of the game. Too often players simply sleepwalk from one game to another. That does not mean that the games aren't competitive, or that the players are not trying exceptionally hard to win. It simply means that skill levels are not high enough or given enough time to develop. It is one of the negative by-products of county cricketers playing too much cricket.

As always seems the case with county cricket, I believe that the domestic structure needs to be looked at. From 2014, one-day county cricket is going to revert back from forty overs to fifty overs, thus mirroring the international game. Many, including me, might be tempted to ask why it didn't mirror the international game in the first place. It seems incongruous to expect your domestic structure to produce excellent international cricketers if you aren't even playing the same game.

The broader problem, however, is one of volume. In what can hardly be described as a radical departure from the past, the latest version of the domestic structure keeps the County Championship at sixteen games (far too many in my opinion), reduces one-day cricket by four games and adds four games into the already bloated Twenty20 league. The overall effect is completely neutral. There will be just as many days of cricket played.

To me, this is the biggest impediment for the domestic game in its quest to produce high-quality international cricketers. The two-division system has worked exceptionally well in producing better-quality and more competitive cricket, and generally counties are making huge strides in terms of their professionalism. What they all have to deal with, though, is the inevitable injuries, drop-off in intensity and lack of proper preparation as the season goes on.

I know that there are plenty of old-school cricketers who will argue that you can only get fit for bowling by bowling, but all the evidence shows that bowling too many overs puts any bowler at an increased risk of injury. Those that tend to make it through the season are the 70–80 mph type of bowlers, who are very useful in English conditions but less so in international cricket, with its better wickets. From a batting point of view, the amount of cricket is arguably more beneficial, especially in the longer form of the game, but the lack of time for high-quality deliberate practice still affects the batsmen's development – particularly in the shorter form of the game.

In England, we should have an advantage over other countries because of our long-established domestic structure. What is desperately needed, in my opinion, is for that structure to move with the times. Administrators need to ask themselves, 'What is the best system for producing excellent England cricketers?', as that is where all the revenues for the game come from, rather than 'What is in the best interests of county members?' Looking at it from that standpoint would result in a very different domestic structure from the one we currently employ.

Having said all that, I do think that Twenty20 cricket has helped players to develop their games. In Twenty20 cricket, regardless of the conditions, batsmen must be capable of either hitting the ball out of the park or playing unorthodox shots to manoeuvre the field. Bowlers are aware that 'change-up' balls, from slower balls to bouncers and even slow-ball bouncers, are a necessity. Innovation is crucial in the shortest form of the game.

It is immensely reassuring to see the likes of Alex Hales and Jos Buttler making their way into the England ranks, alongside the obvious talents of Eoin Morgan and Kevin Pietersen. Players like these can win games for England in any conditions and also make it easier for more traditional players, such as Alastair Cook or Ian Bell, to make a telling contribution.

Perhaps it is not a coincidence that the introduction of Twenty20 cricket in this country has seen a gradual but sustained improvement in England's ODI performance. New players coming into the England side in recent years have generally had a reasonable level of experience in the Twenty20 game and have managed to expand their games accordingly. What remains a problem, though, is that players who are already part of the England set-up do not play a lot of domestic Twenty20 cricket, so ironically their skills do not continue to develop as much as might be the case. For me, it makes the opportunity for England players to compete in the IPL a really important issue.

Going to India, surrounding yourself with the best players in the world and learning how to innovate and adapt in vastly different conditions must surely be of huge benefit to players (not to mention the obvious benefits to their bank accounts). Unfortunately, the IPL teams are reluctant to select England players, knowing that they will not be available for the whole tournament. In addition, the ECB is less than keen to see its best assets wandering off to a foreign domestic tournament when they should be getting invaluable rest. However, if England are serious about being a force in the shorter forms of the game, one thing the administrators have to look at is creating a window to allow our players to participate. The IPL is not going anywhere and we run the risk of slipping behind other teams in both ODI and Twenty20 cricket if our players don't participate.

By far the most common problem that we faced while I was involved in the England ODI set-up was fear. By that I mean fear of failure, fear of playing the wrong shot, fear of losing, fear of being dropped, fear of criticism. It was the elephant in the room in far too many of the ODIs in which I played. Fear is crippling in the shorter form of the game because you cannot hope to live with a confident, fearless team if you are not willing to unshackle yourself and go all out to put them under pressure.

I think it is revealing that my average and strike rate in ODI cricket went from around 31.5 runs per innings and 75 runs per 100 hundred balls to nearly 40 and 86 after I was made captain. As captain, much of the fear that surrounds a player on a day-to-day basis leaves you. For starters, you do not fear for your place in the side, and you also know that it is your responsibility to show the way in terms of the type of cricket you are trying to play. If every player could get into a similar mindset, it would have a tremendous effect on the style and effectiveness of a one-day team.

When looking back at the great ODI teams in the last twenty years, from Sri Lanka in the 1996 World Cup through to the great Australian team in the early 2000s, it is no surprise to see that the teams were settled, with confident players, assured of their places in the side. Clearly, this is one of those chicken-and-egg situations: it is impossible to feel confident and assured of your place in the side if you are not playing well, and vice versa.

When we set out to revamp our ODI cricket in 2009, we wanted players to know that they would be judged on their willingness to play in the right style, rather than solely on their averages. Fear is something that needs to be looked firmly in the eye if it is to be overcome. The England management has to send out the right messages to the players if the effects of fear are to be minimised.

I want to finish this chapter by mentioning very briefly my great optimism regarding England's chances in the 2015 World Cup in Australia.

Many of the problems I have mentioned will be either irrelevant or dealt with by the time the competition starts. The conditions over there are far more suited to England's natural style of cricket and do not put batsmen under nearly so much pressure to score quickly off spin bowlers, another perennial difficulty for English players. In addition, the latest ODI rules, giving bowlers a new ball at each end, definitely give an advantage to teams with strong seam-bowling units. England, in that regard, are a match for anyone. The subcontinental sides, with their reliance on spin and reverse swing, are going to find life far more difficult in that competition if the current rules are retained.

England are closer now to cracking the ODI conundrum than they have been at any stage over the last two decades. To me, it is the final piece in the jigsaw as far as the resurgence of English cricket is concerned. If we were somehow to win the 2015 World Cup, following the considerable feats of getting to number one in the world in Test cricket and winning a World Twenty20, then there are many people involved with English cricket who would deserve a well-earned pat on the back. The one-day riddle would finally have been solved.

17

NUMBER ONE

It is the morning of 10 August 2011 and around me the world is going mad. I have spent most of the last few days watching harrowing scenes of thousands of people, young and old, marauding in the streets of London, smashing shop windows and looting on an unprecedented scale. I can't believe this is happening in England. What started as a protest against the shooting of a Tottenham man by police has rapidly spread throughout the capital, with mobile phones and Twitter being used as rallying calls. Yesterday, I was spellbound as gangs of youths rampaged through Ealing, the London suburb where I lived for over eight years. We still have many friends living there and it felt uncomfortably close to home.

Up here in Birmingham, I am far from unaffected by what is going on. The streets of the city have been ablaze with burning cars, and all night long I've heard the tell-tale sirens of dozens of police cars working to keep the civil unrest from spreading. It is definitely one of those moments when the game of cricket seems to hold no real importance at all.

Somehow, however, the team will need to switch on to play a potentially huge Test match this morning. If we win, we will become the new number-one Test team in the world. This is what we have been working towards for the last two and a half years, and despite all the chaos around us, it is an opportunity we do not want to see slip through our fingers. We have worked too hard.

I open my curtains, still a little unsure whether the game is going ahead today. Looking from the top floor of the Hyatt Hotel, I can see a couple of plumes of smoke in the distance, remnants of arson from the night before. Elsewhere, however, everything looks calm. The disturbances on the streets below have definitely come to a conclusion.

I make my way to the bathroom and start getting myself ready, both physically and mentally, for the day ahead.

The last few months had been full of incident. The summer of 2011 started with the adoption of a novel approach by the ECB of having three separate captains: me for Tests, Alastair Cook for ODIs and Stuart Broad for Twenty20s. Although, in an ideal world, I think that it is better to have only one captain, I didn't believe that there were any strong reasons why this new method wouldn't work. Cook, Broad and I all got on fine, and it allowed each captain to concentrate his attention on the form of the game he was responsible for. I saw it as having some real benefits.

It had still been a difficult and sad decision for me to step down as ODI captain at the end of the World Cup and to retire from ODI cricket. My form had been really strong and during the competition I'd produced probably the best one-day innings of my international career, a score of 158 against India. However, the team's performance had hit me hard. It was my one chance to lead England to World Cup glory, but it was not to be. Once we were on the plane back to the UK, it was clear that it was in the best interests of the team and myself to move on. The end of the World Cup is the end of a cycle, a watershed moment if you like, and without the incentive of going on to play in another World Cup, I don't think I would have been motivated enough to carry on playing ODIs.

Of course, one problem with playing only one form of the game is that you only have one bite of the cherry. If you are playing both formats, a good performance in one can boost your confidence in the other, and also help ward off the vultures in the press, who are always on the lookout for a vulnerable target.

During the first series of the summer against Sri Lanka I felt particularly exposed. Although I had been in good form for Middlesex, with a couple of hundreds, I found that my mind was increasingly unclear while I was in the middle. I was being distracted by the repercussions of the decision I had just made. I found myself under more pressure to perform and there were a few uncomfortable feelings in the back of my mind, questioning whether my career was beginning to wind down.

Needless to say, it was not the right mental recipe for success, and I endured a particularly painful series, registering three single-figure scores in the four innings I played. Fortunately the rest of the team were in better nick than myself, and a miraculous victory in the rain-affected first Test in Cardiff, where we managed to bowl Sri Lanka out in twenty-five overs, was the difference between the two sides.

It also meant that we had won seven out of our last eight

Test series, with only the drawn series against South Africa away from home blotting our copybook. Any team that had enjoyed so much continuous success was entitled to feel very confident every time they walked on the field.

By the start of the India series, which had gained further significance as the battle for the world's best Test team, I had never seen the England cricket team looking and sounding so assured. We were not only extremely comfortable and sure of our methods, but also extremely hungry and motivated to knock the Indians off their perch as world number one.

Thankfully, by that stage of the season I was in a far better place mentally to lead the team, having had a little time to come to terms with my decision to retire from ODI cricket. I had also picked up some useful form by playing a game for Somerset in July against the touring Indian team, scoring an unbeaten century.

It was a one-off situation, in which a quirk in the cricketing calendar meant that Middlesex were without a first-class fixture in the month before the India series because of a glut of Twenty20 matches. However, it is hard to describe quite what a strange experience it was to turn up in Taunton, introduce myself to my team-mates, don my new uniform and then stride out to bat with Arul Suppiah, my opening partner against India.

Despite my awkward feelings, I liked the fact that we had been proactive in trying to find a way for me to play, and I am indebted to Somerset for being so open to the suggestion. It is an excellent club, with some fantastic people at the helm, not least the captain, my old opening partner Marcus Trescothick.

In one regard, the series against India was going to be different from all the series we had played over the previous two years: we were not going to be using the Decision Review System. Initially introduced by the ICC as a means of taking advantage of technology to help make sure that more correct decisions were made, the DRS had become an accepted part of the game in most cricket-playing countries.

I have to admit that I'd had my concerns about the system when it first came in. I wasn't thrilled by the fact that players could refer umpiring decisions to be adjudicated by the third umpire. I thought it had the potential to alter the relationship between the players and the officials, in effect allowing players far more power to question and thereby undermine the authority of the umpires. Yet I had always believed that technology should be used, as it seemed ludicrous that millions of viewers around the world could see that an umpire had made a terrible mistake, but the players still had to live by that mistake. It was far better, in my opinion, that the game should try to get as many decisions as possible right. I suppose in an ideal world I would have liked the umpires to use the technology on their own, without the input of players.

Despite my initial reservations, the new system worked remarkably well. Once the umpires got over the fact that some of their decisions were likely to be reviewed by the players, they responded well to the system, almost seeing it as a back-up in case they didn't get their decision right first time around. Also, in many cases, it actually enhanced the standing of umpires, as the best ones usually had the reviews of their decisions turned down.

It did, however, put captains under increased pressure. In a sense, the captain of the team had to become a de facto umpire in his own right, trying to judge whether the umpire had got the original decision correct or not. With only two reviews per side, you could not afford to waste a review in a futile attempt to overrule an umpire, so you had to judge when to use your reviews very carefully. It was also important to understand the characters of your players when discussing whether to review a decision or not. Like many bowlers, Graeme Swann wasn't always reliable in that regard. Any appeal that was turned down by an umpire was 'absolutely definitely out' in his opinion, and I was always grateful for the more measured and accurate responses from Matthew Prior, the wicketkeeper.

Overall, it was close to irrefutable that more correct decisions were being made as a result of the system. No longer did a batsman, or bowler for that matter, with their international career on the line, have to worry about a shocking decision hammering the final nail in their coffin. It was particularly surprising, therefore, that the Board of Control for Cricket in India (BCCI) and its players were unwilling to use the system. I think they had concerns about the accuracy of the ball-tracking software, but it seemed strange to argue that the eyes of a middle-aged man standing behind the stumps were more likely to be accurate than a combination of high-speed cameras. To me, it didn't make sense.

Nonetheless, the BCCI had managed to ensure that no cricket match in which the Indian team played would have to use the DRS system. Quite what the umpires, who had grown accustomed to using the system at all other times, thought about the situation I don't know, but those were the parameters within which we were forced to work.

If anyone looked at the scorecards of the first two Test matches of the series, they would be forgiven for thinking that the Indian side were steamrollered by a rampant England team flourishing in home conditions. In fact, both games were far closer than first meets the eye. At Lord's, we had to weather particularly difficult conditions early in the game after losing the toss, but the combination of a stupendous double hundred by Kevin Pietersen and an early injury to the fast bowler Zaheer Khan, who looked out of shape physically, swung the match in our favour.

In Nottingham, it was the turn of Stuart Broad to come to the party with an inspired new-ball spell that completely changed the second Test. With India handily placed at 267–4, already 46 runs ahead of our first-innings score, we desperately needed something to happen. Broad delivered with a hat-trick, ensuring a relatively paltry first-innings deficit, before Ian Bell scored a sublime hundred to take the game away from the opposition. At 2–0 up in the series, our dreams of becoming the world number-one side seemed incredibly close to coming to fruition. All we required was one more victory.

* * *

I can't say enough what a pleasure it was to captain the England cricket team during the series against India. I think that I can appreciate what Steve Waugh must have felt like when he was in charge of the rampant Australian side in the early 2000s. We were a side brimming with confidence, full of players who knew their roles and were comfortable with their games. In the unlikely circumstances that we found ourselves in trouble, invariably someone would stand up and deliver. Cook, Pietersen, Trott and Bell were all in sublime form and our bowling attack was a handful for any opposition team. The combination of Anderson, Broad and Swann, backed up by the likes of Bresnan, Finn and Tremlett, was striking fear into opposition batting line-ups.

I think much of our confidence originated in having a strategy that we knew worked for us. Commentators like nothing more than to judge a captain or a team on tactics. They wonder whether he could have an extra slip in place, or if a change of bowler is required. From the decisions that happen out there in the middle, they then deduce whether a team or captain is either positive (i.e. good) or conservative (i.e. bad). From my experience, I think they generally miss the point. Tactics are important, but not nearly as important as having the right strategy and committing to it.

One of the issues we have always grappled with as an England team is that of identity. You could easily define the West Indies by their calypso cricket – flamboyant players, outrageous shots and quick bowling. India have always been associated with spin – either batsmen expertly capable of playing it or beguiling exponents of bowling it. Likewise, you can broadly characterise

South Africa as methodical, Pakistan as mercurial, Australia as domineering and so on. What was England's cricket about, though?

To me, this was a vitally important question, because if we could answer it, we would always have something to fall back on when things were difficult and it would allow us to follow our own path, rather than look towards other countries in an effort to emulate their strengths. There is no doubt that a team's strengths will change over time, according to which players they have at their disposal, but after thinking about it for a while, as well as looking at some really good analysis from Nathan Leamon, it became clear to us where our strengths lay.

Our batting line-up was useful because it was varied. We had myself, Cook and Trott at the top of the order. Our job was to set up the innings for the more explosive middle order of Pietersen, Bell and Prior. In the midst of those three lay Paul Collingwood or later Eoin Morgan, who were both adept at playing in a number of ways, as versatile batsmen. We were then very fortunate to have the likes of Broad and Swann, who could make life difficult for opposition captains with their counterattacking style. All in all, it was a good blend of different styles.

With the ball, however, it took us longer to find our unique style. We had an extremely talented bowling line-up, with James Anderson being the undoubted leader. Stuart Broad was very capable of blowing away opposition teams with an inspired spell of bowling. In addition, we had Steve Finn, full of promise and pace; Chris Tremlett, who possessed awkward bounce and accuracy; as well as Tim Bresnan, who was entirely reliable, swing or no swing. The seamers were backed up by Graeme Swann, who was undoubtedly one of the world's best spin bowlers, able to attack and defend at the same time. All we needed, then, was a method to stick to in order to put opposition teams under pressure.

Over time, it became apparent that the method that worked best for us was one of containment. We were very fortunate that all our bowlers could hold a line or a length for long periods of time. In fact, the more we focused on it, the better they became at it. By concentrating on starving the opposition of runs, they would be able, as a unit, to create enough pressure to induce a batsman into making a mistake. All we had to do was set fields that allowed them to bowl maidens and wait for batsmen to fall into the trap.

In some ways, I was surprised that this strategy worked as well and as consistently as it did, on all sorts of different wickets. Perhaps modern-day batsmen weren't as patient as their ancestors, but time and time again batsmen tried to hit their way out of being strangled, only to fail in their quest. It was often the best players, such as Ponting and Tendulkar, who fell for the trap. Guys who didn't like to be dominated tended to be the most susceptible.

At times, we still had to turn to plan B, which usually involved having to be more active in our search for a wicket, especially against players who were willing to play the waiting game against us. However, on most occasions I preferred to be certain that our plan A wasn't working before looking for other ways of taking wickets.

There will be people out there who say that the method was too staid and predictable, lacking in flair and charisma. I believe, though, that we were merely sticking to what we did best. We had found what the England cricket team's unique strength was, and our results over a three-year period spoke far more loudly than any of the detractors.

Certainly, by the time we reached the third Test against India in August, the method had taken us to the verge of becoming the world's best cricket team.

In this Test series, the Indian cricket team, proud holders of the ICC mace that signifies the world's best Test team, have been undone by a combination of cricketing strengths. The England batsmen have been in form and hungry to make what Graham Gooch, our batting coach, refers to as 'daddy hundreds' – large scores that take the game away from the opposition. Our bowling attack, meanwhile, has been simply too hot to handle. A few of the Indian batsmen, including Yuvraj Singh and Suresh Raina, have looked distinctly uncomfortable against the short ball, while the rest have generally struggled with the swing and seam. Rahul Dravid apart, who once again has proved his excellent all-round qualities, their big-name players have not delivered.

As the tension around the country in the wake of the riots has slowly dissipated, so the pressure on the Indian team has gradually increased. A substandard batting performance on a decent wicket on the first day of the third Test has left India with a mountain to climb with the ball. Without the injured Zaheer Khan, their bowling attack has looked threadbare and all our batsmen have gradually worn them down.

Alastair Cook, in particular, has shown remarkable mental strength in batting for over nine hours for a career-best 294. He will undoubtedly be kicking himself for not going on to get 300, showing that even at your moment of greatest triumph, there are still regrets to be had, but he has batted us into a position of utter dominance. The result of the game is a formality.

Trailing by 486 runs after the first innings, India quickly subsided to 130–7 before a spirited resistance by Dhoni, in particular, has restored a little respectability. Although he has been stuck with an underperforming side in English conditions, I have admired his calm manner and strong leadership. Captaining India, with all the hype and mania that surrounds the side, must be incredibly difficult, but he has handled it all exceptionally well. Nonetheless, they now find themselves on the verge of relinquishing the crown of the world's number-one side.

Tim Bresnan bustles in to the crease, bowling at Sreesanth, the Indian number-eleven batsman. The ball is pitched short of a length, aimed at Sreesanth's ribcage, conforming exactly to our pre-game plan to rough up the tail-enders. Sreesanth is unable to control the steepling bounce and can only fend off the ball, sending it looping towards Kevin Pietersen in the gully.

We all freeze for a moment in anticipation of Pietersen making the catch. There is no way that he can drop it and he duly completes the task. There is pandemonium as we all come together in a huddle, *jumping up and down. We have won the game, the series is ours and, far more importantly, we are now officially the best Test team in the world.*

A goal that started as a pipe dream two and a half years earlier has now been achieved, at least a year and a half earlier than we expected.

That evening, with a few beers down my neck and filled with the unique sensations that accompany a job well done, I couldn't help but think about the journey that we had all been on over the last few years. What started with the ignominy of being bowled out for 51 in Jamaica had ended with us sitting on the top of the pile, as the world's best team.

I spent a little time thinking about the reasons for the turn-around in fortunes. I thought back to the various changes that Andy Flower and I had made to the set-up. None had been exactly revolutionary, and it would be hard to argue that any one thing that we did could explain why we had so much success so quickly.

You could perhaps argue that the sum of the parts added up to something radically different from the past. If you put together the improvements in our statistical analysis, a changed emphasis in practice and a far more wide-ranging preparation process, then what you had was a method that bore no resemblance to the one that Andy and I inherited.

I still don't believe, though, that the answer to our rapid rise lay there. In truth, there was a combination of reasons for our success, ranging from Hugh Morris at the ECB, right through to Mark Saxby, our masseur, and almost everything and everyone in between. There is no way that any one person could take the credit for what happened.

If I were forced to focus on one area, however, it would have to be on the relationships between everyone in the set-up. I don't think that anyone could dispute that the culture in the dressing room had changed significantly, even from when we were beating the Australians in 2005. Of course, some of it was by design, but much of it was the result of people coming together and working towards a common goal.

There was a genuine feeling of togetherness within the group, which kept us going during the tough moments and allowed us to scale new heights when things were going in our favour. Andy Flower and the rest of the management team set a fantastic example in that respect, but the players, who could easily have found themselves being sidetracked by self-interest and personal agendas, did a tremendous job in buying into the idea that the team had to come first.

Corporate consultants would probably look at our group and conclude that there were some strong 'cultural architects', or a 'critical mass' of individuals who policed the side. I prefer to say that there were a bunch of good blokes, who all desperately wanted to be part of something special. Many people go through life not knowing what it is like to be part of a great team. I don't think it happens all that often. I truly believe that we were some of the fortunate ones lucky enough to experience it.

Of course, getting to the top and staying there are two completely different things. I had no idea at that stage quite how difficult the next step of the journey would be, as our status as the world's number-one team, our motivation, our goals and also our togetherness would be tested to the limit over the next twelve months.

India in England 2011 – The Pataudi Trophy

1st Test. Lord's, London. 21–25 July 2011
England 474–8 dec (K.P. Pietersen 202*, M.J. Prior 71*, I.J.L. Trott 70,
A.J. Strauss 22; P. Kumar 5–106) and 269–6 dec (M.J. Prior 103*,
S.C.J. Broad 74*, A.J. Strauss 32; I. Sharma 4–59)
India 286 (R. Dravid 103; S.C.J. Broad 4–37) and 261 (S.K. Raina 78,
V.V.S. Laxman 56; J.M. Anderson 5–65)
England won by 196 runs.

2nd Test. Trent Bridge, Nottingham. 29 July – 1 August 2011
England 221 (S.C.J. Broad 64, A.J. Strauss 32) and 544 (I.R. Bell 159,
T.T. Bresnan 90, M.J. Prior 73, E.J.G. Morgan 70, K.P. Pietersen 63,
A.J. Strauss 16; P. Kumar 4–124)
India 288 (R. Dravid 117, Yuvraj Singh 62, V.V.S. Laxman 54; S.C.J. Broad
6–46) and 158 (S.R. Tendulkar 56; T.T. Bresnan 5–48)
England won by 319 runs.

3rd Test. Edgbaston, Birmingham. 10–13 August 2011
India 224 (M.S. Dhoni 77; S.C.J. Broad 4–53, T.T. Bresnan 4–62) and 244
(M.S. Dhoni 74*; J.M. Anderson 4–85)
England 710–7 dec (A.N. Cook 294, E.J.G. Morgan 104, A.J. Strauss 87,
K.P. Pietersen 63, T.T. Bresnan 53*)
England won by an innings and 242 runs.

4th Test. The Oval, London. 18–22 August 2011
England 591–6 dec (I.R. Bell 235, K.P. Pietersen 175, A.J. Strauss 40)
India 300 (R. Dravid 146) and 283 (f/o) (S.R. Tendulkar 91, A. Mishra
84; G.P. Swann 6–106.)
England won by an innings and 8 runs.

England won the series 4–0.

18

TIME TO GO

I make my way from the outfield at Lord's, head bowed and dejected. I continue up the stairs in front of the pavilion and turn left as I enter the Long Room. I avert my gaze from the inquisitive members as I head for the sanctuary of the dressing room. This is the last time I will make this walk as an England cricketer, although I am far too frustrated, tired and generally hacked off with life for it to be a rousing emotional affair. In any case, I am just about the only one who knows it. No one else in the ground, apart from my wife and Flower, has any idea what is about to happen over the next few days.

I pick my way past the piles of kit littering the dressing-room floor. I find my space in the far corner of the room, near the television set, and sit down. I carefully pack my helmet in my kit bag and then bury my head in my hands. For ten minutes, I just sit there, unable to move. A couple of well-meaning team-mates walk past and give me a consolatory pat on the leg, but I can't even muster the energy to look up. I am caught in a web of conflicting emotions.

I feel incredibly tired, as though I have simply run out of energy – I have nothing more to give. I am also wallowing in a rising tide of sadness. I simply can't believe that I have played my last game of cricket. This is not the way I wanted it to end. Although my contribution to the match is now over,

I still feel unbelievably frustrated at what has happened over the last seven days. What is meant to be one of the great occasions in any cricketer's career, a hundredth Test match, has been marred by events beyond my control. This is no celebration.

It looks almost certain that we will lose the Test match to South Africa, along with both the series and our number-one ranking. My contribution to the game has been insignificant, falling to Morne Morkel yet again in the first innings for 20 and then inexplicably leaving a straight ball from Philander in the second for one. The dismissal showed all the hallmarks of scrambled thinking.

Over the last ten days my mind has been on anything but batting. The England cricket team is in crisis again, featuring once more on the front pages of the newspapers, and Andy Flower and I have found ourselves right in the middle of a destabilising and potentially damaging PR game between Kevin Pietersen, the England cricket team and the ECB.

How did it come to this? Twelve months before, we had been crowned the world's number-one cricket team. We were being fêted wherever we went. Everyone was patting us on the back, telling us what a pleasure it was to see an England sporting team reach the summit. We were crowned 'Team of the Year' at the *BBC Sports Personality of the Year* awards, and both Alastair Cook and I were nominated for the much-coveted main prize. After a hectic eighteen months, we had close to three months off to wallow in the warm feeling of success. Our next assignment, against Pakistan in Dubai, was not going to take place until after New Year.

Perhaps I was too negative, but I couldn't help worrying when everyone, from the media to the person on the street, kept telling us how great we were. It brought back uncomfortable memories of the hubris that affected the team after the 2005 Ashes, and we all know what happened in the twelve months that followed. This time, though, I thought we were in a better position to cope. We were supremely confident, with a very settled side, and there were some excellent people in and around the team, determined to keep everyone's feet on the ground. We knew that our next two series in Dubai and Sri Lanka would test us, as they demanded skill against the spinning ball, but it was exactly the sort of challenge we needed.

The one area we were struggling with was in goal-setting. Up to that point, it was easy for us to understand and commit to a goal. We wanted to be the best team in the world and we could track our progress towards that goal along the way. Now, however, things had become a little less clear. In truth, we became torn between trying to set a challenging new goal for ourselves, taking things to a new level, and consolidating our position, not looking too far ahead.

If, for instance, we decided we wanted to create a legacy for ourselves by dominating Test cricket, it would take a very long time and it would be all but impossible to judge exactly when we had achieved that goal. If, on the other hand, we set ourselves the more modest challenge of still being at the top of the rankings in twelve months' time, then that smacked of just trying to hang on, rather than pushing forward.

Many sports teams and managers in this country have struggled to achieve sustained success. You only have to look at the England rugby union team after the World Cup victory in 2003, or Manchester City after winning the Premiership in 2011–12. Repeating great feats is fiendishly difficult, especially when many members of the team justifiably feel a little satisfied with what they have achieved. What is the point in playing sport if you aren't entitled to enjoy your best moments?

Also, the attitude of other teams changes overnight. Suddenly, you are the hunted, rather than the hunter. Everyone is straining to knock you off your block and will do everything in their power to make sure they are as prepared as you are. If you don't raise things to a new level very quickly, you will find yourselves overtaken before you know it.

It didn't take us long after arriving in Dubai in January 2012 to realise that everything had changed. A couple of sloppy performances in the warm-up games, when players could be forgiven for being a little ring-rusty, were the prelude to a very difficult first Test match against Pakistan. Batting first, on what looked like a good wicket, we were 52–5 at lunch thanks to a combination of nervy batting and excellent spin bowling by Saeed Ajmal. In that first session, we not only batted ourselves out of the game, but we also allowed a particularly worrying mental frailty against spin to develop. By the end of the day, Ajmal had picked up seven wickets on a track that was hardly turning at all, and from that moment on, most of the battles in the series were between our ears, rather than with the Pakistani bowlers.

Our bowlers fought particularly hard to keep us in the first

Test, to no avail, and they actually bettered their performance in the second Test match in Abu Dhabi, leaving us with the fairly routine task of chasing down 145 to level the series. To say that we failed in that regard would be an understatement. We were bowled out for 72, as a mixture of high-quality spin bowling, nerves and poor technique fatally undermined our batsmen.

After three weeks in Dubai, all the back-patting and celebrations at the end of the previous summer seemed like years ago. We were still the number-one team in the world on paper, but we had already lost the series against Pakistan and we all had a huge amount of work to do on how we dealt with spin bowling.

It is fair to say that the DRS had forced players to change their techniques against spin completely. Before the introduction of the technology, batsmen had rarely been given out lbw off the front foot. It was one of those silly conventions of the game, by which the umpires felt bound to give the benefit of any doubt to the batsman. Ball-tracking, however, showed that many balls bowled by spin bowlers were going to hit the stumps and so umpires started raising their fingers more often. Graeme Swann, with his excellent bowling to left-handers in particular, was a grateful beneficiary of this change in interpretation.

Batsmen were faced with a choice. They could either keep playing the way they were accustomed, or find another method that kept their front pad out of the way. It was pretty clear that what we had been doing wasn't working and so hours were spent in the nets in Dubai working on different ways of playing spin. However, the result was that for this series we sometimes found ourselves caught between old and new methods in the middle. Even though the time spent in the nets would help us in the future, it all but ensured a defeat in the final Test, despite our bowlers once again doing the hard work by dismissing Pakistan for 99 in the first innings. A 3–0 series defeat was both unexpected and shocking.

Any team can have a poor series. I don't think it is right to judge a team on only three matches. I was very concerned, though, about the patent lack of confidence in the batting line-up. Players who had been seemingly invincible the previous summer suddenly were suddenly looking nervous and ungainly on the unfamiliar wickets in Dubai. Even Kevin Pietersen, who so often could be relied upon to take the game to the opposition, was struggling with some demons against left-arm spin. It is not uncommon for one or two of a team's batsmen to be going through a barren patch at any one time, but for the whole batting line-up to be struggling with spin did not augur well for the future, especially as our next assignment was in the dust bowls of Sri Lanka.

I was far from immune from the malaise. In fact, my returns since the Australian Ashes tour had been mediocre at best. I was feeling more and more bogged down, as though it took all my mental energy just to get to 30. I kept getting out in the twenties and thirties, without going on to take advantage of doing the hard work. That was all right while we were winning Test matches, but in Dubai, when runs were in short supply for everyone, my form was much more of an issue. It is never fun going through a run of poor form. You are forced to deal with your own negative thoughts as well as increased scrutiny from the media. If you are also captain of the team and heading towards the back end of your career, it becomes extremely difficult.

On top of the normal concerns about technique and mindset, I found myself having to confront far more weighty and less easily answered questions such as 'Am I experiencing a gradual downward spiral as I get older?' and 'Am I still motivated enough to keep doing all of this?' Doubts like that are destructive in the sense that the more you let them invade your mind, the more self-fulfilling they become.

Throughout the winter of 2011–12, I was carrying too much of this mental baggage, not to mention the obvious captaincy issues that were arising as a result of the team losing Test matches.

The tour to Sri Lanka in March 2012 offered us all a chance to shrug off our insecurities against spin and get back to winning ways. A two-Test tour was always going to be over in a flash, so we were under no illusions as to how important the first Test match would be.

Far more thought and practice went into our pre-series preparation this time, in an effort to reconnect with the attitude that had been so successful for us in Australia the previous winter. Two warm-up games gave us two opportunities to win and thereby regain some confidence. In the end, adapting to the extreme humidity and heat was actually far more difficult than the opposition we faced in those warm-up games, but registering two victories was the perfect way to enter a series against a very good team in its home conditions.

Galle, the location for the first Test match, still bears the scars from the devastating tsunami of 2004. Many of the seafront buildings lie derelict as a shocking reminder of the powerful surge from the sea that took so many lives along with it. The ground itself, guarded by a sixteenth-century Portuguese fort, was submerged by three metres of seawater and was rendered unplayable for three years after the event.

Its reputation for being a haven for spin bowlers has not changed, though, and it would provide us with immediate feedback as to whether our work against spin was having any effect. Unfortunately, the answer we received was emphatic. We were defeated by 75 runs as Rangana Herath, the Sri Lankan left-arm spinner, took twelve wickets in the game. It was depressingly similar to our performances in Dubai. The only bright spot came from Jonathan Trott, who played patiently and diligently en route to a defiant century in the fourth innings. He demonstrated that if you just trust your method and remain patient, it is far from impossible to score runs in those conditions.

Trott aside, we were reaching something of a crisis point. Since being crowned as world number one, we had promptly lost four Test matches in a row. While the environment seemed healthy, with players still sticking together and doing plenty of hard work, we had lost the most precious of sporting components, confidence. Our swagger and aura had deserted us, to be replaced by introspection and hesitation. There was only one way to rectify things and that was to dig extremely deep and find a way to win a game of cricket.

The final Test against Sri Lanka saw a welcome return to form, both for the team and myself. In the lead-up, the attention of the media had once more focused on the embattled captain of the side. A couple of twenties in the first Test had done nothing to dispel the notion that my batting was in terminal decline. What started as a couple of whispers had spread to become the main talking point before the game: 'Is Strauss reaching the end?'

The fire in my belly told me the answer to that question. I still had plenty of fight left in me and I was determined to prove everyone wrong. I did, however, recognise the importance of the next match in Colombo. Five losses in a row would pose serious questions of any captain, especially if he was underperforming himself.

Once again, the bowlers did an outstanding job in limiting Sri Lanka to two sub-300 scores, and on this occasion, the batsmen finally stood up and delivered. There were half-centuries for myself, Cook and Trott, while Kevin Pietersen shrugged off his own travails in the most emphatic of styles, scoring 151 in the first innings, followed by a blistering 42 not out in the second, as we chased another potentially difficult target of 94 to win.

We had broken our subcontinental duck and everyone in the squad breathed a great sigh of relief. A series draw in Sri Lanka is no disgrace and the work that had been put in by everyone would surely bear more fruit in the future. In fact, I believe that the Test series win against India later in 2012 can be directly attributed to the excellent work put in by the players and the support staff over those tough months in Dubai and Sri Lanka.

Although I experienced a brief moment of euphoria after the game, I must admit I was still deeply troubled. My half-century had done enough to keep the vultures at bay for the time being, but it was becoming increasingly clear to me that the combination of batting troubles, the constant demands of captaincy and the pressing need for the England team to be pushed forward were beginning to wear me down. I wasn't enjoying my cricket any more. I felt as if I was just hanging on, both with my batting and as a captain. I still believed that the team wanted me in charge, but my enthusiasm for the job was beginning to wane.

I made a silent vow to myself the evening after that second Test that I would not be hounded out by the press. If I went through another bout of poor form the next summer, then I would leave on my own terms. Perhaps I was haunted by the looks on the faces of Michael Vaughan and Nasser Hussain when they relinquished the role of England captain. They both looked completely spent, mentally and physically. I didn't want to leave the England captaincy on those terms. Far better, in my mind, to go when people still wanted you than to overstay your welcome.

When I looked at the schedule for the following summer, it struck me that the series against South Africa might be the perfect opportunity to bring down the curtain on my career. If we were able to win the series, and in doing so underline our pedigree as the world's number-one team, then it would be the ideal time to wander off into the sunset. Lose and relinquish our crown, and it would be a good moment for a new leader to take the team forward.

Having spent a great deal of time in the build-up to the 2012 summer ruminating about these big decisions, I decided to put them to bed for the time being. There was still a lot of difficult cricket ahead of us and as long as I was captain, I needed to go out and do my job. I had no way of knowing just how eventful the next six months were going to be.

The great irony is that, after finally coming to some firm conclusions that the summer of 2012 would probably be my last, I proceeded to score centuries in both of the first two Test matches of the summer, against the West Indies. Perhaps I wasn't trying quite so hard, or more likely it was merely down to the usual ebb and flow of cricketing form, but I must say that it was immensely satisfying to get to twenty and then twenty-one Test hundreds.

I have to say that the reception I received at Lord's when I registered my hundred was one of the real highlights of my career. The crowd rose to its feet and applauded for what seemed like an eternity. Then, just when things started to settle down, a second wave of applause and noise erupted.

I never felt comfortable with the idea of announcing my retirement prior to my final game. I didn't want the team to be distracted by the thought that for me the end was nigh. I suppose it meant that I never got a ceremonial send-off from English cricket supporters. I didn't need one, though, because the reception I received that day at Lord's told me all I needed to know. I got the impression that the crowd wanted to show their appreciation for what we had achieved as a team as much as for my century, and that suited me fine. It will serve as a fitting tribute.

Apart from my two centuries, the three-Test series against the West Indies was low on drama. As expected, we won the first two Tests, before continuous rain wiped out the final match. From that point on, though, my attention, along with that of Andy Flower, shifted towards a crisis that was developing between Kevin Pietersen and the ECB.

I first saw Kevin Pietersen play cricket in a heated County Championship game between Middlesex and Nottinghamshire in 2001. A relative unknown at that stage, he scored a blistering 165 which really made everyone in our team take notice. This guy was seriously good. What also stood out that day was that here was someone who marched to a different tune from most cricketers.

In an attempt to get under his skin, David Nash, the chirpy Middlesex wicketkeeper, knowing that Pietersen was South African, started calling him a 'doos'. Literally the word means 'box' in Afrikaans, but it can have another, much more insulting meaning. Rather than just ignore Nash's attempt to ruffle his feathers, Pietersen stopped the game mid-over, made his way to the square-leg umpire and protested, 'Sorry, umpire, I can't bat. The wicketkeeper has just called me a "doos".' The umpire, not sure what the word even meant, instructed Pietersen to

England v West Indies
(1st Test)

Played at Lord's Cricket Ground, London, on 17–21 May 2012

Umpires:	Aleem Dar & M Erasmus (TV: Asad Rauf)
Referee:	RS Mahanama
Toss:	England

WEST INDIES

AB Barath	c Anderson b Broad	42	c Prior b Bresnan		24
KOA Powell	b Anderson	5	c Bell b Broad		8
KA Edwards	lbw b Anderson	1	run out (Bairstow)		0
DM Bravo	run out (Bell/Prior/Swann)	29	b Swann		21
S Chanderpaul	not out	87	lbw b Swann		91
MN Samuels	c Bairstow b Broad	31	c Swann b Broad		86
D Ramdin†	c Strauss b Broad	6	b Anderson		43
DJG Sammy*	c Bresnan b Broad	17	c Prior b Broad		37
KAJ Roach	c and b Broad	6	c Bell b Broad		4
FH Edwards	c Prior b Broad	2	not out		10
ST Gabriel	c Swann b Broad	0	b Swann		13
Extras	(b 6, lb 8, nb 3)	17	(lb 7, nb 1)		8
Total	(89.5 overs)	243	(130.5 overs)		345

ENGLAND

AJ Strauss*	c Ramdin b Roach	122	c Powell b Roach		1
AN Cook	b Roach	26	c KA Edwards b Sammy		79
IJL Trott	c Ramdin b Sammy	58	(4) c Sammy b Roach		13
KP Pietersen	c Ramdin b Samuels	32	(5) c Ramdin b Gabriel		13
IR Bell	c Powell b Gabriel	61	(6) not out		63
JM Bairstow	lbw b Roach	16	(7) not out		0
MJ Prior†	b Gabriel	19			
TT Bresnan	c Ramdin b Sammy	0			
SCJ Broad	b FH Edwards	10			
GP Swann	b Gabriel	30			
JM Anderson	not out	0	(3) c Ramdin b Roach		6
Extras	(b 9, lb 3, nb 12)	24	(b 4, lb 3, nb 11)		18
Total	(113.3 overs)	398	(for 5 wkts) (46.1 overs)		193

ENGLAND	O	M	R	W	O	M	R	W
Anderson	25	8	59	2	36	11	67	1
Broad	24.5	6	72	7	34	6	93	4
Bresnan	20	7	39	0	36	11	105	1
Swann	18	6	52	0	18.5	4	59	3
Trott	2	0	7	0	6	0	14	0

WEST INDIES	O	M	R	W	O	M	R	W
FH Edwards	25	1	88	1	8	0	24	0
Roach	25	3	108	3	13	2	60	3
Gabriel	21.3	2	60	3	5	1	26	1
Sammy	28	1	92	2	10	1	25	1
Samuels	14	3	38	1	10.1	0	51	0

Fall of wickets:

	WI	Eng	WI	Eng
1st	13	47	36	1
2nd	32	194	36	10
3rd	86	244	36	29
4th	100	266	65	57
5th	181	292	222	189
6th	187	320	261	–
7th	219	323	307	–
8th	231	342	313	–
9th	243	397	325	–
10th	243	398	345	–

Close of play:	Day 1:	WI (1) 243–9 (Chanderpaul 87*, 89.4 overs)
	Day 2:	Eng (1) 259–3 (Strauss 121*, Bell 5*, 80.2 overs)
	Day 3:	WI (2) 120–4 (Chanderpaul 34*, Samuels 26*, 50 overs)
	Day 4:	Eng (2) 10–2 (Cook 0*, Trott 0*, 4 overs)

Man of the match:	SCJ Broad
Result:	**England won by 5 wickets**

On my way to a one-day career-best 158 against India in the 2010–11 World Cup. It was a sad decision to step down as ODI captain after what was a disappointing tournament for England.

Having been hammered by Sri Lanka in the World Cup quarter-final, it was a joy to be greeted at Heathrow by the smiling faces of my sons Sam (*left*) and Luca (*right*).

And then there were three: in 2011 Alastair Cook (*left*) was appointed one-day captain and Stuart Broad (*right*) Twenty20 captain, while I remained as Test captain.

To secure the world No. 1 spot, we needed to beat India at Edgbaston in 2011. Cook's remarkable 294 made the task a great deal easier.

Spirited resistance from captain MS Dhoni in the second innings restored respectability for India, but it would not be enough.

Another victory in the final Test at The Oval makes it 4–0. What a pleasure it was to captain the England team during the 2011 series against India!

Officially the best team in the world: celebrating with Andy Flower in the Oval dressing room with the ICC Test Championship mace.

With Graeme Fowler, director of cricket at Durham in my student days, at a dinner at Lord's in 2011 to mark the award of an honorary doctorate from the university.

Another proud moment. With my wife, Ruth, later the same year, after receiving my OBE from the Princess Royal for services to cricket.

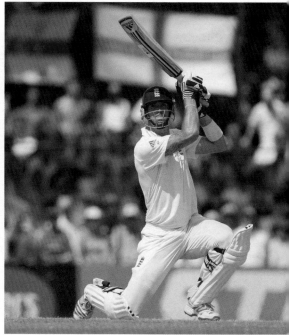

A humbling 3–0 defeat to Pakistan in early 2012 forced us to re-examine our play against spin. Here I watch Monty Panesar in a special nets session in Abu Dhabi.

Kevin Pietersen helps us return to winning ways with an emphatic 151 in the 2nd Test against Sri Lanka at Colombo in April 2012.

In the 1st Test at Galle we had suffered our fourth Test defeat in a row – despite a battling 112 from Jonathan Trott and my satisfying run-out of Suraj Randiv (*below*).

One of the highlights of my career: receiving a standing ovation at Lord's after reaching my century in the 1st Test against the West Indies in 2012.

Waiting for a team photo with James Anderson (*left*) and Kevin Pietersen prior to the 2012 series against South Africa.

Congratulating Hashim Amla on reaching 300 in the 1st Test, which ended as a heavy defeat for England.

Leading the team onto the field for the presentations at Lord's after losing the 3rd Test and the series. It was my 100th and final Test – and the end of a very difficult summer.

Time to go. Announcing my retirement from professional cricket in 2012, as Alastair Cook, the new captain, looks on. I was surprised to be applauded out of the press conference.

Finally the chance for Ruth and me to relax with our sons, Sam and Luca.

get on with it, but the moment stuck with me both for Pietersen's high level of confidence and his unwillingness to get bullied by anyone. He certainly achieved something that very few people have managed, before or since, and that is to get David Nash to shut up.

I find it quite ironic that the word 'doos', so much a part of my first memory of Kevin Pietersen, was also allegedly one of the words that Pietersen used to describe me in his infamous text messages to the South African players in the summer of 2012. The game of cricket certainly goes around in circles.

Over our time together in the England team, KP and I were never really close mates, but we were always on pretty good terms. I think that I understood him reasonably well, possibly because we both had South African roots, and his abrasive nature was far more understandable to a person who had spent a lot of time in the country. I think we both had a fairly high level of respect for each other's games. I was constantly blown away by his incredible confidence in his ability and his insistence on taking the game to the opposition. I think, in return, he enjoyed the fact that I sometimes managed to take the shine off the ball before he got to go in. Either way, we always had some decent banter about the number of Test centuries we had scored. For a long time we were pretty much neck and neck.

I also admired the way he had come back into the team after being deposed as captain in 2009. There is no doubt that the way his stint in charge of the England team ended was a significant assault to his ego, and he could easily have reacted far less graciously to the players, the management and me, his replacement as captain, than he did. He stayed professional, worked hard on his game and used his batting as a way to settle his score with the ECB. I do think, however, that his loyalty to English cricket, and the ECB in particular, was severely affected by the episode.

Perhaps unsurprisingly, the simmering resentment came to the surface during the summer of 2012. For a while Kevin and his representatives had been trying to secure more time for him to play in the IPL. He had just signed a contract with the Delhi Daredevils, reputedly worth two million dollars (certainly not a bad salary for six weeks' work in anyone's language) and he was anxious to make the most of it.

The ECB were unwilling – rightly in my opinion – to let any player either miss or not be properly prepared to play in a Test match in order to fulfil IPL obligations, and so an ugly stand-off ensued between Pietersen and the board, which was probably the backdrop to him suddenly retiring from ODI cricket shortly after the West Indies Test series.

Even his retirement, though, caused trouble, as the conditions of our contracts did not allow a player to retire from ODI cricket but still play Twenty20 cricket. The board were concerned about players picking and choosing the juicy Twenty20 format above the less coveted fifty-over version. So Pietersen found himself pushed into a corner where, in order to retire from ODI cricket, he would have to forgo his opportunity to play in the World Twenty20 later in the summer. Given his history with the board, Pietersen decided that he would prefer to do that rather than back down.

While all this was going on, I largely stayed out of the fight. I had to work with him on a day-to-day basis and I certainly felt that issues between Pietersen and the board should stay exactly that, between Pietersen and the board. Also, I was no longer ODI captain and was therefore less affected by his decision.

I suppose my approach to managing Pietersen was always to let him be himself. His unusual temperament and style was what made him one of the best players I had ever seen and I didn't want to stifle that. Of course, there had to be some boundaries set, as he had a habit of testing the waters. He was never happy merely to go along with the crowd. He wanted to be different and stand out. That was all well and good, in my opinion, as long as he was not directly interfering with or undermining our carefully cultivated team environment.

My involvement in the Pietersen/ECB dispute started just before the start of the South African series in July. I had heard some troubling rumours that he might be preparing to separate himself completely from English cricket after a further attempt by his representatives to get the ECB to yield ground had come to nothing.

At the PCA golf day at the Grove, a few days before the first Test, I took him to one side to ask what was going on. He explained how he was feeling and it was clear that he was far from happy. Some people at the event thought we were arguing in the courtyard of the clubhouse, but nothing was further from the truth. I was merely trying to advise him not to make any hasty decisions about his future. I suppose I challenged him to a certain extent to think about his legacy and the goals that he wanted to reach with the rest of his career. Unfortunately, before our conversation was fully over, we were interrupted and I left him with the words 'Let's finish this chat in the days leading up to the Test match.'

Unfortunately the pre-series preparations got in the way of our continuing the conversation before the first Test match, at The Oval. I don't know whether it would have made any difference if it had reached its conclusion, but it is fair to say that I did not know at the time quite how close to the edge he was.

In any case, the England cricket team had other problems to deal with. Despite playing very well on the opening day of the Oval Test, in what was once again a battle for the number-one spot in the world rankings, we let things slip on the second morning to end up with a slightly substandard score of 385. In reply, South Africa wore down our bowlers on a flat, unresponsive wicket, registering a scarcely believable 637–2. On one of the very few occasions when our efforts to suffocate opposition teams completely backfired, Hashim Amla played magnificently to score an unbeaten triple century, and he was well supported by the two pillars of South African batting, Graeme Smith and Jacques Kallis. After that, the fatigue of spending two days in the field took its toll and we were unable to muster enough energy to hold out for a draw. South Africa had drawn first blood in the most emphatic style.

In the lead-up to the second Test match, at Headingley, the KP issue reared its head once again. On the practice days, he seemed completely withdrawn, as though he was consciously distancing himself from the rest of the team, and on the first day of the game itself, while the rest of us were desperately trying to get back into the series, he seemed determined to let everyone in the ground know just how unhappy he was. As captain, I could not let it go and I called him into a back room to make it clear that his behaviour was unacceptable. I was completely shocked by his lack of contrition and his apparent hostility towards me. It felt as though he was almost deliberately trying to goad me into a confrontation. The whole thing seemed so strange. It was almost as if he was trying to engineer an excuse to turn his back on the team.

Conscious that we still had a vitally important Test match to win, I asked a few of the senior players – Cook, Anderson and Prior – to go in and plead on behalf of his team-mates for him to re-engage in proceedings. To his credit, he did then come out and show far more energy in the field. What's more, he later went out and played one of the most audacious innings I have ever seen from an English player. He pulverised the world's best bowling attack en route to a brilliant 149. You can say what you want about Kevin Pietersen, but you can never doubt his immense ability with the bat in hand.

Despite his hundred, I was still extremely concerned about what he had said to me, and by the fact that he pointedly did not wave his bat in the direction of the dressing room when he reached his hundred. It was clear that things were coming to a head.

Given what had happened that week, I was unsurprised to hear from Rhian Evans, our media relations officer, that Kevin had given a bizarre and disturbing press conference following what was a thrilling drawn Test match. He had basically intimated that the next Test match was likely to be his last for

England and that he was about to 'make some decisions that are going to make me very happy'. What greatly puzzled me, though, was his comment that, 'It's tough being me, playing for England', seemingly implying that he was being treated badly by his team-mates in the dressing room. For me, he had just crossed the line. He seemed to be at best destabilising and at worst undermining the carefully cultivated team environment.

As I was obliged to face the media after the match, I had to fend off a barrage of verbal bouncers from the press corps. I tried as hard as possible not to add fuel to the fire, although I did make the point that 'the team unity over the last three years in this England side has been outstanding. It is something we all pride ourselves on. We always have done and we will continue to do so.' The comment was a direct reaction to what had gone on both in the dressing room and in the press conference.

I know that it later came out that he was upset with the spoof Twitter account, called 'KP genius', that some of the players had followed, and that he even had suspicions that one or more of the players were involved with it. Perhaps he was genuinely upset by the mickey-taking nature of the account, but he had never shown any antipathy towards it before. In fact, I remember him laughing about it at The Oval during the first Test match. In hindsight, perhaps Andy Flower or I should have politely informed the players concerned not to follow the account, but it seemed so innocuous, so in line with the day-to-day banter, that neither of us saw it as a major issue. There was certainly no time while I was captain when I thought that Kevin was being victimised in the dressing room.

As I got into my car for the long journey home after the press conference, I knew that the next nine days, the build-up to my hundredth and probably last Test match, would be as testing as anything I had encountered as captain of the England cricket team.

When Andy Flower and I sat down in a quiet country pub near Oxford a couple of days later to discuss how best to approach the Kevin Pietersen problem, Andy received a call from Hugh Morris to say that Kevin had spoken to him and, after some serious reflection, wanted to recommit himself to the England cricket team. Hugh had suggested a meeting with him and his agent that evening. The call certainly put the cat among the pigeons, as we were already starting to prepare for life without Pietersen in the England ranks. On the surface, KP recommitting himself to English cricket was the best-case scenario, but some serious bridge-building would be required in the dressing room after what had happened in the previous Test match. The meeting that evening was going to be an interesting one.

Before we left the pub to go our separate ways, I felt that it was the right time to tell Andy that, in all likelihood, I was going to retire at the end of the final Test match against South Africa. He was shocked, as he had assumed I was going to carry on until after the twin Ashes series against Australia, but apart from a few exploratory questions about why I thought it was the best time to go, he didn't try and dissuade me. It was my decision to make and he respected it.

I must admit that I felt particularly emotional talking about the prospect of retirement. Up to that point, it had always been an internal dialogue with myself, or with my wife and a couple of close friends. Now that I'd mentioned it to Andy, my long-term confidant but ultimately my coach, it all became much more real. I left saying that I would delay making a final decision until after the Test match. At no stage during that conversation, by the way, was Kevin Pietersen's name mentioned. This was a completely different and separate matter.

Later that day, I had a call from Andy Flower.

'Straussy, I don't know how to tell you this, but I have received some information that KP has sent some text messages to the South African players, criticising you and perhaps even giving them information on how to get you out. A newspaper is apparently in possession of the texts and intends to print them.'

I was completely dumbfounded. I wasn't actually all that bothered about him sending texts to the opposition players. He knew a few of the South African players quite well, after all. I certainly did have some issues with him criticising me to members of the team we were currently playing against. That felt like talking out of school, not to mention giving the opposition a way to drive a wedge between Pietersen and myself and the rest of the team. But if he really had given information about how to get me out, well, that amounted to treachery and I could never forgive him for that.

The sudden text-message saga had certainly put a new complexion on the evening's meeting with KP. When we met, he seemed completely contrite about what had happened the week before and, having had time to consider the repercussions of turning his back on English cricket, he reaffirmed his willingness and commitment to come back into the fold. Without the sudden appearance of those text messages – which had come to light a little too conveniently from a South African point of view for my liking – the matter would have been well on the way to being solved. We could all have forgiven and forgotten.

Unfortunately, without Kevin either refuting that he had sent the messages or, for that matter, apologising for sending them, and letting us know the substance of them, it was impossible to move on. A few gripes at your captain when you are feeling vulnerable might be forgivable, but helping the opposition team to get him out is another matter altogether. The issue was further complicated by the fact that we weren't entirely sure if the newspapers were actually in possession of the text messages or had just been shown them. For some ridiculous and bizarre reason, the contents of a few text messages had become pivotal to KP's further involvement with the England side.

In the meantime, KP and his representatives, mindful of some of the bad PR he had received, had put together a YouTube video, in which he stated his commitment to English cricket. The ECB requested that he delay releasing the video until the text-message saga had been addressed. For whatever reason KP put out the video against the wishes of the ECB, choosing an unfortunate time to do so, while Mo Farah was in the process of winning 5000 metres gold at the Olympics.

From that moment on, clear battle lines were drawn between

Pietersen and the ECB. What began as an issue about IPL participation had apparently turned into a PR/legal battle for both sides to gain public support and cover themselves in case of litigation.

I watched it all unfold, prior to my final Test, and became increasingly tired and exasperated by the legal speak being used. To me, it was a clear case of someone overstepping the boundaries of what was acceptable from a team point of view. If KP wanted to come back into the fold, then he would have to apologise and accept some punishment for his actions. Then we could move on.

The fact that he, and his representatives, were engaging in a deliberate PR damage-limitation exercise worried me greatly. It gave the impression that he was more concerned with coming out of the saga in the best possible light than with doing the right thing by his team-mates.

With the clock ticking down to the start of the Lord's Test, it became apparent that we were not going to get to the bottom of the issue before the start of the game. There was no option, therefore, other than to leave him out of the side.

After all has been said and done, I feel very uncomfortable with the notion that it was issues between KP and myself that led to the whole circus that followed. Up to the Headingley Test match against South Africa, we had never had any significant fall-outs. For sure, the text messages were a big problem, but they actually stemmed from a longstanding and far bigger issue between Kevin and the board.

Subsequent to being dropped for the Test match, he admitted sending 'provocative' text messages and after the match came to my house and sincerely apologised for doing so. I accepted his apology and hold no grudges against him. I am also confident, in retrospect, that he did not give them information to get me out.

The far greater issue, even at the time of the Test match, was one of trust. There were many people involved with English cricket, including myself, who felt particularly let down about a lot of things that had taken place in the previous two weeks. Stuff that should have stayed in the dressing room had been brought out into the open and played out in front of the media. The one nagging frustration I still have is that all of that time, effort and commitment from our players over a three-year period to make our environment special and different was undermined in that one episode.

I am sitting on the balcony as the final wicket at Lord's falls. Steve Finn is well caught by the bucketlike hands of Jacques Kallis at slip. A brilliant rearguard action by Matt Prior, Graeme Swann, Stuart Broad and particularly Jonny Bairstow, who scored two fifties in the match as Pietersen's replacement, has not been enough to stave off defeat. Although we ran the South Africans close, they deserve the 2–0 series win.

Deep down, I am conscious that I have just seen the final action of my career, although I am trying my hardest not to allow my emotions to come to the surface. I lead the team down to the Long Room to shake the South African players by the hand and congratulate them on the win. I negotiate all the usual post-match rigmarole, from the post-match presentation to the press conference, without too much trouble.

When I arrive back in the dressing room, though, things become much tougher. The players have all clubbed together to get me a couple of mementos to recognise the fact that I have just completed my 100th Test match for England. Firstly, Jimmy Anderson stands up and says a few touching words about my contribution to English cricket, before handing over the first twenty of a century of bottles of wine. Shortly afterwards, he is followed by Graeme Swann, who again talks a little about the extent of the achievement and the great career I have had, before presenting me with a painting of the pavilion at Lord's, signed by all the players.

I am the only one in the room, apart from Andy Flower perhaps, who understands the real significance of what is going on. The guys, without knowing it, are saying their goodbyes. Although a part of me wants to tell everyone that I have reached the end of the road, I decided before the Test match that I should give myself at least a couple of days afterwards to see how I feel and let the emotion of the last few weeks subside before committing to a decision. Once you have made it, you can't go back.

Instead, I stand up to thank the players and management for their gifts. I tell them how honoured I feel to have had the oppor-tunity to play for England 100 times. I also mention all the many wonderful moments I have been a part of on the cricket pitch. But the real pleasure has come from the people I have played with. Bonds are formed between groups of men that will never leave you. I tell them how thankful I am to everyone in the room for all the help and support they have given me as captain.

Choking back the tears, I finish by declaring, quite truthfully, that I have never been as proud to lead an England team as I have during this Test match. The way the players reacted to the media storm outside, the way they went about their business on the pitch, their never-say-die attitude, their willingness to stand up for what we believed to be right – this is the ultimate testament to the people sitting in front of me.

I did not finish as England captain with a win, but my final memory will always be a fond one.

England v Pakistan in UAE 2011-12

DICS, Dubai. 17-19 January 2012
England 192 (M.J. Prior 70*, A.J. Strauss 19; Saeed Ajmal 7-55) and 160
(I.J.L. Trott 49, A.J. Strauss 6; Umar Gul 4-63)
Pakistan 338 (Mohammad Hafeez 88, Adnan Akmal 61, Taufeeq Umar
58, Misbah-ul-Haq 52; G.P. Swann 4-107) and 15-0
Pakistan won by 10 wickets.

2nd Test. Sheikh Zayed Stadium, Abu Dhabi. 25-28 January 2012
Pakistan 257 (Misbah-ul-Haq 84, Asad Shafiq 58; S.C.J. Broad 4-47) and
214 (M.S. Panesar 6-62)
England 327 (A.N. Cook 94, I.J.L. Trott 74, S.C.J. Broad 58, A.J. Strauss
11; Saeed Ajmal 4-108) and 72 (A.J. Strauss 32; Abdur Rehman 6-25)
Pakistan won by 72 runs.

3rd Test. DICS, Dubai. 3-6 February 2012
Pakistan 99 (Asad Shafiq 45; S.C.J. Broad 4-36) and 365 (Azhar Ali 157,
Younis Khan 127; M.S. Panesar 5-124)
England 141 (A.J. Strauss 56; Abdur Rehman 5-40) and 252 (A.N. Cook
49, M.J. Prior 49*, A.J. Strauss 26; Umar Gul 4-61, Saeed Ajmal 4-67)
Pakistan won by 71 runs.

Pakistan won the series 3-0.

England in Sri Lanka 2011–12

1st Test. GIS, Galle. 26–29 March 2012

Sri Lanka 318 (D.P.M.D. Jayawardene 180; J.M. Anderson 5–72) and 214
(H.A.P.W. Jayawardene 61*; G.P. Swann 6–82)
England 193 (I.R. Bell 52, **A.J. Strauss 26**; H.M.R.K.B. Herath 6–74) and
264 (I.J.L. Trott 112, **A.J. Strauss 27**; H.M.R.K.B. Herath 6–97)
Sri Lanka won by 75 runs.

2nd Test. P. Sara Oval, Colombo. 3–7 April 2012

Sri Lanka 275 (D.P.M.D. Jayawardene 105, A.D. Mathews 57, T.T.
Samaraweera 54; G.P. Swann 4–75) and 278 (D.P.M.D. Jayawardene 64;
G.P. Swann 6–106)
England 460 (K.P. Pietersen 151, A.N. Cook 94, I.J.L. Trott 64, **A.J. Strauss
61**; H.M.R.K.B. Herath 6–133) and 97–2 (**A.J. Strauss 0**)

England won by 8 wickets.

Series drawn 1–1.

West Indies in England 2012 – The Wisden Trophy

1st Test. Lord's, London. 17–21 May 2012
West Indies 243 (S. Chanderpaul 87*; S.C.J. Broad 7–72) and 345 (S.
Chanderpaul 91, M.N. Samuels 86; S.C.J. Broad 4–93)
England 398 (**A.J. Strauss 122**, I.R. Bell 61, I.J.L. Trott 58) and 193–5
(A.N. Cook 79, I.R. Bell 63*, **A.J. Strauss 1**)
England won by 5 wickets.

2nd Test. Trent Bridge, Nottingham. 25–28 May 2012
West Indies 370 (M.N. Samuels 117, D.J.G. Sammy 106; T.T. Bresnan 4–104)
and 165 (M.N. Samuels 76*; J.M. Anderson 4–43, T.T. Bresnan 4–37)
England 428 (**A.J. Strauss 141**, K.P. Pietersen 80) and 111–1 (**A.J.
Strauss 45**)
England won by 9 wickets.

3rd Test. Edgbaston, Birmingham. 7–11 June 2012
West Indies 426 (D. Ramdin 107*, T.L. Best 95, M.N. Samuels 76; G.
Onions 4–88)
England 221–5 (K.P. Pietersen 78, I.R. Bell 76*, **A.J. Strauss 17**)
Match drawn.

England won the series 2–0.

South Africa in England 2012 – The Basil D'Oliveira Trophy

1st Test. The Oval, London. 19–23 July 2012

England 385 (A.N. Cook 115, I.J.L. Trott 71, M.J. Prior 60, **A.J. Strauss 0**; M. Morkel 4–72) and 240 (I.R. Bell 55, **A.J. Strauss 27**; D.W. Steyn 5–56)

South Africa 637–2 dec (H.M. Amla 311*, J.H. Kallis 182*, G.C. Smith 131)

South Africa won by an innings and 12 runs.

2nd Test. Headingley, Leeds. 2–6 August 2012

South Africa 419 (A.N. Petersen 182, G.C. Smith 52) and 258–9 dec (J.A. Rudolph 69, G.C. Smith 52; S.C.J. Broad 5–69)

England 425 (K.P. Pietersen 149, M.J. Prior 68, **A.J. Strauss 37**) and 130–4 (A.N. Cook 46, **A.J. Strauss 12**)

Match drawn.

3rd Test. Lord's, London. 16–20 August 2012

South Africa 309 (J.P. Duminy 51, V.D. Philander 61; S.T. Finn 4–75) and 351 (H.M. Amla 121; S.T. Finn 4–74)

England 315 (J.M. Bairstow 95, I.R. Bell 58, **A.J. Strauss 20**; M. Morkel 4–80, D.W. Steyn 4–94) and 294 (M.J. Prior 73, I.J.L. Trott 63, J.M. Bairstow 54; V.D. Philander 5–30)

South Africa won by 51 runs.

South Africa won the series 2–0.

19

THE FUTURE

It is important for all cricketers to understand that their lives do not come to an end alongside their careers. Although the great game of cricket has been an immense part of my life for the last fifteen years, I have never felt that it has defined me as a person. My best friends today are the same guys who were my best friends well before I hopped onto the life-changing conveyor belt of international cricket.

Also, while it is impossible to have quite the same relationship with players when you are no longer in the thick of competition, my family, and especially my wife, Ruth, were there before it all started and remain now that it has all finished. In a way, I have lost a little of the intimacy that I had with my cricketing family but regained it with my real family. I know that my boys, Sam and Luca, are particularly pleased to have their dad around a bit more often.

That being said, any professional sportsman or sportswoman has to struggle through some difficult emotions on retirement. It is almost impossible to replace the adrenalin surges that accompany a Test century or an Ashes series win. We all have to come to terms with the fact that life has changed. That is a different matter, though, from admitting that your best days are behind you. At the age of thirty-six, I feel far too young to spend the rest of my life talking about the 2010–11 Ashes as my most significant contribution to the planet. In many ways that would be sadder than retiring.

In the days following the press conference at which I announced my retirement from professional cricket, when I was somewhat surprisingly applauded out of the room by my good old friends in the Fourth Estate, I started to let my mind wander towards the future.

On the immediate horizon was a much-needed holiday, before committing to the hugely challenging and rewarding quest to run the London Marathon with Ruth, to raise some money for the Lord's Taverners. Apart from the obvious good cause, it was an excellent way to remain focused and keep fit. In some ways, it was like preparing for another Test series, and it served to soften the blow of no longer playing and having to endure a winter in the UK for the first time in over a decade. It also proved to be a very enjoyable shared experience with Ruth. I am just grateful that she didn't beat me over the line.

If the truth be known, I am not sure where my path lies in the future. For the time being, I am keen to try out a rich and varied array of opportunities.

Cricket is always likely to play a significant part in my life. The ECB have been good enough to keep me involved with the long-term planning of the English game, which I am both passionate and excited about. Also, I am looking forward to playing a role in the ICC Cricket Committee. In my view, the ICC is a much-maligned organisation, which struggles to lead the world game more because of the undue influence of individual cricketing boards than because of its own inadequacies. Hopefully, I can make some sort of contribution.

Perhaps inevitably, I tried my hand at commentary for Sky TV for the 2013 Ashes series, as well as writing a column for the *Sunday Times*. For a cricket fan like me, the prospect of having the best seat in the house was too hard to resist.

My experiences in the commentary box have definitely allowed me to look at the role of the media from a different point of view. While players get understandably defensive if any criticism comes their way, commentators are often merely reacting to whatever the topic of the day might be. There is actually far more positivity and genuine support for the England team than players think. Although it would never have been feasible, it would have done me good to spend a day or two up in the commentary box while I was still a player. It might have saved me from a little of the stress and frustration I experienced when going through the various dips in my career.

The technicalities of broadcasting certainly took a little getting used to, but I thoroughly enjoyed being part of a team of mainly ex-England captains, who unsurprisingly were just as passionate and intrigued by the game of cricket as I am.

It was also fascinating to watch the 2013 Ashes series unfold while no longer being directly involved in proceedings. Most neutral observers would have predicted an England win, and in that sense the series yielded few surprises. Australia, reeling before the series had even begun after a number of self-inflicted off-field gaffes, as well as suffering the ignominy of a 4–0 whitewash defeat in India earlier in the year, performed better than expected – especially after losing the second Test match at Lord's so heavily.

The eventual 3–0 series result flattered England a little. However, it would be hard to argue that they weren't the better side over the course of the five Test matches. It shows how far the relative fortunes of the sides have changed since 2005 that Australia's defeat was met with some relief by Australian supporters, while England fans were left feeling a little short-changed.

For Alastair Cook, it was the first time he had had to deal with the huge challenges in terms of pressure, expectation and non-stop demands that face any England captain during an Ashes series, and he will be delighted he was able to fulfil the boyhood dream of lifting the Ashes urn at The Oval at the first time of asking. Many past England captains would have given their left arm to match what he and the rest of his players achieved.

As his former opening partner, and a close friend, I was delighted to see him withstand the stress and lead England to victory. With so little time before the return leg starts in Brisbane, he is no doubt preparing himself for a busy winter.

I have to admit that I felt a tinge of jealousy as the players huddled together after securing the series at Durham. There are many things I don't miss about international cricket, but those times as a group, when all the players come together to celebrate a hard-earned victory, are the moments that any player savours. Nothing can replace them.

Aside from cricket, I have a few opportunities in the commercial world that I am keen to follow, including setting up a consultancy business focusing on leadership and performance, called Think Half Full.

In the long term I will be looking to commit my time to one or two of these pursuits but not to all of them. I am not sure it is possible to keep so many balls in the air without one of them dropping.

One new career that has been mooted in the press is as a politician. I have no idea where this idea came from. Perhaps somebody saw my ability to keep talking through a press conference while actually saying nothing of consequence and reckoned that it would transfer well into the world of politics. While I haven't given the idea a lot of thought, it doesn't feel like the right direction for me. If there was one area in the sport that I didn't particularly warm to, it was the politics, both at domestic and international level.

I suppose I still have a little time on my side. While I will now always be an ex-England cricketer, I can never be sure what opportunities lie ahead. If they are anything like the ones I have had so far in my life, I will count myself incredibly fortunate.

In the meantime, my son is nagging me to bowl at him in the garden . . .

CAREER STATISTICS

Compiled by Benedict Bermange

TEST CAREER

Overall record

	M	Inns	NO	Runs	HS	Avge	SR	100	50	Ct
Test matches	100	178	6	7037	177	40.91	48.92	21	27	121

By opponent

	M	Inns	NO	Runs	HS	Avge	SR	100	50	Ct
Australia	20	36	0	1421	161	39.47	50.58	4	7	21
Bangladesh	4	5	0	263	83	52.60	68.31	0	3	7
India	12	22	1	929	128	44.23	42.61	3	3	13
New Zealand	9	16	0	813	177	50.81	47.04	3	4	15
Pakistan	13	24	1	793	128	34.47	51.22	2	3	13
South Africa	16	30	1	1113	147	38.37	47.14	3	3	12
Sri Lanka	8	13	0	297	61	22.84	46.18	0	2	18
West Indies	18	32	3	1408	169	48.55	51.57	6	2	22

By country

	M	Inns	NO	Runs	HS	Avge	SR	100	50	Ct
Australia	10	17	0	554	110	32.58	47.02	1	4	11
England	61	105	3	4045	161	39.65	49.57	10	19	83
India	5	10	1	489	128	54.33	44.45	3	0	4
New Zealand	3	6	0	274	177	45.66	45.36	1	0	6
Pakistan	2	4	0	44	23	11.00	37.60	0	0	1
South Africa	9	17	1	826	147	51.62	50.86	3	2	7
Sri Lanka	2	4	0	114	61	28.50	49.13	0	1	6
United Arab Emirates	3	6	0	150	56	25.00	35.12	0	1	2
West Indies	5	9	1	541	169	67.62	57.37	3	0	1

By continent

	M	Inns	NO	Runs	HS	Avge	SR	100	50	Ct
Africa	9	17	1	826	147	51.62	50.86	3	2	7
Americas	5	9	1	541	169	67.62	57.37	3	0	1
Asia	12	24	1	797	128	34.65	42.48	3	2	13
Australasia	13	23	0	828	177	36.00	46.46	2	4	17
Europe	61	105	3	4045	161	39.65	49.57	10	19	83

Home and away

	M	Inns	NO	Runs	HS	Avge	SR	100	50	Ct
Home	61	105	3	4045	161	39.65	49.57	10	19	83
Away	36	67	3	2842	177	44.40	49.01	11	7	36
Neutral	3	6	0	150	56	25.00	35.12	0	1	2

By year

	M	Inns	NO	Runs	HS	Avge	SR	100	50	Ct
2004	9	18	2	971	137	60.68	50.89	4	4	14
2005	12	22	0	789	147	35.86	52.18	3	1	12
2006	14	26	0	1031	128	39.65	49.97	3	3	16
2007	8	15	0	432	96	28.80	47.21	0	3	9
2008	12	21	1	972	177	48.60	43.54	4	3	15
2009	14	24	2	1172	169	53.27	54.13	4	4	9
2010	12	20	1	657	110	34.57	52.06	1	5	17
2011	8	11	0	316	87	28.72	44.25	0	2	15
2012	11	21	0	697	141	33.19	43.21	2	2	14

By batting position

	Inns	NO	Runs	HS	Avge	SR	100	50	
1	119	4	4381	169	38.09	47.15	11	20	
2	52	2	2360	147	47.20	52.95	9	7	
3	6	0	253	177	42.16	48.74	1	0	
4	1	0	43	43	43.00	36.44	0	0	

By team innings

	Inns	NO	Runs	HS	Avge	SR	100	50	Ct
1	100	1	4394	169	44.38	49.93	13	18	76
2	78	5	2643	177	36.20	47.32	8	9	31

By match innings

	Inns	NO	Runs	HS	Avge	SR	100	50	Ct
1	55	1	2448	169	45.33	51.95	9	4	36
2	45	0	1946	141	43.24	47.61	4	14	40
3	42	0	1638	177	39.00	46.81	7	3	32
4	36	5	1005	106	32.41	48.17	1	6	13

By result

	M	Inns	NO	Runs	HS	Avge	SR	100	50	Ct
Won	47	79	4	3721	177	49.61	52.49	11	19	73
Lost	26	52	0	1312	123	25.23	40.92	2	5	20
Drawn	27	47	2	2004	169	44.53	48.99	8	3	28

By series stage

	M	Inns	NO	Runs	HS	Avge	SR	100	50	Ct
1st Test	30	55	2	2384	137	44.98	49.31	8	7	39
2nd Test	29	50	3	1623	161	34.53	46.31	4	6	41
3rd Test	22	39	0	1552	177	39.79	48.98	5	6	23
4th Test	13	23	1	905	147	41.13	50.30	2	5	11
5th Test	6	11	0	573	142	52.09	53.10	2	3	7

By captain

	M	Inns	NO	Runs	HS	Avge	SR	100	50	Ct
A Flintoff	11	21	0	640	128	30.47	43.74	1	2	11
KP Pietersen	3	6	1	316	123	63.20	45.79	2	1	1
AJ Strauss	50	85	3	3343	169	40.76	50.83	9	14	60
ME Trescothick	2	4	0	227	112	56.75	49.24	1	1	2
MP Vaughan	34	62	2	2511	177	41.85	48.34	8	9	47

As captain/as player

	M	Inns	NO	Runs	HS	Avge	SR	100	50	Ct
As captain	50	85	3	3343	169	40.76	50.83	9	14	60
As player	50	93	3	3694	177	41.04	47.31	12	13	61

Tests – series by series

	M	Inns	NO	Runs	HS	Avge	SR	100	50	Ct
New Zealand in England 2004	3	6	0	273	112	45.50	51.80	1	2	4
West Indies in England 2004	4	8	1	317	137	45.28	47.66	1	1	7
England in South Africa 2004–05	5	10	1	656	147	72.88	50.15	3	1	5
Bangladesh in England 2005	2	2	0	77	69	38.50	62.60	0	1	3
Australia in England 2005	5	10	0	393	129	39.30	57.79	2	0	6
England in Pakistan 2005–06	2	4	0	44	23	11.00	37.60	0	0	1
England in India 2005–06	3	6	0	237	128	39.50	44.13	1	0	4
Sri Lanka in England 2006	3	5	0	156	55	31.20	45.88	0	1	4
Pakistan in England 2006	4	7	0	444	128	63.42	63.70	2	1	5
England in Australia 2006–07	5	10	0	247	50	24.70	42.15	0	1	3
West Indies in England 2007	4	7	0	168	77	24.00	52.01	0	1	5
India in England 2007	3	6	0	211	96	35.16	42.62	0	2	4
England in New Zealand 2007–08	3	6	0	274	177	45.66	45.36	1	0	6
New Zealand in England 2008	3	4	0	266	106	66.50	44.55	1	2	5
South Africa in England 2008	4	7	0	180	58	25.71	38.46	0	1	4
England in India 2008–09	2	4	1	252	123	84.00	44.76	2	0	0
England in West Indies 2008–09	5	9	1	541	169	67.62	57.37	3	0	1
West Indies in England 2009	2	3	1	56	26	28.00	49.12	0	0	4
Australia in England 2009	5	9	0	474	161	52.66	49.84	1	3	4
England in South Africa 2009–10	4	7	0	170	54	24.28	53.79	0	1	2
Bangladesh in England 2010	2	3	0	186	83	62.00	70.99	0	2	4
Pakistan in England 2010	4	7	1	155	53	25.83	50.48	0	1	5
England in Australia 2010–11	5	7	0	307	110	43.85	51.85	1	3	8
Sri Lanka in England 2011	3	4	0	27	20	6.75	38.02	0	0	8
India in England 2011	4	6	0	229	87	38.16	39.14	0	1	5
England v Pakistan in UAE 2011–12	3	6	0	150	56	25.00	35.12	0	1	2
England in Sri Lanka 2011–12	2	4	0	114	61	28.50	49.13	0	1	6
West Indies in England 2012	3	5	0	326	141	65.20	47.59	2	0	5
South Africa in England 2012	3	6	0	107	37	17.83	39.77	0	0	1

Tests – match by match

Start date	Opponent	Venue	Bat posn	How out	Runs	Mins	Balls	Fours	Sixes	Ct
20/5/2004	New Zealand	Lord's	2	c MH Richardson b DL Vettori	112	305	215	13	0	1
			2	run out (CL Cairns)	83	217	171	13	0	0
3/6/2004	New Zealand	Leeds	2	c DR Tuffey b DL Vettori	62	156	114	7	0	1
			2	c NJ Astle b DR Tuffey	10	21	12	2	0	1
10/6/2004	New Zealand	Nottingham	2	c BB McCullum b CL Cairns	0	6	3	0	0	1
			2	lbw b CL Cairns	6	11	12	1	0	0
22/7/2004	West Indies	Lord's	2	c RD Jacobs b OAC Banks	137	298	202	20	0	0
			2	c RR Sarwan b PT Collins	35	133	103	0	0	0
29/7/2004	West Indies	Birmingham	2	c RD Jacobs b JJC Lawson	24	80	40	5	0	0
			2	c RD Jacobs b JJC Lawson	5	39	22	0	0	2
12/8/2004	West Indies	Manchester	2	b DJ Bravo	90	291	227	8	0	2
			2	c S Chanderpaul b PT Collins	12	43	27	2	0	1
19/8/2004	West Indies	The Oval	2	c FH Edwards b JJC Lawson	14	75	44	2	0	2
			2	not out	0	3	0	0	0	0
17/12/2004	South Africa	Port Elizabeth	2	c AB de Villiers b SM Pollock	126	304	228	17	0	2
			2	not out	94	172	134	12	1	0
26/12/2004	South Africa	Durban	2	c M Ntini b N Boje	25	109	69	5	0	0
			2	c M van Jaarsveld b M Ntini	136	381	285	16	0	0
2/1/2005	South Africa	Cape Town	2	b M Ntini	45	144	105	4	0	0
			2	lbw b N Boje	39	136	107	3	0	1
13/1/2005	South Africa	Johannesburg	2	c JH Kallis b SM Pollock	147	355	250	23	1	1
			2	c AB de Villiers b M Ntini	0	5	4	0	0	0
21/1/2005	South Africa	Centurion	2	c MV Boucher b A Nel	44	192	124	5	0	0
			2	c JH Kallis b M Ntini	0	6	2	0	0	0
26/5/2005	Bangladesh	Lord's	2	lbw b Mashrafe Mortaza	69	143	93	10	0	1
					–	–	–	–	–	–
3/6/2005	Bangladesh	Chester-le-Street	2	lbw b Mashrafe Mortaza	8	34	30	1	0	0
					–	–	–	–	–	–
21/7/2005	Australia	Lord's	2	c SK Warne b GD McGrath	2	28	21	0	0	1
			2	c and b B Lee	37	115	67	6	0	0
4/8/2005	Australia	Birmingham	2	b SK Warne	48	113	76	10	0	1
			2	b SK Warne	6	28	12	1	0	0
11/8/2005	Australia	Manchester	2	b B Lee	6	43	28	0	0	0
			2	c DR Martyn b GD McGrath	106	246	158	9	2	0

Start date	Opponent	Venue	Bat posn	How out	Runs	Mins	Balls	Fours	Sixes	Ct
25/8/2005	Australia	Nottingham	2	c ML Hayden b SK Warne	35	99	64	4	0	2
			2	c MJ Clarke b SK Warne	23	68	37	3	0	0
8/9/2005	Australia	The Oval	2	c SM Katich b SK Warne	129	351	210	17	0	2
			2	c SM Katich b SK Warne	1	16	7	0	0	0
12/11/2005	Pakistan	Multan	2	lbw b Mohammad Sami	9	18	14	2	0	1
			2	c Hasan Raza b Danish Kaneria	23	91	61	2	0	0
20/11/2005	Pakistan	Faisalabad	2	b Naved-ul-Hasan	12	57	36	1	0	0
			2	b Naved-ul-Hasan	0	11	6	0	0	0
1/3/2006	India	Nagpur	1	c VVS Laxman b S Sreesanth	28	71	64	5	0	3
			1	c MS Dhoni b IK Pathan	46	129	113	6	0	1
9/3/2006	India	Mohali	1	c MS Dhoni b IK Pathan	18	46	38	1	0	0
			1	c MS Dhoni b A Kumble	13	102	64	0	0	0
18/3/2006	India	Mumbai	1	c MS Dhoni b Harbhajan Singh	128	329	240	17	1	0
			1	c MS Dhoni b MM Patel	4	26	18	0	0	1
11/5/2006	Sri Lanka	Lord's	2	c DPMD Jayawardene b M Muralitharan	48	119	97	9	0	0
					–	–	–	–	–	–
25/5/2006	Sri Lanka	Birmingham	2	run out (TT Samaraweera)	30	95	65	5	0	1
			2	c DPMD Jayawardene b M Muralitharan	16	49	36	2	0	1
2/6/2006	Sri Lanka	Nottingham	2	b WPUJC Vaas	7	37	28	0	0	1
			2	c DPMD Jayawardene b M Muralitharan	55	147	114	6	0	0
13/7/2006	Pakistan	Lord's	2	lbw b Abdul Razzaq	30	60	44	5	0	1
			2	c Imran Farhat b Danish Kaneria	128	300	214	13	0	0
27/7/2006	Pakistan	Manchester	2	c Kamran Akmal b Abdul Razzaq	42	120	85	6	0	1
					–	–	–	–	–	–
4/8/2006	Pakistan	Leeds	2	c Younis Khan b Shahid Nazir	36	75	43	5	0	0
			2	c Kamran Akmal b Mohammad Sami	116	250	171	16	0	0
17/8/2006	Pakistan	The Oval	2	c Kamran Akmal b Mohammad Asif	38	86	57	7	0	2
			2	lbw b Danish Kaneria	54	122	83	9	0	0
23/11/2006	Australia	Brisbane	1	c MEK Hussey b GD McGrath	12	25	21	2	0	1
			1	c b SR Clark	11	51	31	1	0	0
1/12/2006	Australia	Adelaide	1	c DR Martyn b SR Clark	14	63	44	0	0	0
			1	c MEK Hussey b SK Warne	34	125	79	3	0	2
14/12/2006	Australia	Perth	1	c AC Gilchrist b SR Clark	42	101	71	6	0	0
			1	lbw b B Lee	0	2	4	0	0	0
26/12/2006	Australia	Melbourne	1	b SK Warne	50	206	132	1	0	0
			1	c AC Gilchrist b B Lee	31	173	107	2	0	0

Start date	Opponent	Venue	Bat posn	How out	Runs	Mins	Balls	Fours	Sixes	Ct
2/1/2007	Australia	Sydney	1	c AC Gilchrist b B Lee	29	64	52	3	0	0
				lbw b SR Clark	24	68	45	3	0	0
17/5/2007	West Indies	Lord's	1	c DS Smith b DB-L Powell	33	100	70	6	0	0
				c RS Morton b CD Collymore	24	56	55	2	0	2
25/5/2007	West Indies	Leeds	1	c D Ramdin b DB-L Powell	15	35	27	2	0	0
7/6/2007	West Indies	Manchester	1	lbw b JE Taylor	6	11	6	0	0	2
				lbw b FH Edwards	0	2	4	0	0	0
15/6/2007	West Indies	Chester-le-Street	1	c D Ramdin b FH Edwards	77	169	136	11	0	0
				b DB-L Powell	13	33	25	1	0	1
19/7/2007	India	Lord's	1	c RS Dravid b A Kumble	96	256	186	16	0	0
				c SR Tendulkar b Z Khan	18	47	41	3	0	0
27/7/2007	India	Nottingham	1	c SR Tendulkar b Z Khan	4	9	9	1	0	0
				c MS Dhoni b Z Khan	55	198	133	6	0	1
9/8/2007	India	The Oval	1	c S Sreesanth b Z Khan	6	18	13	1	0	2
				c VVS Laxman b RP Singh	32	137	113	6	0	2
5/3/2008	New Zealand	Hamilton	4	b DL Vettori	43	130	118	5	0	1
			3	c BB McCullum b KD Mills	2	30	16	0	0	2
13/3/2008	New Zealand	Wellington	3	c MS Sinclair b KD Mills	8	39	33	1	0	0
			3	lbw b JDP Oram	44	137	88	3	0	0
22/3/2008	New Zealand	Napier	3	c JM How b TG Southee	0	8	6	0	0	2
				c MD Bell b JS Patel	177	481	343	25	0	1
15/5/2008	New Zealand	Lord's	1	lbw b JDP Oram	63	231	174	6	0	1
23/5/2008	New Zealand	Manchester	1	c BB McCullum b IE O'Brien	60	174	140	5	0	0
5/6/2008	New Zealand	Nottingham	1	c LRPL Taylor b IE O'Brien	106	278	186	12	0	0
				c LRPL Taylor b KD Mills	37	122	97	5	0	1
10/7/2008	South Africa	Lord's	1	lbw b M Morkel	44	179	131	6	0	1
18/7/2008	South Africa	Leeds	1	c MV Boucher b M Morkel	27	102	65	4	0	0
				c MV Boucher b M Ntini	0	14	13	0	0	1
30/7/2008	South Africa	Birmingham	1	hit wicket b A Nel	20	92	67	2	0	0
				c JH Kallis b M Morkel	25	95	65	5	0	0
7/8/2008	South Africa	The Oval	1	c GC Smith b M Ntini	6	16	20	1	0	1
				c GC Smith b PL Harris	58	164	107	6	0	1

Start date	Opponent	Venue	Bat posn	How out	Runs	Mins	Balls	Fours	Sixes	Ct
11/12/2008	India	Chennai	1	c and b A Mishra	123	356	233	15	0	0
			1	c VVS Laxman b Harbhajan Singh	108	397	244	8	0	0
19/12/2008	India	Mohali	1	lbw b Z Khan	0	1	3	0	0	0
			1	not out	21	103	83	1	0	0
4/2/2009	West Indies	Kingston	1	c D Ramdin b JE Taylor	7	20	15	1	0	0
			1	c D Ramdin b JE Taylor	9	69	50	0	0	0
13/2/2009	West Indies	North Sound	1	not out	6	14	8	0	0	0
					—	—	—	—	—	—
15/2/2009	West Indies	St John's	1	c and b FH Edwards	169	346	278	24	1	0
			1	c DS Smith b FH Edwards	14	23	21	2	0	0
26/2/2009	West Indies	Bridgetown	1	b DB-L Powell	142	249	210	18	1	0
			1	b CH Gayle	38	101	72	5	0	1
6/3/2009	West Indies	Port-of-Spain	1	b FH Edwards	142	368	271	11	0	0
			1	c and b CH Gayle	14	25	18	2	0	1
6/5/2009	West Indies	Lord's	1	c D Ramdin b JE Taylor	16	32	24	2	0	0
			1	not out	14	29	24	2	0	2
14/5/2009	West Indies	Chester-le-Street	1	c D Ramdin b CH Gayle	26	95	66	4	0	0
					—	—	—	—	—	—
8/7/2009	Australia	Cardiff	1	c MJ Clarke b MG Johnson	30	90	60	4	0	2
			1	c BJ Haddin b NM Hauritz	17	78	54	1	0	1
16/7/2009	Australia	Lord's	1	b BW Hilfenhaus	161	370	268	22	0	0
			1	c MJ Clarke b NM Hauritz	32	62	48	4	0	0
30/7/2009	Australia	Birmingham	1	c GA Manou b BW Hilfenhaus	69	175	134	11	0	0
7/8/2009	Australia	Leeds	1	c MJ North b PM Siddle	3	16	17	0	0	1
			1	lbw b BW Hilfenhaus	32	97	78	4	0	0
20/8/2009	Australia	The Oval	1	c BJ Haddin b BW Hilfenhaus	55	128	101	11	0	0
			1	c MJ Clarke b MJ North	75	226	191	8	0	1
16/12/2009	South Africa	Centurion	1	b M Ntini	46	138	87	6	0	0
			1	c MV Boucher b M Morkel	1	5	3	0	0	0
26/12/2009	South Africa	Durban	1	b M Morkel	54	80	67	9	0	1
					—	—	—	—	—	—
3/1/2010	South Africa	Cape Town	1	c MV Boucher b M Morkel	2	3	6	0	0	1
			1	c HM Amla b PL Harris	45	166	107	7	0	1
14/1/2010	South Africa	Johannesburg	1	c HM Amla b DW Steyn	0	1	1	0	0	1
			1	lbw b WD Parnell	22	59	45	3	0	0

Start date	Opponent	Venue	Bat posn	How out	Runs	Mins	Balls	Fours	Sixes	Ct
27/5/2010	Bangladesh	Lord's	1	b Mahmudullah	83	192	129	8	1	2
			1	c Mushfiqur Rahim b Shakib Al Hasan	82	112	88	6	0	2
4/6/2010	Bangladesh	Manchester	1	c Imrul Kayes b Shafiul Islam	21	46	45	4	0	1
					–	–	–	–	–	0
29/7/2010	Pakistan	Nottingham	1	c Kamran Akmal b Mohammad Aamer	45	107	75	6	0	1
			1	c Kamran Akmal b Mohammad Aamer	0	2	3	0	0	0
6/8/2010	Pakistan	Birmingham	1	c Zulqarnain Haider b Mohammad Aamer	25	62	40	2	0	1
			1	not out	53	152	114	4	0	3
18/8/2010	Pakistan	The Oval	1	c Kamran Akmal b Wahab Riaz	15	50	34	3	0	0
			1	c Yasir Hameed b Mohammad Aamer	4	3	4	1	0	0
26/8/2010	Pakistan	Lord's	1	b Mohammad Asif	13	54	37	0	0	0
					–	–	–	–	–	0
25/11/2010	Australia	Brisbane	1	c MEK Hussey b BW Hilfenhaus	0	2	3	0	0	1
			1	st BJ Haddin b MJ North	110	267	224	15	0	1
3/12/2010	Australia	Adelaide	1	b DE Bollinger	1	4	3	0	0	0
					–	–	–	–	–	1
16/12/2010	Australia	Perth	1	c BJ Haddin b RJ Harris	52	125	102	8	0	0
			1	c RT Ponting b MG Johnson	15	39	35	3	0	0
26/12/2010	Australia	Melbourne	1	c MEK Hussey b PM Siddle	69	232	167	5	0	1
					–	–	–	–	–	1
3/1/2011	Australia	Sydney	1	b BW Hilfenhaus	60	92	58	8	1	2
					–	–	–	–	–	0
26/5/2011	Sri Lanka	Cardiff	1	c DPMD Jayawardene b RAS Lakmal	20	79	47	2	0	1
					–	–	–	–	–	3
3/6/2011	Sri Lanka	Lord's	1	lbw b UWMBCA Welagedara	4	14	12	1	0	2
			1	lbw b UWMBCA Welagedara	0	1	2	0	0	0
16/6/2011	Sri Lanka	Southampton	1	c NT Paranavitana b UWMBCA Welagedara	3	10	10	0	0	1
					–	–	–	–	–	0
21/7/2011	India	Lord's	1	c I Sharma b Z Khan	22	107	83	2	0	1
			1	lbw b Harbhajan Singh	32	98	70	4	0	0
29/7/2011	India	Nottingham	1	c SK Raina b P Kumar	32	166	98	4	0	0
			1	c MS Dhoni b S Sreesanth	16	84	52	1	0	1
10/8/2011	India	Birmingham	1	b A Mishra	87	231	176	13	0	1
					–	–	–	–	–	1
18/8/2011	India	The Oval	1	c MS Dhoni b S Sreesanth	40	183	106	5	0	0
					–	–	–	–	–	0

Start date	Opponent	Venue	Bat posn	How out	Runs	Mins	Balls	Fours	Sixes	Ct
17/1/2012	Pakistan	Dubai	1	b Saeed Ajmal	19	85	43	1	0	0
			1	c Adnan Akmal b Umar Gul	6	24	16	0	0	0
25/1/2012	Pakistan	Abu Dhabi	1	c Asad Shafiq b Mohammad Hafeez	11	53	42	1	0	1
			1	lbw b Abdur Rehman	32	106	100	3	0	0
3/2/2012	Pakistan	Dubai	1	st Adnan Akmal b Abdur Rehman	56	226	150	5	0	1
			1	lbw b Abdur Rehman	26	101	76	2	0	0
26/3/2012	Sri Lanka	Galle	1	lbw b HMRKB Herath	26	61	40	2	0	1
			1	c TM Dilshan b HMRKB Herath	27	64	60	2	0	1
3/4/2012	Sri Lanka	Colombo-PSS	1	c HAPW Jayawardene b TM Dilshan	61	202	126	4	0	2
			1	b TM Dilshan	0	2	6	0	0	2
17/5/2012	West Indies	Lord's	1	c D Ramdin b KAJ Roach	122	382	258	19	0	1
			1	c KOA Powell b KAJ Roach	1	5	7	0	0	0
25/5/2012	West Indies	Nottingham	1	c D Ramdin b DJG Sammy	141	434	303	22	0	1
			1	c DM Bravo b MN Samuels	45	91	72	7	0	0
7/6/2012	West Indies	Birmingham	1	c DM Bravo b TL Best	17	70	45	1	0	3
					–	–	–	–	–	0
19/7/2012	South Africa	The Oval	1	lbw b M Morkel	0	3	4	0	0	0
			1	c VD Philander b Imran Tahir	27	126	80	2	0	0
2/8/2012	South Africa	Leeds	1	c AB de Villiers b DW Steyn	37	154	106	7	0	0
			3	c and b J-P Duminy	22	45	33	2	0	0
16/8/2012	South Africa	Lord's	1	b M Morkel	20	46	36	2	0	0
			1	lbw b VD Philander	1	18	10	0	0	1

Test centuries

	Opponent	Venue	Season
177	New Zealand	Napier	2007–08
169 (c)	West Indies	St John's	2008–09
161 (c)	Australia	Lord's	2009
147	South Africa	Johannesburg	2004–05
142 (c)	West Indies	Port-of-Spain	2008–09
142 (c)	West Indies	Bridgetown	2008–09
141 (c)	West Indies	Nottingham	2012
137	West Indies	Lord's	2004
136	South Africa	Durban	2004–05
129	Australia	The Oval	2005
128 (c)	Pakistan	Lord's	2006
128	India	Mumbai	2005–06
126	South Africa	Port Elizabeth	2004–05
123	India	Chennai	2008–09
122 (c)	West Indies	Lord's	2012
116 (c)	Pakistan	Leeds	2006
112	New Zealand	Lord's	2004
110 (c)	Australia	Brisbane	2010–11
108	India	Chennai	2008–09
106	New Zealand	Manchester	2008
106	Australia	Manchester	2005

How he scored his runs

	Number	Runs
Singles	1920	1920
Twos	538	1076
Threes	161	483
Fours	867	3468
Fives	6	30
Sixes	10	60

Batting record against different types of bowling

	Runs	Balls	Fours	Sixes	Outs	Avge	SR
Right-arm seam	4453	9229	593	5	95	46.87	48.25
Left-arm seam	655	1408	88	0	24	27.29	46.52
Off-breaks	739	1679	77	0	22	33.59	44.01
Leg-breaks	467	868	46	2	16	29.19	53.80
Slow left-arm	673	1129	56	3	13	51.77	59.61
Slow left-arm chinamen	50	72	7	0	0		69.44

Bowlers dismissing Andrew Strauss in Tests most often

	Times	Matches
SK Warne	8	10
M Morkel	8	11
M Ntini	7	11
Z Khan	6	6
BW Hilfenhaus	6	9
B Lee	5	10
FH Edwards	5	13
Mohammad Aamer	4	4
SR Clark	4	7
DB-L Powell	4	8
JE Taylor	4	9
JJC Lawson	3	2
Abdur Rehman	3	3
M Muralitharan	3	3
UWMBCA Welagedara	3	3
KD Mills	3	6
Danish Kaneria	3	7
Harbhajan Singh	3	7
GD McGrath	3	8
DL Vettori	3	8
S Sreesanth	3	8
CH Gayle	3	15

Manner of dismissal

	Times
Bowled	25
Caught wicketkeeper	45
Caught fielder	72
Lbw	25
Run out	2
Stumped	2
Other	1

Batting partners in Tests

	Inns	Unb	Runs	Best	Avge	100	50
AN Cook	132	2	5253	229	40.40	14	21
ME Trescothick	52	1	2670	273	52.35	8	12
IR Bell	30	1	1168	187	40.27	3	6
IJL Trott	26	1	1165	181	46.60	4	4
KP Pietersen	36	0	965	144	26.80	1	6
MP Vaughan	23	0	807	142	35.08	1	4
PD Collingwood	17	0	604	214	35.52	2	1
RWT Key	8	0	589	291	73.62	2	1
OA Shah	3	1	438	178	219.00	3	0
GP Thorpe	4	1	382	177	127.33	1	2
A Flintoff	4	0	200	143	50.00	1	0
MA Butcher	6	0	194	86	32.33	0	1
RS Bopara	5	0	147	58	29.40	0	1
N Hussain	1	0	108	108	108.00	1	0
MJ Prior	4	0	72	28	18.00	0	0
TR Ambrose	1	0	63	63	63.00	0	1
GO Jones	2	0	55	47	27.50	0	0
SCJ Broad	2	0	46	31	23.00	0	0
TT Bresnan	1	0	27	27	27.00	0	0
EJG Morgan	2	0	17	13	8.50	0	0
GP Swann	1	0	12	12	12.00	0	0
MJ Hoggard	1	0	9	9	9.00	0	0
JM Anderson	1	0	8	8	8.00	0	0
JM Bairstow	1	0	8	8	8.00	0	0
LE Plunkett	1	0	3	3	3.00	0	0

Tests as captain

Start date	Opponent	Venue	Toss	Decision	Result
13/7/2006	Pakistan	Lord's	Won	Bat	Drawn
27/7/2006	Pakistan	Manchester	Lost	Bat	Won
4/8/2006	Pakistan	Leeds	Won	Bat	Won
17/8/2006	Pakistan	The Oval	Lost	Bowl	Won
17/5/2007	West Indies	Lord's	Lost	Bowl	Drawn
4/2/2009	West Indies	Kingston	Won	Bat	Lost
13/2/2009	West Indies	North Sound	Lost	Bowl	Drawn
15/2/2009	West Indies	St John's	Lost	Bowl	Drawn
26/2/2009	West Indies	Bridgetown	Won	Bat	Drawn
6/3/2009	West Indies	Port-of-Spain	Won	Bat	Drawn
6/5/2009	West Indies	Lord's	Lost	Bowl	Won
14/5/2009	West Indies	Chester-le-Street	Won	Bat	Won
8/7/2009	Australia	Cardiff	Won	Bat	Drawn
16/7/2009	Australia	Lord's	Won	Bat	Won
30/7/2009	Australia	Birmingham	Lost	Bat	Drawn
7/8/2009	Australia	Leeds	Won	Bat	Lost
20/8/2009	Australia	The Oval	Won	Bat	Won
16/12/2009	South Africa	Centurion	Won	Bowl	Drawn
26/12/2009	South Africa	Durban	Lost	Bat	Won
3/1/2010	South Africa	Cape Town	Won	Bowl	Drawn
14/1/2010	South Africa	Johannesburg	Won	Bat	Lost
27/5/2010	Bangladesh	Lord's	Lost	Bowl	Won
4/6/2010	Bangladesh	Manchester	Won	Bat	Won
29/7/2010	Pakistan	Nottingham	Won	Bat	Won
6/8/2010	Pakistan	Birmingham	Lost	Bat	Won
18/8/2010	Pakistan	The Oval	Won	Bat	Lost
26/8/2010	Pakistan	Lord's	Lost	Bowl	Won
25/11/2010	Australia	Brisbane	Won	Bat	Drawn
3/12/2010	Australia	Adelaide	Lost	Bat	Won

16/12/2010	Australia	Perth	Won	Bowl	Lost
26/12/2010	Australia	Melbourne	Won	Bowl	Won
3/1/2011	Australia	Sydney	Lost	Bat	Won
26/5/2011	Sri Lanka	Cardiff	Lost	Bat	Won
3/6/2011	Sri Lanka	Lord's	Lost	Bowl	Drawn
16/6/2011	Sri Lanka	Southampton	Won	Bowl	Drawn
21/7/2011	India	Lord's	Lost	Bowl	Won
29/7/2011	India	Nottingham	Lost	Bowl	Won
10/8/2011	India	Birmingham	Won	Bowl	Won
18/8/2011	India	The Oval	Won	Bat	Won
17/1/2012	Pakistan	Dubai	Won	Bat	Lost
25/1/2012	Pakistan	Abu Dhabi	Lost	Bat	Lost
3/2/2012	Pakistan	Dubai	Lost	Bat	Lost
26/3/2012	Sri Lanka	Galle	Lost	Bat	Lost
3/4/2012	Sri Lanka	Colombo-PSS	Lost	Bat	Won
17/5/2012	West Indies	Lord's	Won	Bowl	Won
25/5/2012	West Indies	Nottingham	Lost	Bat	Won
7/6/2012	West Indies	Birmingham	Won	Bowl	Drawn
19/7/2012	South Africa	The Oval	Won	Bat	Lost
2/8/2012	South Africa	Leeds	Won	Bowl	Drawn
16/8/2012	South Africa	Lord's	Lost	Bat	Lost

Test captaincy summary

Played	Won	Lost	Drawn	%Won	Toss won	Toss lost	TW bat	TW bowl	TL bat	TL bowl
50	24	11	15	48	27	23	18	9	13	10

ONE-DAY INTERNATIONAL CAREER

Overall record

	M	Inns	NO	Runs	HS	Avge	SR	100	50	Ct
ODIs	127	126	8	4205	158	35.63	80.99	6	27	57

By opponent

	M	Inns	NO	Runs	HS	Avge	SR	100	50	Ct
Australia	36	36	1	979	87	27.97	76.36	0	8	18
Bangladesh	8	8	1	610	154	87.14	103.38	2	3	4
India	11	11	2	387	158	43.00	81.81	1	2	2
Ireland	2	2	0	38	34	19.00	76.00	0	0	0
Netherlands	1	1	0	88	88	88.00	106.02	0	1	0
New Zealand	7	7	0	183	61	26.14	62.88	0	2	3
Pakistan	15	15	0	625	126	41.66	86.20	1	5	9
Scotland	1	1	0	61	61	61.00	141.86	0	1	0
South Africa	13	13	1	247	46	20.58	65.00	0	0	7
Sri Lanka	9	9	0	157	45	17.44	67.09	0	0	7
West Indies	19	18	2	725	105	45.31	81.09	2	5	7
Zimbabwe	5	5	1	105	33	26.25	71.42	0	0	0

By country

	M	Inns	NO	Runs	HS	Avge	SR	100	50	Ct
Australia	17	17	0	372	63	21.88	72.79	0	3	11
Bangladesh	1	1	0	18	18	18.00	58.06	0	0	0
England	54	54	4	2235	154	44.70	85.27	4	14	27
India	14	14	1	601	158	46.23	85.00	1	5	4
Ireland	1	1	0	4	4	4.00	30.76	0	0	0
Pakistan	5	5	0	143	94	28.60	78.14	0	1	1
Scotland	1	1	0	61	61	61.00	141.86	0	1	0
South Africa	14	14	1	224	35	17.23	64.55	0	0	9
Sri Lanka	2	2	0	8	5	4.00	28.57	0	0	0
West Indies	14	13	1	459	105	38.25	77.66	1	3	5
Zimbabwe	4	4	1	80	33	26.66	68.37	0	0	0

By continent

	M	Inns	NO	Runs	HS	Avge	SR	100	50	Ct
Africa	18	18	2	304	35	19.00	65.51	0	0	9
Americas	14	13	1	459	105	38.25	77.66	1	3	5
Asia	22	22	1	770	158	36.66	81.13	1	6	5
Australasia	17	17	0	372	63	21.88	72.79	0	3	11
Europe	56	56	4	2300	154	44.23	85.91	4	15	27

Home and away

	M	Inns	NO	Runs	HS	Avge	SR	100	50	Ct
Home	54	54	4	2235	154	44.70	85.27	4	14	27
Away	57	56	4	1498	158	28.80	76.93	2	9	22
Neutral	16	16	0	472	88	29.50	75.64	0	4	8

By year

	M	Inns	NO	Runs	HS	Avge	SR	100	50	Ct
2003	1	1	0	3	3	3.00	33.33	0	0	0
2004	21	20	4	655	100	40.93	75.28	1	4	3
2005	22	22	2	713	152	35.65	81.29	1	3	8
2006	20	20	1	592	78	31.15	76.48	0	6	11
2007	14	14	0	276	55	19.71	65.71	0	1	6
2009	21	21	1	647	105	32.35	78.14	1	4	10
2010	14	14	0	806	154	57.57	95.95	2	6	11
2011	14	14	0	513	158	36.64	89.37	1	3	8

By competition

	M	Inns	NO	Runs	HS	Avge	SR	100	50	Ct
World Cup	11	11	0	417	158	37.90	86.33	1	1	3
ICC Champions Trophy	11	11	1	266	56	26.60	71.89	0	3	6
Other matches	105	104	7	3522	154	36.30	81.17	5	23	48

By batting position

	Inns	NO	Runs	HS	Avge	SR	100	50
1	64	2	2422	158	39.06	83.80	4	18
2	19	1	631	152	35.05	82.16	1	3
3	13	0	395	94	30.38	73.14	0	3
4	29	5	731	100	30.45	75.36	1	3
5	1	0	26	26	26.00	108.33	0	0

By match innings

	Inns	NO	Runs	HS	Avge	SR	100	50	Ct
Batting first	63	0	1962	154	31.14	77.39	3	12	38
Batting second	63	8	2243	158	40.78	84.41	3	15	19

By result

	M	Inns	NO	Runs	HS	Avge	SR	100	50	Ct
Won	55	55	7	2270	154	47.29	84.92	3	16	29
Tied	3	3	0	162	158	54.00	100.00	1	0	1
No result	4	3	1	27	25	13.50	84.37	0	0	3
Lost	65	65	0	1746	105	26.86	75.09	2	11	24

By captain

	M	Inns	NO	Runs	HS	Avge	SR	100	50	Ct
A Flintoff	14	14	0	289	61	20.64	66.58	0	3	7
AJ Strauss	62	62	2	2367	158	39.45	86.54	4	16	37
ME Trescothick	8	8	0	279	98	34.87	82.05	0	2	1
MP Vaughan	43	42	6	1270	152	35.27	75.46	2	6	12

As captain/as player

	M	Inns	NO	Runs	HS	Avge	SR	100	50	Ct
As captain	62	62	2	2367	158	39.45	86.54	4	16	37
As player	65	64	6	1838	152	31.68	74.80	2	11	20

Bowling

Opponent	Balls	Mdns	Runs	Wkts	BB	Avge	4w	5w	SR Econ
Zimbabwe	6	0	3	0	–	–	–	–	– 3.00

ODIs – series by series

	M	Inns	NO	Runs	HS	Avge	SR	100	50	Ct
England in Sri Lanka 2003–04	1	1	0	3	3	3.00	33.33	0	0	0
England in West Indies 2003–04	5	4	0	172	67	43.00	74.78	0	2	1
NatWest Series in England 2004	5	5	1	256	100	64.00	77.34	1	1	1
India in England 2004	3	3	1	45	41	22.50	69.23	0	0	0
ICC Champions Trophy in England 2004	4	4	1	102	52	34.00	80.31	0	1	1
England in Zimbabwe 2004–05	4	4	1	80	33	26.66	68.37	0	0	0
England in South Africa 2004–05	7	7	1	104	35	17.33	63.41	0	0	4
NatWest Series in England 2005	7	7	1	378	152	63.00	101.88	1	2	2
Australia in England 2005	3	3	0	88	41	29.33	55.34	0	0	1
England in Pakistan 2005–06	5	5	0	143	94	28.60	78.14	0	1	1
England in India 2005–06	6	6	1	174	74	34.80	75.32	0	2	0
England in Ireland 2006	1	1	0	4	4	4.00	30.76	0	0	0
Sri Lanka in England 2006	5	5	0	133	45	26.60	83.64	0	0	5
Pakistan in England 2006	5	5	0	165	78	33.00	81.68	0	2	3
ICC Champions Trophy in India 2006–07	3	3	0	116	56	38.66	68.63	0	2	3
Commonwealth Bank Series in Australia 2006–07	10	10	0	193	55	19.30	65.64	0	1	4
World Cup in West Indies 2006–07	4	4	0	83	46	20.75	65.87	0	0	2
England in West Indies 2008–09	5	5	1	204	105	51.00	86.80	1	1	2
West Indies in England 2009	2	2	0	56	52	28.00	68.29	0	1	2
Australia in England 2009	7	7	0	267	63	38.14	81.40	0	2	1
ICC Champions Trophy in South Africa 2009–10	4	4	0	48	25	12.00	64.86	0	0	2
England in South Africa 2009–10	3	3	0	72	32	24.00	66.05	0	0	3
England in Scotland 2010	1	1	0	61	61	61.00	141.86	0	1	0
Australia in England 2010	5	5	0	191	87	38.20	78.27	0	2	5
Bangladesh in England 2010	3	3	0	237	154	79.00	111.26	1	1	1
Pakistan in England 2010	5	5	0	317	126	63.40	93.23	1	2	5
England in Australia 2010–11	7	7	0	179	63	25.57	82.48	0	2	7
World Cup in Bangladesh/ India/Sri Lanka 2010–11	7	7	0	334	158	47.71	93.55	1	1	1

CAREER STATISTICS

ODIs – match by match

	Opponent	Venue	Bat posn	How out	Runs	Mins	Balls	Fours	Sixes	Ct
18/11/2003	Sri Lanka	Dambulla	2	c and b KADM Fernando	3	14	9	0	0	0
18/4/2004	West Indies	Georgetown	3	b DJ Bravo	29	62	46	5	0	0
24/4/2004	West Indies	Port-of-Spain	3							
1/5/2004	West Indies	Gros Islet	3	b M Dillon	10	43	16	1	0	0
2/5/2004	West Indies	Gros Islet	3	lbw b CH Gayle	67	110	82	7	0	1
5/5/2004	West Indies	Bridgetown	3	b IDR Bradshaw	66	124	86	4	0	0
27/6/2004	West Indies	Nottingham	4	c RD Jacobs b DJ Bravo	43	94	63	6	0	0
29/6/2004	New Zealand	Chester-le-Street	4	c JDP Oram b JEC Franklin	8	37	29	0	0	0
1/7/2004	West Indies	Leeds	4	not out	44	51	37	9	0	0
4/7/2004	New Zealand	Bristol	4	c NJ Astle b IG Butler	61	117	86	7	0	1
6/7/2004	West Indies	Lord's	4	c DJ Bravo b CH Gayle	100	183	116	8	2	0
1/9/2004	India	Nottingham	4	not out	41	74	52	6	0	0
3/9/2004	India	The Oval	4	c SC Ganguly b V Sehwag	2	10	9	0	0	0
5/9/2004	India	Lord's	4	lbw b IK Pathan	2	10	4	0	0	0
10/9/2004	Zimbabwe	Birmingham	4	c T Taibu b EC Rainsford	25	48	30	2	0	0
17/9/2004	Sri Lanka	Southampton	4	run out (MF Maharoof)	7	30	22	0	0	0
21/9/2004	Australia	Birmingham	4	not out	52	69	42	6	0	0
25/9/2004	West Indies	The Oval	4	run out (DJ Bravo)	18	45	33	2	0	1
28/11/2004	Zimbabwe	Harare	4	c and b S Matsikenyeri	8	12	14	0	0	1
1/12/2004	Zimbabwe	Harare	4	b GM Ewing	33	68	52	2	0	0
4/12/2004	Zimbabwe	Bulawayo	4	not out	22	33	34	2	0	0
5/12/2004	Zimbabwe	Bulawayo	4	c E Chigumbura b S Matsikenyeri	17	14	17	3	0	0
30/1/2005	South Africa	Johannesburg	4	c JM Kemp b A Nel	15	28	26	0	0	1
2/2/2005	South Africa	Bloemfontein	4	c MV Boucher b AJ Hall	2	11	9	0	0	0
4/2/2005	South Africa	Port Elizabeth	4	c AG Prince b SM Pollock	35	42	40	3	0	1
6/2/2005	South Africa	Cape Town	4	c AG Prince b A Nel	17	48	25	2	0	0
9/2/2005	South Africa	East London	4	run out (MV Boucher)	20	43	29	0	0	0
11/2/2005	South Africa	Durban	4	not out	0	1	0	0	0	0
13/2/2005	South Africa	Centurion	4	c MV Boucher b A Nel	15	42	35	2	0	3
16/6/2005	Bangladesh	The Oval	2	not out	82	104	77	10	1	0
19/6/2005	Australia	Bristol	2	b GD McGrath	16	40	23	3	0	0
21/6/2005	Bangladesh	Nottingham	2	lbw b Nazmul Hossain	152	207	128	19	0	1
23/6/2005	Australia	Chester-le-Street	2	b B Lee	3	17	13	0	0	0
26/6/2005	Bangladesh	Leeds	2	b Manjural Islam Rana	98	149	104	7	1	0

Date	Opponent	Venue	Bat posn	How out	Runs	Mins	Balls	Fours	Sixes	Ct
28/6/2005	Australia	Birmingham	2	c JN Gillespie b GD McGrath	25	25	18	5	0	0
2/7/2005	Australia	Lord's	2	b B Lee	2	21	8	0	0	1
7/7/2005	Australia	Leeds	2	c AC Gilchrist b GB Hogg	41	110	84	2	0	1
10/7/2005	Australia	Lord's	2	b MS Kasprowicz	11	32	25	1	0	0
12/7/2005	Australia	The Oval	2	c AC Gilchrist b MS Kasprowicz	36	81	50	5	0	0
10/12/2005	Pakistan	Lahore	3	c Salman Butt b Danish Kaneria	94	122	98	6	0	0
12/12/2005	Pakistan	Lahore	3	c Kamran Akmal b Shoaib Akhtar	0	3	4	0	0	0
15/12/2005	Pakistan	Karachi	3	lbw b Mohammad Sami	23	49	23	3	0	0
19/12/2005	Pakistan	Rawalpindi	3	lbw b Naved-ul-Hasan	0	1	1	0	0	1
21/12/2005	Pakistan	Rawalpindi	3	st Kamran Akmal b Arshad Khan	26	72	57	3	0	0
28/3/2006	India	Delhi	1	c MS Dhoni b IK Pathan	0	1	2	0	0	0
31/3/2006	India	Faridabad	1	b RR Powar	61	137	85	6	0	0
3/4/2006	India	Margao	1	c MS Dhoni b IK Pathan	7	14	13	1	0	0
6/4/2006	India	Kochi	1	lbw b IK Pathan	7	12	11	1	0	0
12/4/2006	India	Jamshedpur	1	retired hurt	74	137	85	10	0	0
15/4/2006	India	Indore-TG	1	c KD Karthik b S Sreesanth	25	41	34	5	0	0
13/6/2006	Ireland	Belfast	3	c AC Botha b KJ O'Brien	4	16	13	1	0	0
17/6/2006	Sri Lanka	Lord's	2	c KC Sangakkara b CRD Fernando	12	33	16	1	0	2
20/6/2006	Sri Lanka	The Oval	2	c M Muralitharan b MF Maharoof	18	42	23	2	0	1
24/6/2006	Sri Lanka	Chester-le-Street	2	lbw b WPUJC Vaas	32	55	44	3	0	1
28/6/2006	Sri Lanka	Manchester	4	c KC Sangakkara b TM Dilshan	45	56	44	5	0	0
1/7/2006	Sri Lanka	Leeds	4	c KC Sangakkara b SL Malinga	26	43	32	1	0	1
30/8/2006	Pakistan	Cardiff	2	c Shahid Afridi b Mohammad Asif	2	16	14	0	0	0
2/9/2006	Pakistan	Lord's	2	c Kamran Akmal b Shoaib Akhtar	0	3	1	0	0	0
5/9/2006	Pakistan	Southampton	2	c Kamran Akmal b Abdul Razzaq	50	67	46	8	0	0
8/9/2006	Pakistan	Nottingham	1	b Mohammad Hafeez	78	124	100	9	0	2
10/9/2006	Pakistan	Birmingham	1	c Kamran Akmal b Iftikhar Anjum	35	41	41	8	0	1
15/10/2006	India	Jaipur	1	c RS Dravid b IK Pathan	10	54	32	1	0	2
21/10/2006	Australia	Jaipur	1	c AC Gilchrist b A Symonds	56	178	90	6	0	1
28/10/2006	West Indies	Ahmedabad	1	b CH Gayle	50	60	47	8	0	0
12/1/2007	Australia	Melbourne	1	c ML Hayden b NW Bracken	12	20	20	1	0	0
16/1/2007	New Zealand	Hobart	1	lbw b JEC Franklin	28	79	58	3	0	0
19/1/2007	Australia	Brisbane	1	c BJ Hodge b GD McGrath	18	56	37	3	1	0
23/1/2007	New Zealand	Adelaide	1	lbw b JEC Franklin	19	37	33	3	0	1
26/1/2007	Australia	Adelaide	1	c AC Gilchrist b MG Johnson	17	49	32	2	0	0
30/1/2007	New Zealand	Perth	4	st BB McCullum b DL Vettori	12	30	20	0	0	1

	Opponent	Venue	Bat posn	How out	Runs	Mins	Balls	Fours	Sixes	Ct
2/2/2007	Australia	Sydney	5	c SR Clark b NW Bracken	26	25	24	3	0	0
6/2/2007	New Zealand	Brisbane	4	b SB Styris	55	120	63	3	1	0
9/2/2007	Australia	Melbourne	4	lbw b NW Bracken	0	3	2	0	0	2
11/2/2007	Australia	Sydney	4	c AC Gilchrist b NW Bracken	6	6	5	0	0	0
8/4/2007	Australia	North Sound	3	b SW Tait	7	11	10	2	1	2
11/4/2007	Bangladesh	Bridgetown	3	lbw b Syed Rasel	23	41	37	2	1	0
17/4/2007	South Africa	Bridgetown	3	c GC Smith b JH Kallis	46	113	67	2	1	0
21/4/2007	West Indies	Bridgetown	1	c DS Smith b CD Collymore	7	10	12	1	0	2
20/3/2009	West Indies	Providence	1	c DJ Bravo b DB-L Powell	15	33	23	1	0	0
22/3/2009	West Indies	Providence	1	b KA Pollard	105	204	129	7	0	0
27/3/2009	West Indies	Bridgetown	1	c CH Gayle b FH Edwards	2	25	18	0	0	0
29/3/2009	West Indies	Bridgetown	1	not out	79	85	61	9	1	0
3/4/2009	West Indies	Gros Islet	1	c DJ Bravo b R Rampaul	3	5	4	0	0	1
24/5/2009	West Indies	Bristol	1	c DJG Sammy b JE Taylor	4	29	16	0	0	1
26/5/2009	West Indies	Birmingham	1	st D Ramdin b SJ Benn	52	103	66	4	0	0
4/9/2009	Australia	The Oval	1	c CL White b B Lee	12	20	14	2	0	0
6/9/2009	Australia	Lord's	1	c and b NM Hauritz	47	78	53	6	0	0
9/9/2009	Australia	Southampton	1	c MJ Clarke b NM Hauritz	63	97	72	7	0	0
12/9/2009	Australia	Lord's	1	c NW Bracken b NM Hauritz	63	104	75	8	0	0
15/9/2009	Australia	Nottingham	1	lbw b NM Hauritz	35	56	38	6	0	0
17/9/2009	Australia	Nottingham	1	c TD Paine b B Lee	0	1	2	0	0	1
20/9/2009	Australia	Chester-le-Street	1	c BW Hilfenhaus b NM Hauritz	47	88	74	4	0	2
25/9/2009	Sri Lanka	Johannesburg	1	c SHT Kandamby b KMDN Kulasekara	9	34	25	1	0	0
27/9/2009	South Africa	Centurion	1	c MV Boucher b WD Parnell	25	51	37	5	0	0
29/9/2009	New Zealand	Johannesburg	1	c BB McCullum b KD Mills	0	1	2	0	0	0
2/10/2009	Australia	Centurion	1	c JR Hopes b PM Siddle	14	9	10	1	1	0
22/11/2009	South Africa	Centurion	2	c AB de Villiers b CK Langeveldt	16	31	26	3	0	2
27/11/2009	South Africa	Cape Town	1	c MV Boucher b M Morkel	24	39	24	4	0	0
29/11/2009	South Africa	Port Elizabeth	2	lbw b J Botha	32	71	59	6	0	1
19/6/2010	Scotland	Edinburgh	1	c NFI McCallum b RM Haq	61	56	43	12	0	0
22/6/2010	Australia	Southampton	1	c TD Paine b RJ Harris	10	14	11	2	0	1
24/6/2010	Australia	Cardiff	1	c and b NM Hauritz	51	79	56	3	2	0
27/6/2010	Australia	Manchester	1	c TD Paine b RJ Harris	87	182	121	8	0	3
30/6/2010	Australia	The Oval	1	c TD Paine b SW Tait	37	61	45	5	0	1
3/7/2010	Australia	Lord's	1	b SW Tait	6	20	11	1	0	0
8/7/2010	Bangladesh	Nottingham	1	run out (Mahmudullah)	50	50	37	7	0	0

Date	Opponent	Venue	Bat posn	How out	Runs	Mins	Balls	Fours	Sixes	Ct
10/7/2010	Bangladesh	Bristol	1	c Jahurul Islam b Rubel Hossain	33	32	36	4	1	0
12/7/2010	Bangladesh	Birmingham	1	c Shakib Al Hasan b Rubel Hossain	154	201	140	16	5	1
10/9/2010	Pakistan	Chester-le-Street	1	b Saeed Ajmal	41	53	45	3	2	0
12/9/2010	Pakistan	Leeds	1	lbw b Saeed Ajmal	126	184	134	10	1	2
17/9/2010	Pakistan	The Oval	1	b Umar Gul	57	83	54	8	0	1
20/9/2010	Pakistan	Lord's	1	c Fawad Alam b Shoaib Akhtar	68	105	72	8	0	2
22/9/2010	Pakistan	Southampton	1	c Kamran Akmal b Shoaib Akhtar	25	48	35	2	1	0
16/1/2011	Australia	Melbourne	1	c MJ Clarke b B Lee	63	87	65	6	0	0
21/1/2011	Australia	Hobart	1	lbw b DE Bollinger	19	35	28	2	0	1
23/1/2011	Australia	Sydney	1	run out (DJ Hussey)	23	39	27	2	0	0
26/1/2011	Australia	Adelaide	1	c BJ Haddin b B Lee	8	13	10	1	0	2
30/1/2011	Australia	Brisbane	1	c SPD Smith b DE Bollinger	3	24	16	0	0	2
2/2/2011	Australia	Sydney	1	c DJ Hussey b SPD Smith	63	87	69	6	0	1
6/2/2011	Australia	Perth	1	b SW Tait	0	1	2	0	0	1
22/2/2011	Netherlands	Nagpur-J	1	c TLW Cooper b Mudassar Bukhari	88	113	83	9	0	0
27/2/2011	India	Bangalore	1	lbw b Z Khan	158	188	145	18	1	0
2/3/2011	Ireland	Bangalore	1	b GH Dockrell	34	61	37	2	1	0
6/3/2011	South Africa	Chennai	1	c AB de Villiers b RJ Peterson	0	1	3	0	0	0
11/3/2011	Bangladesh	Chittagong-D	1	c Junaid Siddique b Naeem Islam	18	48	31	2	0	0
17/3/2011	West Indies	Chennai	1	c CH Gayle b AD Russell	31	50	39	3	1	1
26/3/2011	Sri Lanka	Colombo-RPS	1	b TM Dilshan	5	30	19	0	0	0

ODI centuries

	Opponent	Venue	Season
158 (c)	India	Bangalore	2010–11
154 (c)	Bangladesh	Birmingham	2010
152	Bangladesh	Nottingham	2005
126 (c)	Pakistan	Leeds	2010
105 (c)	West Indies	Providence	2008–09
100	West Indies	Lord's	2004

How he scored his runs

	Number	Runs
Singles	1482	1482
Twos	304	608
Threes	48	144
Fours	454	1816
Fives	1	5
Sixes	25	150

Batting record against different types of bowling

	Runs	Balls	Fours	Sixes	Outs	Avge	SR
Right-arm seam	2671	3293	320	16	62	43.08	81.11
Left-arm seam	576	745	79	1	20	28.80	77.32
Off-breaks	446	617	24	1	23	19.39	72.29
Leg-breaks	186	192	14	1	2	93.00	96.88
Slow left-arm	326	346	17	6	5	65.20	94.22
Slow left-arm chinamen	0	2	0	0	1	0.00	0.00

Bowlers dismissing Andrew Strauss in ODIs most often

	Times	Matches
NM Hauritz	6	11
B Lee	6	25
IK Pathan	5	9
SW Tait	4	8
NW Bracken	4	13
Shoaib Akhtar	4	13
JEC Franklin	3	7
A Nel	3	8
GD McGrath	3	15
CH Gayle	3	19
Rubel Hossain	2	3
RJ Harris	2	4
MS Kasprowicz	2	4
Saeed Ajmal	2	5
S Matsikenyeri	2	5
TM Dilshan	2	9
DE Bollinger	2	11
DJ Bravo	2	18

Manner of dismissal

	Times
Bowled	21
Caught wicketkeeper	29
Caught fielder	44
Lbw	16
Run out	5
Stumped	3
Other	0

Batting partners in ODIs

	Inns	Unb	Runs	Best	Avge	100	50
ME Trescothick	28	1	1230	192	45.55	3	7
IR Bell	22	0	961	170	43.68	3	4
IJL Trott	17	0	842	250	49.52	2	3
KP Pietersen	20	1	765	105	40.26	1	6
A Flintoff	13	2	718	226	65.27	2	2
PD Collingwood	17	1	680	210	42.50	2	2
RS Bopara	13	0	531	108	40.84	1	3
MP Vaughan	17	1	502	84	31.37	0	3
MJ Prior	20	1	432	66	22.73	0	2
SM Davies	7	0	390	113	55.71	1	2
C Kieswetter	9	0	337	121	37.44	1	1
VS Solanki	9	0	310	64	34.44	0	4
JL Denly	8	0	268	106	33.50	1	1
EC Joyce	5	0	152	43	30.40	0	0
GO Jones	3	0	120	82	40.00	0	1
EJG Morgan	4	0	111	57	27.75	0	1
OA Shah	6	0	106	50	17.66	0	1
MB Loye	3	0	87	52	29.00	0	1
AD Mascarenhas	1	0	59	59	59.00	0	1
RWT Key	2	0	49	27	24.50	0	0
SJ Harmison	1	0	44	44	44.00	0	0
LJ Wright	2	0	41	41	20.50	0	0
R Clarke	1	0	23	23	23.00	0	0
GJ Batty	1	0	17	17	17.00	0	0
MH Yardy	3	0	15	6	5.00	0	0
SCJ Broad	1	0	12	12	12.00	0	0
A McGrath	2	0	9	7	4.50	0	0

ODIs as captain

	Opponent	Venue	Toss	Decision	Result
12/4/2006	India	Jamshedpur	Lost	Bat	Won
15/4/2006	India	Indore-TG	Lost	Bowl	Lost
13/6/2006	Ireland	Belfast	Won	Bat	Won
17/6/2006	Sri Lanka	Lord's	Won	Bowl	Lost
20/6/2006	Sri Lanka	The Oval	Lost	Bat	Lost
24/6/2006	Sri Lanka	Chester-le-Street	Won	Bat	Lost
28/6/2006	Sri Lanka	Manchester	Lost	Bat	Lost
1/7/2006	Sri Lanka	Leeds	Won	Bat	Lost
30/8/2006	Pakistan	Cardiff	Lost	Bowl	No Res
2/9/2006	Pakistan	Lord's	Lost	Bowl	Lost
5/9/2006	Pakistan	Southampton	Lost	Bowl	Lost
8/9/2006	Pakistan	Nottingham	Lost	Bat	Won
10/9/2006	Pakistan	Birmingham	Won	Bowl	Won
20/3/2009	West Indies	Providence	Won	Bat	Won
22/3/2009	West Indies	Providence	Lost	Bat	Lost
27/3/2009	West Indies	Bridgetown	Lost	Bowl	Lost
29/3/2009	West Indies	Bridgetown	Won	Bowl	Won
3/4/2009	West Indies	Gros Islet	Lost	Bowl	Won
24/5/2009	West Indies	Bristol	Won	Bowl	Won
26/5/2009	West Indies	Birmingham	Lost	Bowl	Won
4/9/2009	Australia	The Oval	Won	Bowl	Lost
6/9/2009	Australia	Lord's	Won	Bowl	Lost
9/9/2009	Australia	Southampton	Won	Bat	Lost
12/9/2009	Australia	Lord's	Won	Bat	Lost
15/9/2009	Australia	Nottingham	Won	Bat	Lost
17/9/2009	Australia	Nottingham	Lost	Bat	Lost
20/9/2009	Australia	Chester-le-Street	Won	Bowl	Won
25/9/2009	Sri Lanka	Johannesburg	Won	Bowl	Won
27/9/2009	South Africa	Centurion	Won	Bat	Won
29/9/2009	New Zealand	Johannesburg	Lost	Bowl	Lost
2/10/2009	Australia	Centurion	Won	Bat	Lost
22/11/2009	South Africa	Centurion	Won	Bowl	Won
27/11/2009	South Africa	Cape Town	Lost	Bat	Lost
29/11/2009	South Africa	Port Elizabeth	Lost	Bat	Won
19/6/2010	Scotland	Edinburgh	Lost	Bat	Won
22/6/2010	Australia	Southampton	Lost	Bat	Won
24/6/2010	Australia	Cardiff	Lost	Bat	Won
27/6/2010	Australia	Manchester	Won	Bowl	Won
30/6/2010	Australia	The Oval	Won	Bowl	Lost
3/7/2010	Australia	Lord's	Lost	Bat	Lost
8/7/2010	Bangladesh	Nottingham	Lost	Bat	Won
10/7/2010	Bangladesh	Bristol	Won	Bowl	Lost
12/7/2010	Bangladesh	Birmingham	Lost	Bowl	Won
10/9/2010	Pakistan	Chester-le-Street	Lost	Bowl	Won
12/9/2010	Pakistan	Leeds	Lost	Bat	Won
17/9/2010	Pakistan	The Oval	Lost	Bat	Lost
20/9/2010	Pakistan	Lord's	Lost	Bat	Lost
22/9/2010	Pakistan	Southampton	Won	Bat	Won
16/1/2011	Australia	Melbourne	Won	Bat	Lost
21/1/2011	Australia	Hobart	Won	Bowl	Lost
23/1/2011	Australia	Sydney	Won	Bat	Lost
26/1/2011	Australia	Adelaide	Won	Bat	Won
30/1/2011	Australia	Brisbane	Lost	Bat	Lost
2/2/2011	Australia	Sydney	Won	Bat	Lost
6/2/2011	Australia	Perth	Lost	Bat	Lost
22/2/2011	Netherlands	Nagpur-J	Lost	Bat	Won
27/2/2011	India	Bangalore	Lost	Bat	Tied
2/3/2011	Ireland	Bangalore	Won	Bat	Lost

	Opponent	Venue	Toss	Decision	Result
6/3/2011	South Africa	Chennai	Won	Bat	Won
11/3/2011	Bangladesh	Chittagong-D	Lost	Bowl	Lost
17/3/2011	West Indies	Chennai	Won	Bat	Won
26/3/2011	Sri Lanka	Colombo-RPS	Won	Bat	Lost

ODI captaincy summary

Played	Won	Lost	Tied	NR	%Won	Toss won	Toss lost	TW bat	TW bowl	TL bat	TL bowl
62	27	33	1	1	43.54	31	31	18	13	20	11

TWENTY20 RECORD

T20s – match by match

	Opponent	Venue	Bat posn	How out	Runs	Mins	Balls	Fours	Sixes	Ct
13/6/2005	Australia	Southampton	7	b JN Gillespie	18	15	16	1	0	0
15/6/2006	Sri Lanka	Southampton	2	b CRD Fernando	33	33	21	6	0	1
28/8/2006	Pakistan	Bristol	4	c Kamran Akmal b Mohammad Asif	0	2	2	0	0	0
15/3/2009	West Indies	Port-of-Spain	6	run out (S Chanderpaul)	22	25	25	2	0	0

INDEX

An invitation from the publisher

Join us at www.hodder.co.uk, or follow us
on Twitter @hodderbooks to be a part of
our community of people who love the very
best in books and reading.

Whether you want to discover more about a book
or an author, watch trailers and interviews, have the
chance to win early limited editions, or simply browse
our expert readers' selection of the very best books,
we think you'll find what you're looking for.

And if you don't, that's the place to tell us what's missing.

We love what we do, and we'd love you to be a part of it.

www.hodder.co.uk

 @hodderbooks

HodderBooks

HodderBooks